COMPUTER BOOK SERIES FROM IDG

Setting Up An Inte[rnet Site] For Dummies, 3r[d Ed.]

M000311349

Domain Information

Write the indicated reference information for your Internet domain in the second column.

Domain Name

IP Address

Primary DNS Server

Secondary DNS Server

Technical Contact Name

Technical Contact E-Mail Address

Technical Contact NIC Handle

Administrative Contact Name

Administrative Contact E-Mail Address

Administrative Contact NIC Handle

Billing Contact Name

Billing Contact E-Mail Address

Billing Contact NIC Handle

SMTP Relay Host

Default Internet Gateway

Useful Keywords for Internet Queries

Use the following terms in searching the Internet for more information:

- ✔ Setting Up an Internet Site
- ✔ Creating an Internet Site
- ✔ Setting Up Shop on the Internet
- ✔ Internet Publishing
- ✔ Providing Information on the Internet
- ✔ Internet Programming
- ✔ WinSock
- ✔ MacTCP

- ✔ Internet Commerce
- ✔ Internet Security
- ✔ Internet Server
- ✔ Virtual Server
- ✔ Mail Server
- ✔ FTP Server
- ✔ Server Software
- ✔ Internet Advertising
- ✔ Internet Presence

IDG BOOKS WORLDWIDE™

...For Dummies: #1 Computer Book Series for Beginners

COMPUTER
BOOK SERIES
FROM IDG

Setting Up An Internet Site For Dummies, 3rd Edition

Cheat Sheet

Site Information

Write the URL or service address for each service your Internet site offers.

Service	Address
Home Page URL	
POP Server Address	
List Server Address	
FTP Server URL	
IRC Server Address	
E-Mail Information Server	
Internet BBS Address	
NNTP Server URL	
Gopher URL	

Emergency Contact Information

Type	Contact Name	URL
Police	CERT: Computer Emergency Response Team	http://www.cert.org/
Medical	McAfee Anti-Virus	http://www.mcafee.com/
Network	Service Provider	
Network	Service Provider	

Resources for Site Developers

Resource	URL
SCIENCE.ORG Setting Up an Internet Site page	http://computers.science.org/internet/site/setup/
Web66 Internet Server Cookbook	http://web66.coled.umn.edu/Cookbook/
Apple and the Internet	http://applenet.apple.com/
Building Internet Servers	http://www.cybergroup.com/html/servers.html
WinHTTPd/WebSite Central	http://website.ora.com/
MacHTTP Home Page	http://www.starnine.com/software/
WinSMTP Home Page	http://www.seattlelab.com/
Internet Servers via MacOS	http://www.pism.com/
The InterNIC	http://www.internic.net/

...For Dummies: #1 Computer Book Series for Beginners

SETTING UP AN INTERNET SITE

FOR

DUMMIES®

3RD EDITION

SETTING UP AN INTERNET SITE FOR DUMMIES®

3RD EDITION

by Jason Coombs, Ted Coombs, David Crowder, & Rhonda Crowder

IDG BOOKS WORLDWIDE

IDG Books Worldwide, Inc.
An International Data Group Company

Foster City, CA ♦ Chicago, IL ♦ Indianapolis, IN ♦ Southlake, TX

Setting Up An Internet Site For Dummies,® 3rd Edition

Published by
IDG Books Worldwide, Inc.
An International Data Group Company
919 E. Hillsdale Blvd.
Suite 400
Foster City, CA 94404
www.idgbooks.com (IDG Books Worldwide Web site)
www.dummies.com (Dummies Press Web site)

Library of Congress Catalog Card No.: 98-84490

ISBN: 0-7645-0358-8

Printed in the United States of America

10 9 8 7 6 5 4 3 2 1

3B/RZ/QT/ZY/IN

Distributed in the United States by IDG Books Worldwide, Inc.

Distributed by Macmillan Canada for Canada; by Transworld Publishers Limited in the United Kingdom; by IDG Norge Books for Norway; by IDG Sweden Books for Sweden; by Woodslane Pty. Ltd. for Australia; by Woodslane Enterprises Ltd. for New Zealand; by Longman Singapore Publishers Ltd. for Singapore, Malaysia, Thailand, and Indonesia; by Simron Pty. Ltd. for South Africa; by Toppan Company Ltd. for Japan; by Distribuidora Cuspide for Argentina; by Livraria Cultura for Brazil; by Ediciencia S.A. for Ecuador; by Addison-Wesley Publishing Company for Korea; by Ediciones ZETA S.C.R. Ltda. for Peru; by WS Computer Publishing Corporation, Inc., for the Philippines; by Unalis Corporation for Taiwan; by Contemporanea de Ediciones for Venezuela; by Computer Book & Magazine Store for Puerto Rico; by Express Computer Distributors for the Caribbean and West Indies. Authorized Sales Agent: Anthony Rudkin Associates for the Middle East and North Africa.

For general information on IDG Books Worldwide's books in the U.S., please call our Consumer Customer Service department at 800-762-2974. For reseller information, including discounts and premium sales, please call our Reseller Customer Service department at 800-434-3422.

For information on where to purchase IDG Books Worldwide's books outside the U.S., please contact our International Sales department at 650-655-3200 or fax 650-655-3295.

For information on foreign language translations, please contact our Foreign & Subsidiary Rights department at 650-655-3021 or fax 650-655-3281.

For sales inquiries and special prices for bulk quantities, please contact our Sales department at 650-655-3200 or write to the address above.

For information on using IDG Books Worldwide's books in the classroom or for ordering examination copies, please contact our Educational Sales department at 800-434-2086 or fax 817-251-8174.

For press review copies, author interviews, or other publicity information, please contact our Public Relations department at 650-655-3000 or fax 650-655-3299.

For authorization to photocopy items for corporate, personal, or educational use, please contact Copyright Clearance Center, 222 Rosewood Drive, Danvers, MA 01923, or fax 978-750-4470.

is a trademark under exclusive license to IDG Books Worldwide, Inc., from International Data Group, Inc.

About the Authors

Jason Coombs (jason@science.org) and **Ted Coombs** (tedc@ science.org) lead an independent research and development laboratory called science.org (located on the Web at www.science.org/). Together, they've cowritten six books about computer technology, including three in the ...*For Dummies* series published by IDG Books WorldWide, Inc. (www.dummies.com/) and numerous magazine articles. They live and work near the Pacific Ocean in Encinitas, California, where they surf, scuba dive, and ocean kayak with the local dolphins. (And yes, in case you're wondering, they're father and son. Ted Coombs is the father and Jason is the son.)

David and Rhonda Crowder were selling hypertext systems in the days when you had to explain to people what the word *hypertext* meant. They have been involved in the online community for over a decade, when David was SysOp for the FidoNet BBS, Taliesin's Dream. They created the award-winning LinkFinder (http://www.linkfinder.com/) and NetWelcome (http://www.netwelcome.com/) sites. LinkFinder holds a four-star rating from *NetGuide* magazine, and NetWelcome is the recipient of several awards, including *NetGuide*'s Gold Site Award. David founded three Internet mailing lists that are now owned and run by Ziff-Davis. David and Rhonda have coauthored three other computer books. They live with their cats in Miami, Florida.

ABOUT IDG BOOKS WORLDWIDE

Welcome to the world of IDG Books Worldwide.

IDG Books Worldwide, Inc., is a subsidiary of International Data Group, the world's largest publisher of computer-related information and the leading global provider of information services on information technology. IDG was founded more than 25 years ago and now employs more than 8,500 people worldwide. IDG publishes more than 275 computer publications in over 75 countries (see listing below). More than 60 million people read one or more IDG publications each month.

Launched in 1990, IDG Books Worldwide is today the #1 publisher of best-selling computer books in the United States. We are proud to have received eight awards from the Computer Press Association in recognition of editorial excellence and three from *Computer Currents'* First Annual Readers' Choice Awards. Our best-selling ...For Dummies® series has more than 30 million copies in print with translations in 30 languages. IDG Books Worldwide, through a joint venture with IDG's Hi-Tech Beijing, became the first U.S. publisher to publish a computer book in the People's Republic of China. In record time, IDG Books Worldwide has become the first choice for millions of readers around the world who want to learn how to better manage their businesses.

Our mission is simple: Every one of our books is designed to bring extra value and skill-building instructions to the reader. Our books are written by experts who understand and care about our readers. The knowledge base of our editorial staff comes from years of experience in publishing, education, and journalism — experience we use to produce books for the '90s. In short, we care about books, so we attract the best people. We devote special attention to details such as audience, interior design, use of icons, and illustrations. And because we use an efficient process of authoring, editing, and desktop publishing our books electronically, we can spend more time ensuring superior content and spend less time on the technicalities of making books.

You can count on our commitment to deliver high-quality books at competitive prices on topics you want to read about. At IDG Books Worldwide, we continue in the IDG tradition of delivering quality for more than 25 years. You'll find no better book on a subject than one from IDG Books Worldwide.

John Kilcullen
CEO
IDG Books Worldwide, Inc.

Steven Berkowitz
President and Publisher
IDG Books Worldwide, Inc.

*Eighth Annual
Computer Press
Awards ≥1992*

WINNER

*Ninth Annual
Computer Press
Awards ≥1993*

WINNER

WINNER

*Tenth Annual
Computer Press
Awards ≥1994*

WINNER

*Eleventh Annual
Computer Press
Awards ≥1995*

Dedication

For Olga Samper

— David and Rhonda Crowder

Authors' Acknowledgments

Thanks are due to all the many people who made this book possible. Our agent, Chris Van Buren of Waterside Productions, was always ready with timely advice and encouragement. Camila Payan rendered invaluable assistance when our backs were against the wall. Jill Pisoni, Susan Pink, Colin Banfield, Heather Dismore, and the rest of the editorial and production staff at IDG worked their daily miracles, each and every one adding a part of themselves to make this a better book than we could have accomplished alone.

— David and Rhonda Crowder

Publisher's Acknowledgments

We're proud of this book; please register your comments through our IDG Books Worldwide Online Registration Form located at http://my2cents.dummies.com.

Some of the people who helped bring this book to market include the following:

Acquisitions, Development, and Editorial

Project Editor: Susan Pink

Acquisitions Editor: Jill Pisoni

Media Development Manager: Joyce Pepple

Permissions Editor: Heather H. Dismore

Technical Editor: Colin Banfield

Editorial Manager: Mary C. Corder

Editorial Assistant: Donna Love

Production

Project Coordinator: Valery Bourke

Layout and Graphics: Steve Arany, Lou Boudreau, Angela F. Hunckler, Drew R. Moore, Brent Savage, M. Anne Sipahimalani

Proofreaders: Kelli Botta, Sally Burton, Michelle Croninger, Rachel Garvey, Rebecca Senninger, Carrie Voorhis, Janet M. Withers

Indexer: Liz Cunningham

Special Help

Constance Carlisle, Carmen Krikorian, Paula Lowell, Joell Smith, Suzanne Thomas, Phil Worthington, Access Technology

General and Administrative

IDG Books Worldwide, Inc.: John Kilcullen, CEO; Steven Berkowitz, President and Publisher

IDG Books Technology Publishing: Brenda McLaughlin, Senior Vice President and Group Publisher

Dummies Technology Press and Dummies Editorial: Diane Graves Steele, Vice President and Associate Publisher; Mary Bednarek, Director of Acquisitions and Product Development; Kristin A. Cocks, Editorial Director

Dummies Trade Press: Kathleen A. Welton, Vice President and Publisher; Kevin Thornton, Acquisitions Manager

IDG Books Production for Dummies Press: Beth Jenkins Roberts, Production Director; Cindy L. Phipps, Manager of Project Coordination, Production Proofreading, and Indexing; Kathie S. Schutte, Supervisor of Page Layout; Shelley Lea, Supervisor of Graphics and Design; Debbie J. Gates, Production Systems Specialist; Robert Springer, Supervisor of Proofreading; Debbie Stailey, Special Projects Coordinator; Tony Augsburger, Supervisor of Reprints and Bluelines; Leslie Popplewell, Media Archive Coordinator

Dummies Packaging and Book Design: Patti Crane, Packaging Specialist; Kavish + Kavish, Cover Design

◆

The publisher would like to give special thanks to Patrick J. McGovern, without whom this book would not have been possible.

◆

Contents at a Glance

Cartoons at a Glance

By Rich Tennant

page 271

page 127

page 63

page 225

page 7

Fax: 978-546-7747 • **E-mail:** the5wave@tiac.net

Table of Contents

Introduction

*T*his book shows you everything you need to know to set up your own Internet site. Whatever kind of site you want, from running an FTP server out of your office to utilizing virtual Web servers clear across the world, you'll find clear and simple directions here on how to do it.

Should You Read This Internet Book?

Setting Up An Internet Site For Dummies, 3rd Edition, is the ideal book for anyone who wants to create a permanent Internet presence for personal or business purposes. Whether you're an experienced (or travel-weary) Internet navigator or just beginning to explore what the Internet can do for you, this book can serve as a valuable guide.

Above all, this book is for people who believe that providing interactive resources and doing business on the Internet should be simple, effective, and fun — not technical, time-consuming, and dull. Buy this book if you want to do something with the Internet. We designed this book to meet the needs of the following three types of readers:

- ✔ People who already use the Internet and want to turn it into a more useful tool
- ✔ Anyone who wants to provide information on the Internet for a business or for personal goals
- ✔ Experienced Web publishers who want to get the most out of the World Wide Web

In this book, we assume that you're a relatively experienced computer user. We make no attempt to explain files, icons, mouse actions, or any other basic computer concept. If you're new to computers, you need to pick up some basic training before this book makes much sense to you. For that basic training, check out one of the *Windows For Dummies* books by Andy Rathbone or *The Internet For Dummies,* 5th Edition, by John Levine, Carol Baroudi, and Margaret Levine Young (both by IDG Books Worldwide, Inc.).

How to Use This Book

If you've ever used a *...For Dummies* book before, you'll feel right at home here. That's because the clever folks at IDG have standardized things to make life easier for you. When there's a line of program code, it appears in a monospaced type, like this:

```
rm .vacation.msg
```

Anything that appears in code font should be typed letter for letter. Stuff in code in *italics* is a placeholder, and you should substitute a value for it. For example, in the following line of code:

```
mv TextFile .vacation.msg
```

you would type **mv** and **.vacation.msg**, but substitute the name of your text file for *TextFile*.

The instructions in a numbered list are in bold print. If there's anything in those instructions that you need to type, it stands out because it isn't bold, like this:

2. Type howdydoody **in the File text box.**

And just to cover all the bases, placeholders are in italics in numbered lists, too. For example:

3. Type htpasswd -c *pathname username.*

In this example, you would type **htpasswd -c** but when you came to *pathname,* you'd replace it with the name of the password file. Likewise, you'd replace *username* with the name the user will use.

Then there's the bit about arrows and underlined keys. For instance, you'll find sentences such as "In the Pegasus program, choose Tools⇨Mail filtering rules⇨Edit new mail filtering rules." The arrows show the flow of the menus as you choose them. In this example, when you click the Tools menu, one of the choices you get is Mail filtering rules. When you click that choice, one of the choices on the new menu that pops up is Edit new mail filtering rules. Note that we underline the hot keys you can use to select menu commands from the keyboard, so if you don't feel like giving your mouse a workout, you can limber up your fingers and press the keys instead.

URLs are listed like this:

```
http://netwinsite.com/dnews.htm
```

All the URLs in this book are accurate at the time of this writing. Because the Internet is a dynamic medium, however, a few may be inaccessible when you try them.

 Be sure to visit the *...For Dummies* home page at www.dummies.com and click the Really Useful Extras link in the Contents at a Glance column. The Really Useful Extras page contains links to all the Web sites mentioned in the book, so you won't even have to type them yourself.

Organization of This Book

We did organize this book — we promise. In fact, we organized the book well enough to divide its text into parts, chapters, sections, paragraphs . . . just to keep everything from spilling out all over the place. The following sections describe the five parts in this book.

Part I: Laying the Foundation of an Internet Site

Anyone who builds a physical structure knows that it needs a solid foundation. Setting up an Internet site is no different. The better your foundation, the more effective your site. Part I guides you away from weak materials and toward those that make your Internet site strong and vibrant.

This part also presents the basic concepts you need to understand as you prepare to follow the instructions in this book. As a provider of Internet resources, you need to know some things that the average Internet user doesn't. This part also walks you through the first steps that everyone needs to take in setting up an Internet site: getting a domain name and establishing a presence on the Internet.

Part II: Publishing Information on the Internet

The World Wide Web has become a popular electronic-publishing medium. Chapters 5 and 6 give you the lowdown on Web publishing. The Internet offers many other efficient and useful means of providing information, such as Internet newsgroups. Chapter 7 covers what you need to publish information by setting up your own news server.

Part III: Setting Up Basic Internet Services

Part III shows you how to set up the most important basic resources. As you discover throughout this book, good software tools turn your Internet site into something special. The tools that this part covers include File Transfer Protocol (FTP), e-mail service, and mailing lists.

Part IV: Site Builder Skills for Today's Internet

Life on the Internet is what you make of it. Every site developer should know how to obtain publicity for an Internet site and create a secure environment in which to conduct electronic commerce. Part IV gives you the basic skills that everyone who runs an Internet site needs.

Part V: The Part of Tens

You know you have a ...*For Dummies* book when you get to The Part of Tens. And, if you're like us, it's the first part you read (except for the cartoons). Dive into ten technology add-ons, ten things your Web site can't live without, ten tools for Web development, and lots of other decimal lists.

Icons Used in This Book

This book has icons in the margins — okay, we admit they're not as fascinating as James Dean or Marilyn Monroe, but you should pay attention to these icons because they guide you to specific points that can enhance your Internet site, lessen your workload, and keep you out of trouble.

If you see this icon, you find in the accompanying text information about the software or hardware you need to accomplish the tasks we describe in this book. If you have the right stuff, you face no limits to what you can accomplish.

This icon suggests ways in which you can use the technology described in this book to start an Internet business. The Internet is an evolving landscape of opportunity. New products and services that use Internet technology or help other users are always emerging. Many such businesses exist only on the Internet, having no real-world business location.

This icon points out the hidden wisdom of Internet veterans. Next to this icon, you find insights and war stories from the electronic frontier so that you can benefit from the experience of others.

Watch out — the Information Superhighway is still under construction, and it has a few potholes. This icon points them out to help you avoid trouble.

Sometimes we forget things, so we use this icon to point out important things you want to remember. You probably don't forget things, but humor us if you see this icon.

Most of the technical stuff in this book appears in a simple, readable, entertaining format right in the main text. This icon points out *really* technical things that require a college education to even think about. You can read this stuff, or you can skip it — without hurting our feelings.

We use this icon to mark items contained in the *Setting Up An Internet Site For Dummies* CD-ROM.

About the CD-ROM

We put together a CD-ROM full of the programs you need to set up and maintain an Internet site. Some of the programs included on the *Setting Up An Internet Site For Dummies* CD-ROM are shareware, so after you set up your site and start using the software, you need to send license fees to the authors of that software.

Other programs on the CD-ROM are demo versions of software that we find useful. Try these programs to determine which ones give you the options you need to create a compelling, useful Internet site. If you find that some demos are just what you need, contact the creators of the software to discover how you can purchase production versions of the software.

Finally, still other programs on the CD-ROM are freeware, which means you just plug 'em in and enjoy. Still, it's nice to drop the developers a note saying how much you like their software. You just might make their day.

Part I
Laying the Foundation of an Internet Site

The 5th Wave   By Rich Tennant

"HOW SHOULD I KNOW WHY THEY TOOK IT OFF THE LIST? MAYBE THERE JUST WEREN'T ENOUGH MEMBERS TO SUPPORT AN 'AIREDALES FOR ELVIS' BULLETIN BOARD."

In this part . . .

By the time you finish with this part, you'll know what Cat 5 means and what you do with an EtherNet hub. You'll know how to use virtual Web servers and be able to penetrate the mysteries of domain name registration. But the Internet is more than just hardware and software. The most important thing you'll find in this part is how to put your stamp on your site, showcasing your own unique style.

Chapter 1

Setting the Tone of Your Site

● ●

In This Chapter

▶ Determining the tone for your site

▶ Tailoring the subject and theme for your audience

▶ Authoring a workable Web site

▶ Updating your material and links

● ●

*E*very computer that communicates on the Internet is part of some Internet site. An *Internet site* is a collection of computers that are all permanently connected to the Internet and that appear to the outside world to be related to one another. Your personal computer becomes a temporary part of somebody else's Internet site if you connect to an Internet service provider using a modem. Every Web page lives on a computer that is part of somebody's Internet site. Every piece of e-mail that is sent to you moves through the network and hops from one Internet site to another until it ends up on your computer for you to read. Everything that happens on the Internet begins with the construction of an Internet site.

Some Internet sites are built by large companies, government agencies, military installations, schools, and power companies; others are built by small companies, families, individuals, and even Internet-book authors. All Internet sites need electricity and a permanent connection to the Internet, but beyond these two things, every Internet site is different. The needs and preferences of the site builder determine the exact nature of a particular Internet site. Some sites, such as those built by Internet service providers, have a way to give customers access to the Internet in exchange for a monthly service fee. Other sites don't provide services to customers but do provide information in the form of Web pages, for example. You are free to do whatever you want or need to do with your Internet site, and this simple fact is what has caused the Internet to grow.

Before you can make the switch from Net surfer to site builder, you must acquire a deeper understanding of the Internet. If you just surf the Net, the nuances that make up the various parts of the Internet make little difference to your overall experience. If you build an Internet site, however, understanding those nuances can make the difference between a useful and appealing site and a mediocre one.

The choices you make regarding design and editorial content will set the tone of your site. Whatever you do will attract some people and repel others, and the decisions you make will depend more on your audience than on your subject matter. In this chapter, we cover how to use words and other content to appeal to the appropriate audience for you, and how to keep your site fresh and up-to-date. For layout and graphic design considerations, check out Chapter 6.

Tuxedoes and T-Shirts

When you consider the tone you want to set for your site, formality is a prime consideration. Do you prefer to establish a respectful distance between yourself and your visitors? Or do you want 'em to kick off their shoes and flop down on the couch? A site designed to attract clients to a prestigious law firm will have a radically different approach than one that's meant to give groupies a list of all the cities where their favorite band will play during their new world tour.

What we're talking about here is image — not the pictures you put on your site, but the way the world perceives you. As any advertising professional can tell you, image can be even more important than substance in this world. That doesn't mean you can get away with a flashy, cool site that has nothing real to offer. You may cause a stir with such an empty site, but it won't have any staying power.

Every site has some purpose, some reason for being there. You may be planning a commercial enterprise, an informational site, an entertainment site, or a personal one. Here are some reasons why people have created Internet sites:

- To sell products
- To raise money for a charity
- To lobby for or against a cause
- To post their resumes in hopes of getting their dream jobs
- To provide public health information
- To advertise a company's services
- To help locate lost pets
- To provide a meeting place for hobbyists
- To give the public access to official documents

Whatever your purpose, you'll need to gear everything toward supporting it. If you're pushing entertainment, make your site as fun as possible. If you're promoting information, make it as compelling and useful as possible. Remember, whatever you're doing, lots of other people will be competing for your audience. Give it everything you've got if you expect to keep 'em coming back for more.

Man, That's Deep

How deeply will you dig into the subject matter? If you have a site dealing with Web design, are you going to stop at how to add horizontal lines or will you get into Java animation? If you're talking about Christopher Columbus, are you going to tell the kindergarten story about how the people of his time thought the world was flat, or will you detail the savants' debate about the distance between Europe and China? Basically, you need to determine your intended audience — who they are, what they know, and what they'll consider worthwhile.

Focus is the name of the game. If you want to reach mid-level executives, for instance, you need to put together information that would be of interest to them, such as stock options, personnel law, and BMW maintenance. The trick is to *limit* what you handle. It's unlikely that any site could possibly cover everything there is to say about any one subject. Even if you could manage it, you'd be likely to end up with an unwieldy and useless site. What makes a site useful is its focus on only the important elements. What's important? That depends entirely on what you're dealing with and who's using your site.

To make the task easier on yourself, just break your topic down into three categories. Call the categories something like *simple, moderate,* and *complex* or *beginning, intermediate,* and *advanced.* It helps to think of both your site and your intended audience in these arbitrary terms. They'll give you a framework within which you can make rational decisions. If you develop an advanced site and your audience falls under the beginning category, you're asking for trouble; if the situation is the reverse, you'll lose the respect of your audience. Match the people and the material and you'll be on the right track.

Let It Flow

Language is the number one way to lock in a particular feeling at your site. Regardless of the subject matter you're covering, stilted, dry, or dead wording will drive away everyone but a fanatical visitor. Put your passion into your words. Put *yourself* into them. Show the world that what you have to say matters. After all, if it doesn't matter to you, why should it matter to them?

This doesn't mean your visitors have to salivate over every paragraph, or that a site dedicated to the analysis of metal alloys has to sound like a romance novel. But if metal alloys is the most interesting thing in your life, make it the most interesting thing on the Internet, too. Remember the old saying about learning? There are no boring subjects, only boring teachers. Well, apply it to your site work, too. Don't take something interesting and fascinating and turn it into a sleeping pill.

Think about elements (such as presentation or depth of subject matter) that attract you to your favorite sites and incorporate these elements in your own site. You should think like a surfer when creating the content of your site.

Like wording, grammar can make an important difference. It's important to make a literate presentation so that you will be taken seriously. However, don't get so hung up over the placement of a comma that you lose sight of your ultimate goal, which is the presentation of meaningful information in a useable format. Grammar is somethin' but it ain't everythin'.

Face it. Most people have no idea whether the correct word is *sank* or *sunk*, anyway, and if you ask them what *past perfect* means, you'll get a blank look or nostalgic reminiscences. If you're reasonably well-educated and read even moderately (no, technical manuals and *Dilbert* don't count), you'll get close enough to be understood. If the exact phrasing is important and you're in doubt, check with a good reference book such as Strunk and White's *Elements of Style* or Gordon's oddly-named but useful book *The Transitive Vampire*. Better yet, post a message in the alt.english.usage newsgroup or use one of the other online resources listed in Table 1-1.

Keepin' Up with the Joneses

Like Alice in Wonderland said (or maybe it was Alvin Toffler), "It takes all the running I can do just to stay in the same place." Or something to that effect. As the world changes around you and the subject matter of your site becomes outdated (probably about the time you finish it), you'll need to update it. Updating is a critical part of maintaining a credible site. A news site that doesn't have the latest scandal or crisis won't be visited the next time a story breaks. People will remember and go to the site that had the information they wanted when they wanted it.

Table 1-1	Online Grammar and Style Resources
Title	*Web Address*
alt.english.usage FAQ	`http://www.cis.ohio-state.edu/hypertext/faq/usenet/alt-usage-english-faq/faq.html`
Basic Prose Style and Mechanics	`http://www.rpi.edu/dept/llc/writecenter/web/text/proseman.html`
Common Errors in English	`http://www.wsu.edu:8080/~brians/errors/errors.html`
Grammar and Style Notes	`http://www.english.upenn.edu/~jlynch/grammar.html`
Mama's Hot 100 Grammar Goofs	`http://www.unl.edu/mama/grammar/college.htm`
Roget's Thesaurus	`http://humanities.uchicago.edu/forms_unrest/ROGET.html`
WWWebster Thesaurus	`http://www.m-w.com/thesaurus.htm`
WWWebster Dictionary	`http://www.m-w.com/cgi-bin/dictionary`

Your updating needs probably aren't as frantic and time-intensive as CNN's (see Figure 1-1), but you still need to establish a regular schedule for checking your material, and also be ready to jump in at a moment's notice and update ahead of schedule. Keep yourself up-to-date in your field so that you'll be able to recognize what needs changing.

One of the most important parts to keep up-to-date is links to other resources. After all, the Web is composed of many strands. People surfing to Web sites expect to find links to related material, and they aren't fond of sites that have none.

Your links page doesn't have to be a one-way street out of your site. When you put in a link to someone else's site, contact their Webmaster (an e-mail link is usually at the bottom of the index page) to see whether he or she will add a link back to your site. That's called *reciprocal linking,* and it's a common practice on the World Wide Web.

Links to other sites need constant monitoring. Ones that were fine yesterday may lead nowhere tomorrow. Other sites move or shut down, almost always without notification. Manually checking every link every day would take a lot of your time. Fortunately, you have two easy alternatives.

Figure 1-1:
Some sites
need to be
updated
more
frequently
than others.

The first is to let your users do the testing for you. Put a message like this one on your links page:

> Although we do the best we can to keep our links up-to-date, we would appreciate it if you would let us know when you find a broken link so that we can take appropriate action and continue to give you the best service on the Web.

Make sure that you add a `mailto:` link in the message to make it easy for users to report broken links (`mailto:` links are covered in Chapter 8).

Unfortunately, you can't necessarily count on other people doing your job for you, but there is one other thing you can do. Several programs, such as InfoLink (see Figure 1-2), solve the broken-link problem automatically. Just feed them the URL of the Web page or site you want checked and they're off and running, checking every link on the page and then generating a report.

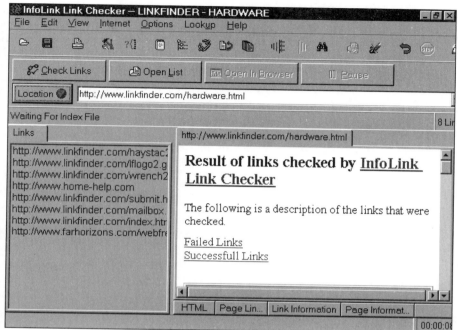

Figure 1-2:
InfoLink
checks for
broken links
automatically.

The report tells you which pages have moved, which are just plain gone, and which are on servers that are having problems. You simply look at the links that didn't make proper connections and drop from your site those you don't want. Table 1-2 lists the URLs of several such programs. Some also do other things, such as build site maps or spell-check your HTML pages. Download these programs and give them a try. They'll make your life a lot easier.

Table 1-2	Link-Checking Programs
Program	*Web Address*
Astra SiteManager	`http://www.merc-int.com/products/astrasmguide.html`
CyberSpyder	`http://www.cyberspyder.com/index.html`
InfoLink	`http://www.biggbyte.com/`
Linkbot	`http://www.tetranetsoftware.com/`
SiteCHECK	`http://www.pcworld.com/software_lib/data/articles/internet/3409.html`

And, if you don't want to be bothered even with running a program, a service called Inspector Web will do your checking for you for a fee. The service has different rates for one-shot, weekly, or monthly reports, and you can even run a free sample check of your Web site of up to 800 links. The Inspector Web site is located at http://www.greenpac.com/.

Chapter 2
Internetworking

. . . .

In This Chapter
▶ Understanding networks
▶ Comparing site options
▶ Creating your own computer network

. . . .

Don't skip this chapter! You may be thinking that this chapter is not for you because you have only one PC sitting on your desk, not a network. Not true. A *network* is simply one computer connected to another, and the Internet is a big network of computers. Therefore, setting up an Internet site means setting up your computer, no matter what kind it is, as part of the network. Even if you have only one computer initially, if you turn that one computer into the foundation of an Internet site, you need to know about networking.

Internetworking Is for Everyone

The Internet is just a large computer network that, aside from its size, is no different than a network you'd have in your office or possibly at home. As with all networks, on the Internet you can do more than just send and receive information. Any computer on the Internet can share resources with other computers via the network. Here are some of the resources that users commonly share across a network:

- ✔ Printers
- ✔ Disk drives and files
- ✔ Modems
- ✔ Backup tape or cartridge devices (such as Iomega Jaz or Zip drives)
- ✔ Company databases

One of the main reasons people started connecting personal computers with networks was to share printers. In a network, all the computers in an office can use the same printer. The time and money that network-printer sharing save, more than pays for the cost of the network.

Only recently, however, did people become aware that their networks were capable of doing much more than just sharing printers. Networks can also be used to share disk drives, company databases, modems, backup tapes, and (most recently) a single dedicated connection to the Internet.

A computer that provides resources (such as a database or a printer) to other computers over a network is said to be providing a network *service* and is often referred to as a *server*. The computers that use the services of a server are called *clients*. The idea that clients and servers work together to accomplish things that neither could do alone is an important technical feature of computer use on the Internet. This approach to computer networking has proven to be so valuable that it has been given a special technical term: *client/server computing*.

All the shared devices or software services that server computers provide on a network must have unique names so that client computers can refer to them without ambiguity. A variety of methods are used to give unique names to network services, but the one that has gained the most popularity is the now-common *URL* (Uniform Resource Locator) for identifying services on the Internet.

If you build a computer network of your own and connect it to the Internet, every machine and every device on your network can provide services. At the same time, each computer can also be a client, using the services that are available on the network. Your computer systems may not be powerful supercomputers, but that doesn't matter much on the Internet. Even personal computers can provide sophisticated services, ranging from running Web server software and providing Web pages to clients all the way up to serving the commerce infrastructure of a business.

Which Way to Go?

You can follow one of four basic approaches to establish an Internet site:

- ✔ Build your own Internet site from scratch
- ✔ Use an ISP
- ✔ Lease a virtual server
- ✔ Lease a dedicated server

Each approach has its own benefits and drawbacks. If you're a real do-it-yourself type with very deep pockets, go with option one. The other three all give you various levels of compromise between the freedom (and drudgery) of true hands-on operation and the deeply fulfilling task of finding out how to cope with bureaucracy.

Connecting with your inner gadget freak

Setting up your own Internet site has distinct advantages. For one, the only way to have complete control of the technology that your Internet site uses is to set up everything yourself. If anything goes wrong with your Internet site's hardware or software, you can experience the joy of dropping everything else you're doing and fixing the problem yourself. If you want to use a new hardware or software technology, you can personally discover the irony of the word *compatible*.

If you're going to take this route, you need a high-speed Internet connection. This type of connection costs a lot more than the low-speed dial-up telephone line that Internet users generally use for Internet access. But, as a site builder, your purpose on the Internet is different than that of a user. Your site provides resources for other people to use (many people, we hope), and requires dedicated, high-speed Internet access to accommodate all your users around the clock. Of course, you and everyone in your organization have dedicated high-speed Internet access as well. Therefore, it is both a drawback because it costs more and a benefit because you and all the other members of your company can surf the Net at high speed.

Running your own dedicated connection to the Internet enables you to experiment with new and interesting technologies. Ultimately, you must decide whether your plans for your Internet site justify the expense for a dedicated connection. If the price of a dedicated connection falls (as we think that it must over the next few years), this decision is easier to make. Several industries are working to give everyone, everywhere a dedicated Internet connection known as an *Internet dial tone*. They recognize how important it is for anyone to be able to use data-communications technology with the same freedom and flexibility that people now use the telephone.

Why own when you can rent?

There's an alternative method for setting up an Internet site: renting services from an Internet service provider. Creating a Web site by using a Web-publishing service provider is always less expensive than setting up an Internet site and running your own Web server software. If you don't build your Web site yourself, you may sacrifice the freedom to choose the technology that you could use to build the site. Unless you have some really strange requirements, however, any of the major Web server software products will do just fine, and you can bet the farm that any ISP worth its salt is using one of them.

The real kicker here is that even if you build your own site on your own turf with your own gear and software, you'll have to go through an ISP anyway. That dedicated high-speed connection that you're paying a fortune for doesn't run out through your wall and disappear. It's connected to the Internet, right? Guess where? An ISP. Don't let 'em fool you even if they call themselves by some other fancy name. (Even ISPs have ISPs that provide *their* connections.)

ISPs can provide you with everything you can do on your own, from Web presence to anonymous FTP directories. They can, but they may not want to. The reason for this is that two types of ISPs exist. You can call them *incoming* ISPs and *outgoing* ISPs.

Your typical ISP — the one you use for your personal connection from home and your private e-mail account, the one whose system you run your Web browser through — is an outgoing ISP. That is, the ISP's income depends on local users dialing up and surfing the Web, sending e-mail, and so on. Each person uses a very small amount of the ISP's resources. It takes at least a thousand users for outgoing ISPs to break even. Although they do provide their users with space for Web sites and other needs, and are even willing to accept a commercial site on their equipment (for an extra fee), *they do not want your site to be a success.* This is not because they are evil trolls who are out to get you; it's because a successful site brings a lot of incoming traffic that ties up lots more resources than a casual user does. The result for the ISP is either higher costs or degraded service, and they don't want to deal with either.

Most ISPs also limit the types of programs you can run on their machines or require that you submit the program to their own staff for approval — for good reason. If you create a program that has bugs and ultimately crashes, it could disable an ISP's entire machine, interrupting Internet service for many people. It is also possible that an improperly written program could cause a serious security problem, allowing unscrupulous people to gain control of their system. Although the ISPs have good and justifiable reasons for these limitations, they can be devastatingly restrictive to your site-building effort. For example, if you are developing or modifying a CGI program (see Chapter 10) using Windows, but your site is on a machine using UNIX, you'll want to test the program on the UNIX box, doubtlessly tweaking and nudging it several times before you're finally satisfied with it. If you have to submit the program for approval every time you make a minor change and then wait until one of the ISP's programmers looks it over — and you may have to pay for each analysis, too — it'll take forever to do the simplest thing.

Make sure to verify that you have the capability to run programs using the Common Gateway Interface (CGI) — it's called *CGI access* — before you sign on with an ISP. Without it, your site will be extremely limited. Thousands of free or low cost CGI programs are available that can add lots of functionality to your site. You can also develop your own and sell them to other site builders.

The best of both worlds

The other type of ISP, the *incoming* variety, doesn't operate in the same way as the outgoing kind. They don't have any local users; all they do is support sites. They understand that this means lots of incoming traffic, but they don't mind because it's what they do for a living. Because they don't have to cater to the needs of local dial-up traffic, they want to help you win.

Usually, the incoming ISP offers *virtual servers,* which are functionally identical to having your own computer system with a dedicated connection. The servers are called *virtual* because they use software that fools the Internet into thinking that a single computer is several different ones. This lets the ISP put many different sites on one system, which saves everybody money. Your site, however, is separate from all the others on their system, just as if it were on a separate, dedicated computer. You have a unique domain name (see Chapter 3). You can set up and run whatever programs you want, and twiddle and tweak them to your heart's desire. The ISP usually even helps you out for free, unless you want something complicated. Then, of course, as with any other ISP, you have to pay for the work.

Virtual servers come in a variety of sizes and prices. In addition to the Web server, they include e-mail boxes, autoresponders, and (usually) mailing list software (see Chapter 8), as well as FTP servers. Some ISPs give you a small number of e-mail boxes to start with and then charge you more for extra mailboxes; others have an unlimited number of mailboxes. You can start out small and cheap and get more storage space as you need it. Some ISPs offer virtual servers with as small as 5MB (megabytes) of storage space, which is plenty for a simple Web site. Increasing your storage space usually costs only about a half a buck to a buck extra per megabyte a month. Chapter 4 goes into more detail on using virtual servers.

Because virtual servers share a high-speed line, they have one problem: They can comfortably handle only about 30,000 visitors per day to your site. If you need to handle more than that, look into a dedicated server. A dedicated server is an entire computer that has nothing but your site on it. Unlike virtual servers, it has its own dedicated high-speed line, which it does not share with any other sites, so that it can handle just about any load you can throw at it.

Both virtual and dedicated servers are rented on a monthly basis, and while you have full control over them, the ISP takes care of all the drudgery, such as maintenance and backups, thus freeing you for more creative work. The ISP also bears the responsibility and expense of upgrading the equipment and software as new technological developments affect the Internet.

You can administer a virtual or dedicated server anywhere in the world, regardless of where you are located. All you need is local Internet access.

If you'd like to actually own the equipment, some ISPs offer a *co-location service,* in which you buy a computer that you want to connect to the Internet and then locate it physically at the office of the ISP. The ISP can usually get the equipment for you at a substantial discount, so make sure that you discuss this with them before purchasing it on your own. With this type of service, the computer has a dedicated and fast Internet connection at a low monthly rate, and you own and control the computer. The only drawbacks are that someone has to drive to the remote site to perform maintenance or fix a hardware failure, and you are responsible for your own upgrades. Also, unlike the virtual server option, you must deal with a local ISP.

Linking Computers

The Internet is just a large network of computer networks. Anyone can build a computer network easily and quickly without spending a great deal of money. The most popular type of local computer network today is the *Ethernet* network. Installing an Ethernet network involves installing an Ethernet adapter in each computer that's part of your Internet site (see Appendix B) as well as connecting all your computers with network cable so that they can communicate by using the Ethernet protocol.

Building a computer network — even a small one in your home — opens new doors. Many products just plug into your Ethernet network and go to work for you. Printers, data-storage devices, CD-ROM jukeboxes, modems, fax systems, Internet servers, and many other products don't require you to open your computer to install new hardware; instead, you just plug the equipment into the network and start using it. After your network is connected to the Internet, you can even use the equipment from a remote location.

To take advantage of this exciting new area of technology (and to set up your own Internet site), prepare each of your computers to work on a network as described in Appendix B and then use the following guidelines to link the computers in a typical Ethernet network:

✔ You need a piece of hardware called a *network hub,* which you can buy at most computer stores. You need to purchase a network hub that matches the network adapters you installed. If you installed network adapters that have transfer rates (throughput) of 10 Mbps (megabits per second), you need a 10 Mbps hub. Some network adapters (called *Fast Ethernet adapters*) and hubs also operate at speeds of 100 Mbps, but they cost more the 10 Mbps versions. You'll need to decide whether speed or economy is your most important factor.

✔ You need to purchase network cabling. The most commonly used type of cabling for Ethernet networks is *unshielded twisted-pair (UTP) cable,* or twisted-pair cable for short. The official designation is *10baseT* and *100baseT* for 10 Mbps and 100 Mbps networks, respectively. Twisted-pair cable comes in different thicknesses, or *categories.* The most popular thickness is Category 5 (usually called Cat 5). Some adapters and hubs use an alternative type of cabling known as *thin coaxial.* Some network adapters enable you to use either type of cabling, but 10baseT and now 100baseT are by far the most common. Basically, unless you have to connect dozens of computers or have to connect computers on opposite sides of major sports stadiums, go with twisted-pair cable.

✔ Connect the cables from the network adapter in each computer to the network hub.

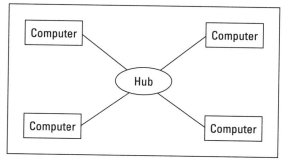

Figure 2-1:
A typical
Ethernet
network.

A feature of most hubs is a status light above each connector. If the connection is made to a computer with a network adapter and the computer is turned on, the status light glows. This feature helps you troubleshoot network problems. If the light is not glowing, you can look for a problem with the physical connection between the network hub and the network adapter. If this connection is okay, the network adapter's connection with the computer may be a problem (the card may not be seated correctly in the card slot), or the network adapter may be defective.

If you create networks that have considerable distance between the computers and the hub, refer to your hub's manual for the maximum distance possible between computer and hub. If you need to exceed that distance, you can purchase an additional piece of hardware known as a *network repeater*. A network repeater simply amplifies the signal it receives from a computer and passes that signal farther down the network.

For more detail on using networks, refer to *Networking For Dummies,* 3rd Edition, by Doug Lowe (published by IDG Books Worldwide, Inc.).

Chapter 3
What's in a Name?

*O*ne of the first things a child learns is her name — and then she bestows names on everything important to her. Favorite toys have names. Pets have names. And now, computers have names, too. In this chapter, you find out why giving your Internet site a name (called a *domain name*) is important and how to apply for one.

Every computer connected to the Internet has a unique numerical address, called the *IP address*. This addressing scheme enables computers to easily identify and communicate with each other. But we're not computers, and humans prefer names to numbers. You can give a name, such as Buzz or InfoDroid or Walnut, to any computer connected to a network. Your computer's name is known as its *host name*.

Network software, such as a Web browser, enables a user to identify a computer by using the computer's name instead of its IP address. For instance, *dummies.com* is the host name for the computer at IP address 206.80.51.139. Each computer still has an IP address that another computer must use to communicate with it via the network, but people don't need to worry about translating computer names into IP addresses.

The Domain Name System in a Nutshell

Just as a king and queen manage a royal domain, a network server that keeps track of all the host names and IP addresses for a network also is said to manage a domain. A network domain may consist of a single network or several networks within an organization. And, just as in those days of old when each ruler's domain had a name, each network domain has its own name, which is known, naturally enough, as a *domain name*.

You refer to an individual computer by its host name. You refer to an entire network by its domain name. To refer to an individual computer within a domain, you use its host name followed by its domain name; that combination is called its fully-qualified domain name. (Call it the FQDN if you want to amaze your friends with your network savvy.)

Suppose, for example, that you name a computer Bruin and that your domain name is `football.com`. The fully-qualified domain name of the host computer, therefore, would appear as follows:

```
bruin.football.com
```

In the early days of the Internet (at the time called *ArpaNet*), special text files called *host files* tracked all computer host names. Any computer connected to the Internet needed a host file that listed every other computer on the network by name. In the 1970s, only a few hundred computers were connected to the Internet, so maintaining a host file wasn't a huge chore. As the number of computers connected to the Internet began to grow rapidly, however, the problems inherent in using the host file system for keeping track of host names quickly became evident. A new system was devised, known as the *domain name system,* or *DNS.*

DNS is a method of managing domain names on the Internet. DNS groups hosts into a *hierarchy of authority* (which is actually a hierarchy of responsibility, as you find in most corporations), enabling the distribution of addresses and host information to special name databases around the globe. The software that computers use to manage these databases, which map IP addresses to domain names, is known as a *name server.*

Computers all across the Internet employ name servers, although not every computer has such a program installed. Computers contact name servers while looking up domain names. The name servers, which distribute domain-name information among themselves, direct the request for information to the name server designated as responsible for keeping track of a particular domain name-IP address.

The domain name hierarchy begins with a *root domain.* In Figure 3-1, the root domain appears at the top of the hierarchy tree. Similar to the root directory of a file system (much like the one on your hard drive), the root domain appears in the hierarchy represented as a backslash. Domains that appear directly beneath the root domain are known as *top-level domains.* The top-level domains include the COM, EDU, NET, MIL, GOV, ORG, and two-letter country domains, such as US. An organization known as the *InterNIC* (Internet Network Information Center) is responsible for managing the root domain and several of the top-level domains. *Domain registries* manage the other top-level domains. Table 3-1 lists the major top-level domains, including a few country domains. More than 250 different country domains currently exist.

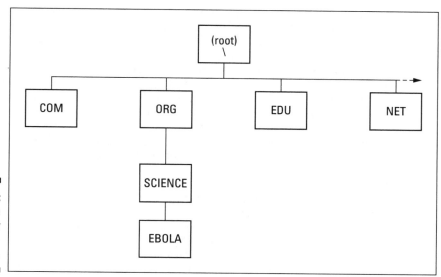

Figure 3-1:
The domain
hierarchy
for ebola.
science.org.

Table 3-1   Some Top-Level Domains and Their Descriptions

Top-Level Domain	Description
COM	Commercial organizations
EDU	Educational institutions
ORG	Nonprofit organizations
MIL	Military agencies for the United States
GOV	Government agencies for the United States
NET	Networks that provide Internet access or other services
AU	Australia
CA	Canada
IL	Israel
IN	India
US	United States
CA.US	California, United States (Labels exist for all 50 states.)

Don't confuse the two-letter country code domain for Canada with the
second-level domain for the state of California. Telling them apart is easy.
The US country code (US) domain name always follows the letters CA if the
latter stand for California.

Domain registries are responsible for knowing where the primary name servers are for all domains within a top-level domain. (Registrars are the people who manage these registries.) Primary name servers are sometimes called *authoritative name servers* because these servers have the authority and responsibility for mapping host names to IP addresses for every computer within a particular domain. If a computer on the network needs to know what the IP address is for a host in a domain, that computer may contact the primary name server for the domain to ask for the address. If the primary name server were the only computer in the world that could answer such a query, however, significant bottlenecks and lots of unnecessary network traffic would result whenever one computer wanted to communicate with another.

Instead, every name server around the world automatically keeps a copy of the host name and IP address information it obtains from another name server. So if the primary name server for a domain stops functioning for a while, many Internet users don't even notice the interruption. Additionally, each domain has an official *secondary name server* that maintains complete copies of the database from the primary server. If you add a new domain to a top-level domain, the domain registry for that top-level domain adds an entry to its database for the primary name server and for all the secondary name servers for the new domain.

Remember that computers know how to deliver information only to IP addresses — not to domain names. For example, Aardvark.com contacts the local name server and asks it to provide the IP address associated with Zebra.com. If the local name server knows that information, the server immediately responds by providing the IP address. If the local name server can't resolve the name Zebra.com to an IP address, it must find the name server that can resolve the domain name. This process is a little like playing the card game Fish. One player asks another for a certain card. If the player has the requested card, he or she hands the card over to the requesting player; if not, the player says, "Go fish!" The player then starts searching for the necessary card.

The local name server then contacts a different name server, one that knows about a greater number of domains. If that name server doesn't know the answer, it bumps the request up to the next level until, finally, the primary name server is consulted if necessary. The primary name server is the ultimate authority for a domain and can normally map the domain name to the IP address for any host within the domain. If the local name server contacts the primary name server and the latter can't provide an IP address for a host name, the local server considers that answer *authoritative* and the host name invalid. After receiving an authoritative answer that a host does not exist, the local name server no longer attempts to contact other name servers.

In other words, the authoritative primary name server has the last word. Either it returns an IP address after another name server asks about a host in its domain, or it indicates that the host does not exist. Because the primary server has the last word, network software knows that asking any other name servers about the host is pointless. If the primary name server can return a valid address, the IP address passes back through the name servers until it finally returns to Aardvark.com, which uses the IP address to communicate with Zebra.com.

The top-level domain COM contains many domains, such as Zebra.com, which in turn can contain many other domains, called *subdomains*. Zebra.com may be the network server of an office in Africa, for example, which may include a subdomain such as Corporate.Zebra.com, whereas the Zebra.com marketing department in New York may use something such as Marketing.Zebra.com. Each of these example subdomains can contain many hosts, including President.Corporate.Zebra.com to identify the president's computer in Africa.

Registering Your Own Domain Name

Every domain name in the entire world is unique. Some domain names may be similar to one another, but no two domain names are identical. The first step on the road to having your own domain name is to find the registrar who manages the registry that will contain your domain name. (You find more information on this point in the following section.) The InterNIC (at http://rs.internic.net) is the primary registrar. You can find contact information for all other registrars on this site.

The next step is the fun one: coming up with a domain name. In choosing a domain name, you should search the registrar's database to determine whether the domain name you want is already in use. Most registrars provide a mechanism for searching their databases, and some even have a Web query form like the one Internic provides at http://www.rs.internic.net/cgi-bin/whois.

Work up several variations on your domain name before you get started. That way, if the one you want most is taken, you have something to fall back on. You probably won't have too much trouble if you want a domain name like schnitzelfrugel.com, but if you're going to base your domain name on some common and obvious term such as *money* or *net* or *web,* you'll have to struggle to come up with anything that isn't already in use.

Choosing a domain registry

The InterNIC manages the COM, EDU, ORG, GOV, and NET top-level domains. The InterNIC thus keeps track of any information about these domains (all that end with .com, .edu, .org, .gov, and .net), including contact information and primary and secondary (backup) name servers. Oddly, however, InterNIC and other domain registries aren't responsible for knowing a domain's IP addresses. Instead, the domain registry keeps track of the name servers and the people responsible for knowing the IP addresses that a domain uses. Knowing this fact, you can better understand that one of the steps in applying for a domain name is setting up primary and secondary name servers for the new domain. If you're using someone else's service, such as an ISP or virtual server provider, the name servers will already be in place and you can get the necessary information from them. Otherwise, you'll have to set up the name servers yourself. You then need to provide the IP address of each name server for your new domain at the time you apply to a domain registry. This procedure may seem a little confusing. Suppose that your administrative assistant is the only one who knows the phone number that someone can reach you on at any one time. The admin assistant becomes like your name server. Anyone who wants to contact you by phone first must contact your admin assistant to retrieve the phone number where you are. As you change numbers, your admin assistant (who keeps track of these things) gives out a new phone number. So anyone who wants to contact you needs to keep track only of your admin assistant's phone number. The admin assistant is then responsible for keeping track of the individual whereabouts of the people for whom the assistant is responsible.

Before you can begin the process of choosing and obtaining a domain name, you need to know where to register, as well as what rules the registrar may have for creating and registering domain names. Each country has its own domain registrar. Table 3-2, later in this chapter, lists some countries, their country codes, and contact information.

To determine which organization you need to contact to register a domain name, consider the following points:

✔ If you're in the United States and you want a domain name that ends in COM, EDU, ORG, GOV, or NET, contact InterNIC directly.

✔ If you're in the United States and want a domain name that ends with US, you need to contact the .US Domain Registry.

✔ If you're outside the United States, you need to contact the registry for your country. In this chapter, we provide registration information for Canada and many other countries.

✔ If you're a U.S. military organization, contact the Department of Defense.

In this chapter, we mainly offer details on registering a domain name with the InterNIC. The InterNIC has the responsibility of managing the root domain and the NET, COM, EDU, ORG, and GOV top-level domains. You generally find, however, that most registrars in the world require similar information and require its submission using a template similar to the InterNIC's template. Fees and regulations vary with each registrar. Contact the registrars directly for more information. (We include contact information in Table 3-2.)

You can search the InterNIC database by using the *Whois utility.* To access a Whois utility, you can telnet to `rs.internic.net` and use the Whois utility on that site as follows:

1. **In Windows 95 or Windows NT, choose Start⇨Run.**

   The Run dialog box appears.

2. **In the Open text box, type** telnet.

3. **Click OK.**

   The telnet program window then appears.

4. **Choose Connect⇨Remote System.**

   The Connect dialog box appears.

5. **In the Host Name text box, type** rs.internic.net.

6. **Click the Connect button.**

   You get a UNIX prompt that looks like this:

   ```
   InterNIC >.
   ```

Domain levels

You can register only secondary-level domain names, such as *mysite*.com with the InterNIC. The registrar doesn't create new top-level domains, such as COM or EDU, for you. That's the job of the *Internet Engineering Task Force* (IETF). Many new top-level domains are currently under consideration. One of the interesting top-level domains in the works is NUM, for using phone numbers as domain names (for example, 6195551212.NUM). For more information on proposals to the IETF for new top-level domains, you can contact the IETF Web site at the following URL:

`http://www.ietf.org/`

Whether you connect to the InterNIC by using telnet or you have access to a UNIX machine connected to the Internet, use the built-in Whois utility by typing the following command:

```
whois mydomain.com
```

Follow the command, **whois**, with the name of the domain name that interests you. This name could be the domain name you're interested in registering or any domain name about which you'd like more information. We use this tool to contact people who manage other domains. Most recently, we used it to track down someone sending malicious e-mail. If you're using telnet, you can now close the telnet window by choosing Connect⇨Exit from the telnet menu bar.

If you'd rather do it the easy way, you can always use the World Wide Web Whois utility provided by InterNIC at the following address:

```
http://rs.internic.net/cgi-bin/whois
```

The Whois Web page has a single field in which you enter the domain name you want to register. If Whois finds a match for a domain name, the display tells you that information. If no one has that name currently registered, the Whois program returns a NO MATCH message. A search on toymouse.com, for example, returns the following message:

```
No match for "TOYMOUSE.COM".
```

If you want to see a tutorial on using the InterNIC Whois Web interface, you can access it at

```
http://rs.internic.net/tools/whois.html
```

Note: Not finding a match in the InterNIC domain database is not a guarantee that your desired domain name is available. A certain name may not appear for several reasons. Perhaps the name is already applied for but not yet activated. Or the name may be in dispute and therefore removed from the database until the dispute is settled.

Becoming a domain contact

Only official contacts may change or remove a domain name. The InterNIC is cautious about enabling just anyone to request domain name changes. For this reason, the registry has devised a foolproof security system, known as *Guardian.* You're not required to use Guardian to apply for and maintain your domain name, but for security reasons, we highly recommend that you do. The upcoming section "The InterNIC Guardian" describes how to use Guardian for registering yourself as a contact.

Each domain has the following three kinds of contacts:

- **Administrative contact.** The administrative contact is the official representative of an organization. These contacts don't need to have technical knowledge; they just must to be able to answer questions about the organization's use of the domain name.

- **Billing contact.** Quite simply, the billing contact gets the bill. Registering domain names with the InterNIC involves paying an annual registration fee. The billing contact is responsible for seeing that the fees are paid.

- **Technical contact.** The technical contact is usually the person who manages the primary name server for your domain. Often, this contact is actually your Internet service provider. If your organization runs its own name server, however, whoever manages this software is probably the technical contact.

If you are the person in charge, pay the bills, and manage your company name server, you can be any or all three of these contacts.

You and your NIC handle

The InterNIC gives contacts a special identification number, known as an *NIC handle*. This situation is a little like that of CB radio, where everyone has a handle. ("This is the Boll Weevil. What's your 20, good buddy?") Unfortunately, NIC handles aren't quite as fanciful and fun as CB handles.

The InterNIC assigns you an NIC handle that consists of your first and last initials and a sequential number. The sequential number follows the last person to register as a contact who had your initials. If you do a Whois search on the name Coombs, for example, you see that Ted Coombs has an NIC handle of TC150. That means that Ted was the 150th person with the initials TC to get a handle. Jason Coombs, on the other hand, has an NIC handle of JC, because Jason was the first JC in the InterNIC database and therefore doesn't have a sequential number.

Registering as a contact

You can register as a contact in two ways. The simplest way, but also the least secure, is to add contact information into your application for a domain name. Registering in this fashion doesn't enable you to register your domain name in a secure fashion or to secure your entry from changes by unauthorized and devious people. A much safer choice is to register yourself as a contact before registering your domain name.

To apply as a contact or to modify existing contact information, you simply fill out a request, which you format by using a contact registration template that InterNIC provides. The simplest way is to use the Web form at

```
http://rs.internic.net/itts/handle
```

If you don't have Web access, you can download a copy of the template from the following site:

```
ftp://rs.internic.net/templates/contact-template.txt
```

If you use the FTP and e-mail approach, you must make the request in ASCII text format. In other words, you can't submit a request in Microsoft Word format or in WordPerfect format. However, most word-processing programs, including the two we just mentioned, can save files in text (TXT) format.

If you want to refer to an already completed sample template, you can download it from the following URL:

```
ftp://rs.internic.net/templates/contact-template-
examples.txt
```

If you want your contact information to remain private, you can make this request during your contact registration. The last question on the contact registration template asks whether you want your information publicly accessible.

The InterNIC offers an additional security feature to protect your domain record from accidental or nefarious changes as part of the contact registration. One question you should answer Yes to is the one that asks whether you want to receive notification of all change requests made to your domain record. This feature may keep you from scratching your head one day, wondering why the Whois lookup for your domain shows someone else's name on it.

After you complete the request, answering all the questions in the template, you must secure it in one of the ways described in the section "The InterNIC Guardian" later in this chapter. Then you can e-mail your request to the InterNIC registrar. The registrar's e-mail address is as follows:

```
hostmaster@internic.net
```

Applying to InterNIC

The instructions we offer for registering a domain name are specific to InterNIC. If you register with any other domain registry, you need to contact that registrar for more information about its registration procedures. With the exception of the Guardian security system, most domain registries use the same application template and similar application procedures.

Registering a domain name is quite simple. Prepare your application; secure it by using one of the procedures discussed in the section "The InterNIC Guardian" later in this chapter; e-mail your application — and wait. You receive notification by e-mail after your domain name is registered. This process usually takes a few days.

Registering a domain name does not give you any legal right to that name. To guarantee your right to a domain name, you must trademark the name. At the same time you perform your search to find out whether a domain name is available, you also should try to determine whether the name is trademarked. If you apply for a particular domain name, you must certify that, to the best of your knowledge, the name you want to register isn't trademarked by another person or company. If you violate someone's trademark, you could be in for an expensive legal battle. Check out `http://www.micropat.com/` for a Web-searchable trademark database.

Preparing your application

Preparing your application for a domain name is similar to registering as a contact. You must follow the registration template exactly. Of course, you can use the online form at the InterNIC Web site, and your completed registration request is e-mailed back to you, formatted correctly.

Follow these steps to prepare your application:

1. **Make sure that you've arranged for both a primary and secondary name server.**

   The InterNIC requires that you (or your service provider) have both name servers configured at the time you submit your application. If you are using an ISP or a virtual server, check with the server administrator to find out the IP addresses of the name servers.

2. **Register the administrative, billing, and technical contacts.**

   See the section "Becoming a domain contact" earlier in this chapter for details.

3. **Choose a domain name.**

   See the section "Registering Your Own Domain Name" earlier in this chapter. Make sure that you first check the registry's Whois database to ensure that the domain name you want is available.

4. **Create a text file and import the empty template or access the Web registration form.**

   You can open the template in a text editor such as Notepad or WordPad. Make changes and save the template as an ASCII text file. The alternative to this procedure is to use the Web form on the InterNIC site. You get the correctly formatted text file through e-mail. To use the Web form, go to the following URL:

```
http://rs.internic.net/cgi-bin/domain
```

Simply filling in the Web registration form doesn't complete your application for a domain name. InterNIC e-mails a completed and correctly formatted application to you. You *must* e-mail this application back to InterNIC to complete your registration process. Otherwise, you could wait forever, believing that the wheels of progress turn slowly, when actually you need to take the next step.

The InterNIC Guardian

To keep your domain name record safe from unscrupulous people or even accidental changes, InterNIC uses a system by which it accepts applications and updates only from an authenticated contact. The default method for determining whether a modification is legitimate is to simply make sure that the request comes from the e-mail address of either the technical contact or administrative contact. Guardian contact authentication gives you two more options to ensure that only authorized representatives can make changes to a company's domain record. It also enables you to specify that you should be contacted if anyone attempts to modify your domain record. To update your contact information and utilize the Guardian system, fill out the form at

```
http://rs.internic.net/itts/handle
```

The Guardian system consists of the following three contact authentication methods, also called *authorization schemes:*

✔ **Mail-from.** InterNIC checks the From field of any e-mail message sent to the registry against the From field of the e-mail message that contains the contact registration form. Be warned, however, that altering the contents of a From field *is* possible in many e-mail client programs, enabling others to pretend that they are you by doing so. This authorization scheme is the least secure and is also the default scheme used if you request no other scheme.

✔ **Crypt-password.** This authorization scheme employs a password that you encrypt by using the UNIX crypt program. (The InterNIC Web site provides a Web interface for the crypt program.) You supply your password whenever you send correspondence to InterNIC requesting changes to a domain record. This password is the one you submitted as part of the contact registration process.

✔ **PGP.** Pretty Good Privacy is a program that enables you to digitally sign any correspondence sent to InterNIC by using public-key cryptography. This scheme affords the highest degree of security and is the one we recommend.

Choose which authorization scheme you want to use by entering a choice in the AUTH-SCHEME field of any templates you submit to InterNIC.

Make sure that you remember what authorization scheme you request as part of your contact registration. This scheme is the one the InterNIC expects you to use in any future correspondence. Not using the scheme you originally selected results in the InterNIC ignoring your correspondence — and may even cause the InterNIC to send a warning message to the domain contacts, telling them that someone has tried to send correspondence using an incorrect authorization scheme. (If InterNIC doesn't send such a warning, it should.)

Paying for Your Domain Name

No such thing as a free lunch? Well, the same goes for free domain names. You must pay $50 per year to maintain a domain name with InterNIC. At the time you first register a domain name, the registry bills you for two years — $100. You don't need to pay right at the time you register, however; InterNIC generously bills you or your billing contact within a few months, and the bill is due 30 days after the invoice date. After two years, the invoice comes annually, either by postal mail or e-mail, whichever you chose when you first registered.

InterNIC accepts several payment methods. If you want to use a credit card, you can use your MasterCard, Visa, American Express, Diners Club/Carte Blanche, or Discover/NOVUS. You can pay also by check or money order. And now, you can even use First Virtual's Virtual PIN to pay your InterNIC fees. Some people feel more comfortable using a First Virtual PIN instead of entering their credit card number. For a small fee of $2 a year, you can maintain a First Virtual account. You can apply for your First Virtual PIN at the following URL:

```
http://rs.internic.net/cgi-bin/fv/apply
```

If you're a school (with an EDU label) or a government agency (with a GOV label), InterNIC picks up the tab. (The plan is that, at some time in the future, government agencies will pay their own way.) Military agencies (MIL) register by using a different service, and the U.S. Department of Defense pays all fees. If you are going to be registering tons and tons of domain names, you can set up a debit account with InterNIC.

If you're curious about the anniversary date for your domain name, you can find this information by performing a Whois search on the domain name. Remember that you receive your bill every year around the domain's anniversary. What an anniversary present!

Where does the money go?

You may be happy to know that a full 30 percent of the money you send to InterNIC goes toward building the intellectual infrastructure of the Internet. InterNIC uses the other 70 percent to support its network services. This money goes to cover the cost of staffing, hardware, software, and all normal overhead. The U.S. National Science Foundation (NSF) controls the amount of money that InterNIC can charge. Back when the NSF operated the InterNIC, domain-name registration was free. The NSF isn't in the business of operating public data networks, however, so the foundation contracted out the duties of running InterNIC to a private company, Network Services.

What happens if you don't pay

If problems arise — as they often do — make sure that you contact InterNIC as soon as possible. You're better off starting a dialog instead of ignoring the problem and letting your domain name expire. The registry's rules are stringent. You must have your payment in no later than midnight of the due date. (You find the due date on your invoice.) If you don't make that date, all contacts receive a 15-day deactivation notice, sent by e-mail and also by regular mail to the domain name user. Many times, however, the user of the domain name is not the contact person. This situation occurs mainly if Internet service providers register the domain names for their customers. If you receive one of these notices, you have 15 days to get your payment to the InterNIC. If you miss this date, the registry removes your domain name from its database.

Even if InterNIC deactivates your domain name, you haven't lost the name yet. You have an additional 60 days to get your money to InterNIC to reactivate your domain name. After 60 days, the registry returns your (former) domain name to the pool of available domain names for someone else to snatch up.

Accessing your account information

What good would having a computer connected to the Internet be if you couldn't check the status of your InterNIC account online? Doing so is simple enough. Contact the InterNIC's Web-tracking system by using the tracking number found in your latest correspondence from the registry.

You can find the Web-based tracking system at the following URL:

```
http://rs.internic.net/cgi-bin/finger
```

If you have trouble using the Web form, don't know your tracking number, or need additional information not found online, you may send an e-mail requesting additional information to mailto:billing@internic.net.

Sending in your payment

When paying your InterNIC invoice, send your payment to the following address:

Network Solutions, Inc.
P.O. Box 17305
Baltimore, MD 21297-0525
USA

If you're making a payment that's not from an invoice, you need to use a different P.O. box number and zip code, as follows:

Network Solutions, Inc.
P.O. Box 17304
Baltimore, MD 21297-0524
USA

If you're paying by credit card, you can save the stamp and just call the phone number on your invoice. The phone number works 24 hours a day, 7 days a week. It's automated, and unlike most such systems, it's easy to use and well designed. You just follow the instructions and punch in the requested information on your telephone keypad. When you're finished, you'll receive an approval code. Make sure to write that code down! It's your only proof that you paid your bill if anything goes wrong. We've never known anything to go wrong, but it's a good idea to cover your sitzfleisch just in case.

Making Changes to Your Domain

Things change. That's both the nature of life and, possibly, of your Internet domain name or company information. You need to update your domain name record with the InterNIC whenever you change name servers, corporate information, or contact information. (You may wonder why you'd ever want to change name servers. Because Internet service providers run most name servers, you're likely to need to change name servers if you ever change Internet service providers.)

To minimize your amount of downtime in making such server changes, coordinate the change in your name server carefully between your existing name service provider and the new name service provider.

You're unlikely to need to change information very often, but if you do, you must make all changes to your domain name record by using a template similar to the one you use to register your domain name.

Registering a US domain

The .US Domain Registry administers the .US Domain Registration Services at the Information Sciences Institute of the University of Southern California (USC), under the Internet Assigned Numbers Authority (IANA). You can find its Web site at the following URL:

```
http://www.isi.edu/in-notes/usdnr/
```

The US domain is a top-level domain the same as that of any other country domain in the InterNIC registry. Using the US domain is a little different than using a COM or an ORG domain. The US domain uses second- and third-level domains. The last row of Table 3-1, earlier in this chapter, shows an example of a second-level domain that the US domain uses. Second-level domains consist primarily of two-letter state labels, such as TX for Texas or CA for California. In addition to states, the second-level domain can be FED, STATE, K12, LIB, CC, TEC, GEN, DST, COG, MUS, ISA, and NSN. Figure 3-2 illustrates part of the US domain hierarchy.

The third-level domain specifies a specific locality. IBM, for example, maintains offices all across the United States. You can easily determine which office uses which domain name by its second- and third-level domains. IBM.Armonk.NY.US, for example, could be the domain name for the IBM Armonk, New York, office. The locality can also be the name of a county or a city. If a domain name uses a county name, a fourth-level domain label, CO, precedes the county name. The label CI precedes city names. CO.SanDiego.CA.US is an example of a possible county domain name.

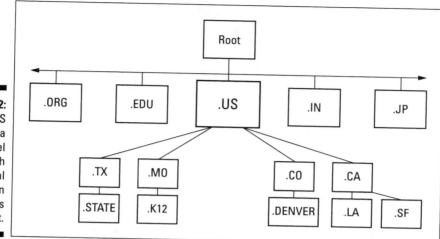

Figure 3-2:
The US domain is a top-level domain with several domain levels beneath it.

All domain names must be unique, because every domain name eventually points to a single IP address. Every computer connected to the Internet has at least one unique IP address.

Applying for a US domain name

You can request a template for applying for a US domain by sending an e-mail request to the US Domain Registrar at the following address: us-domain@isi.edu. You're likely also to be applying for a domain name within a specific locality, also known as a *delegated branch*. You need to look up the delegated branch contact information by pointing your Web browser to the following URL:

```
http://www.isi.edu/in-notes/us-domain-delegated.txt
```

This Web page contains contact information for every single delegated branch in existence. If you apply for a location that's not currently delegated, you can fill in the Web page form found at the following address:

```
http://www.isi.edu/cgi-bin/usdomreg/template.pl
```

You can also find a text version of the template on the US domain's home page.

Currently, the US domain administrator charges no fee for delegating a locality or other branch of the US domain at that level.

Paying for a US domain name

The delegated branch managers determine the amount of the registration fee. Most of them currently do not charge for this service. If the branch in which you're interested does charge, the fee is usually nominal. Regulations don't prohibit a branch manager from charging a fee — requiring only that the fee is fair and applies equally to all customers.

If you apply for a locality-level domain, you may be relieved to know that the US domain registrar does not currently charge a fee for its services.

Registering a Canadian domain name

CA is the two-letter country code for Canada. The .CA Domain Committee and the University of British Columbia administer the CA domain. The process for applying for a domain name in Canada is a little different than applying through the InterNIC or the US domain registrar.

The structure of the CA domain is similar to the that of US domain. Figure 3-3 shows the CA domain as a top-level domain, with all the other domain levels beneath it.

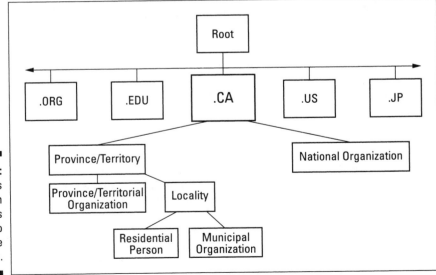

Figure 3-3:
Canada's
CA domain
structure is
similar to
that of the
US domain.

Applying for a CA domain name

When applying for a CA domain name, make sure that the domain name you want to register is available. The .CA Domain Registrar maintains a list of domain names in Gopherspace. (Gopher is an Internet information-publishing system similar to the WWW.) Contact the following URL in your Web browser to search the list of domain names already in use:

```
gopher://nstn.ns.ca:7006/7
```

In applying for a Canadian domain name, you work with a member of the domain committee who helps you with your application. The committee member then checks the application by submitting it to the following URL:

```
mailto:ca-domain-checker@relay.cdnnet.ca
```

A syntax checker looks for errors in the application. After the application is error free, it's sent along to the committee for approval.

The committee takes about a week to either approve or deny an application and may contact the applicant for further information. On approval of the application, the registry registers the domain name and the committee notifies the applicant.

The application template is located at the following URL:

```
http://www.canet.ca/canet/templates/ca-
            domain.application.template
```

The template appears with sample registration information. You simply replace the sample information with your own. Complete instructions for completing this template are online at the following URL:

```
http://www.cdnnet.ca/
```

Contacting the .CA Domain Registrar

For information regarding an application for a Canadian domain name, you can contact the .CA Domain Registrar at the following postal or e-mail address or the listed phone or fax number:

Department of Computer Science
University of British Columbia
Vancouver, BC, Canada V6T 1Z4
Tel: +1 604-822-6724
Fax: +1 604-822-5485
E-mail: ca-registrar@cdnnet.ca

Registering domain names around the world

In most countries of the world, domain registrars are available to accept your domain name registration. Some smaller countries work directly through the InterNIC or one of the larger European domain registrars.

RIPE (Réseaux IP Européens) is a European organization dedicated to the administration and technical coordination necessary for a European IP network. The organization's home page URL is as follows:

```
http://www.ripe.net/
```

The RIPE Network Coordination Centre has utilities for searching the RIPE domain name database. The organization offers a Web-based Whois utility as well as an interface to WAIS (Wide Area Information Service). The RIPE Network Coordination Centre does not register domain names. You must apply with the particular country's domain registrar. Table 3-2 lists contact information for many of the countries of the world.

Table 3-2	Domain Registrar Contact Information
Country	*Contact Information*
AT — AUSTRIA	mailto:domain-admin@univie.ac.at
BE — BELGIUM	http://www.dns.be
BG — BULGARIA	http://www.digsys.bg/bg-nic/
CZ — CZECH REPUBLIC	mailto:ors@eunet.cz
DK — DENMARK	http://www.nic.dk/
FO — FAROE ISLANDS	http://www.nic.fo/
FR — FRANCE	http://www.nic.fr/
GA — GABON	mailto:dfk@ripe.net
DE — GERMANY	mailto:dolderer@nic.de
GR — GREECE	mailto:pr@forthnet.gr
GL — GREENLAND	http://www.nic.gl/
HU — HUNGARY	mailto:hostmaster@nic.hu
IS — ICELAND	mailto:hjons@isnet.is
IE — IRELAND	mailto:hostmaster@ucd.ie
IL — ISRAEL	http://www.isoc.org.il/

Country	Contact Information
IT — ITALY	http://www.nis.garr.it/netdoc/TLD-RA/
JO — JORDAN	http://www.nic.gov.jo/
LV — LATVIA	http://www.nic.lv
LI — LIECHTENSTEIN	mailto:huber@switch.ch
LT — LITHUANIA	mailto:daiva@sc-uni.ktu.lt
LU — LUXEMBOURG	http://www.dns.lu/
MD — MOLDOVA	mailto:domain-admin@roearn.ici.ro
MC — MONACO	mailto:noc@rain.fr
NL — NETHERLANDS	mailto:hostmaster@cwi.nl
NO — NORWAY	mailto:hostmaster@uninett.no
PL — POLAND	http://www.nask.pl/
PT — PORTUGAL	http://ww.dns.pt/dns/
RO — ROMANIA	http://www.rnc.ro/
RU — RUSSIAN FEDERATION	http://www.ripn.net/
SM — SAN MARINO	mailto:lvianello@intelcom.sm
SK — SLOVAKIA (Slovak Republic)	http://www.eunet.sk/sk-nic/
ES — SPAIN	http://www.nic.es/whois
SE — SWEDEN	mailto:ber@sunet.se
CH — SWITZERLAND	mailto:schneider@switch.ch
TN — TUNISIA	mailto:hostmaster@Tunisia.EU.net
TR — TURKEY	mailto:hostmaster@knidos. cc.metu.edu.tr
YU — YUGOSLAVIA	http://ubbg.etf.bg.ac.yu/yu-tld/

Setting Up a DNS Server

As we mention in the section "The Domain Name System in a Nutshell" earlier in the chapter, most organizations depend on their Internet service providers to maintain a DNS server and provide domain name service to the organization. Some advantages to running your own DNS server do exist, however. The two main reasons to do so are for greater flexibility and lower cost.

If you are not going to set up your own complete, independent network with high-speed lines, routers and the like, you can skip this section.

Running your own DNS server enables you to maintain complete control over your domain names. This situation is known as *managing your domain name space* or, more commonly, as *managing a zone.* When you're ready to register a domain name, you can quickly add the domain name to your DNS server (which you must do before registration). This way, you can avoid the hassle and wait of having your ISP add a domain name to its own DNS server. But with a halfway decent ISP, the wait shouldn't be over 24 hours. Unless you're routinely in a tremendous hurry, this is fast enough.

Most ISPs charge a monthly fee for managing a domain name (even though the word *managing* is a bit of an overstatement). The ISP performs no additional work on a monthly basis to maintain a domain name in its DNS database; once the name is in there, it's in there. The only time they have to do anything about it is if you change to another ISP. Ironically, this is the one time they won't charge you. Many ISPs charge per domain name. If your organization maintains several domain names, monthly fees can become costly. Maintaining your own DNS server enables you to avoid any additional charges beyond possible annual fees to a domain name registrar such as the InterNIC.

What is a DNS server?

The first section of this chapter, "The Domain Name System in a Nutshell," gives you a detailed overview of what a domain name is and how name servers work to map domain names to IP addresses. The heart of the DNS service is the *DNS server,* or simply the *name server.*

Name servers are specialized databases of zone information. Name server databases contain records, known as *resource records,* that specify many different types of domain information. Table 3-3 lists most currently used resource record types and a brief description of each one.

Table 3-3	Resource Record Types
Record Type	*Description*
AA host	Address.
AFSDB	Special name service specifier for the Andrew File System.
CNAME	Canonical name for an alias.
HINFO	Text string specifying the operating system and CPU type for a particular domain name.

Record Type	Description
ISDN	Direct dial-in ISDN number for a given domain name.
MB	Mailbox domain name.
MG	Member of a mail group.
MINFO	Domain name specifying a mailbox responsible for a mailing list and a mailbox responsible for receiving error messages.
MR	Domain name that specifies the new name of a renamed mailbox.
MX	Domain name of a host serving as a mail exchange.
NS	Domain name of the authoritative name server.
NULL	Null resource record. (Nothing is in this record.)
PTR	Pointer domain name. PTR points to some domain name within the domain name space.
RP	Domain name that specifies the mailbox of a responsible person. You can also query related TXT records by specifying the domain containing the TXT resource records.
RT	Intermediate domain names to reach a host, with an integer specifying the priority.
SOA	Start of Authority record, which is a complex record specifying the server name of the data source for this zone, the mailbox of the person responsible for the zone, the version number of this copy of the zone information, the refresh rate, retry rate, expiration date, and the minimum Time to Live (TTL).
TXT	Text comment.
WKS	Address of a Well-Known Service.
X.25	PSDN (Public Switched Data Network) address.

Other databases share the information of a zone database. This sharing of information is what makes the DNS system distributed. One DNS server shares its zone information with every other DNS server. The capability of a DNS server to query another's zone database determines the method the databases and servers use in sharing this information. You can see from Table 3-3 that a DNS server's database can contain all types of information, including other name servers, names of persons responsible for the databases, mail exchangers, and, of course, the IP addresses of hosts within the server's domain space (zone).

Configuring a DNS server

If you use Windows NT Server, you can access a DNS server that's already installed in your operating system. To do so, click the Start button and choose Programs➪Administrative Tools (Common)➪DNS Manager from the menus that appear. This sequence starts the Domain Name Service Manager (DNS Manager), as shown in Figure 3-4.

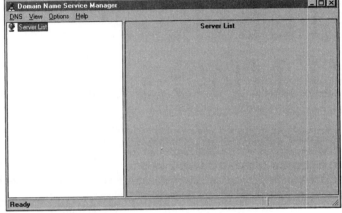

Figure 3-4:
You use the DNS Manager to configure the name server.

In the DNS Manager, choose DNS➪New Server from the menu bar to open the Add DNS Server dialog box. Then enter the Name or IP address of the DNS server in the appropriate text box in this dialog box. Click OK.

If you see an icon with a red X through it in the Domain Name Service Manager Window, the DNS Manager was unable to connect to the DNS service on the server you specified. You can delete a server that you may have entered incorrectly by right-clicking the icon and choosing Delete from the pop-up menu that appears.

After the DNS Manager connects to your DNS server, statistics information appears in the list box on the right side of the Manager window (see Figure 3-5). At this point, you can begin setting the properties for your name server. To do so, choose DNS➪Properties from the Manager's menu bar. You see the IP address of the name server in the Server Properties dialog box. To set the DNS server's properties, follow these steps:

1. **In the Server Properties dialog box, select the Interfaces tab.**

2. **Type the IP address of the name server you're adding in the text box.**

3. **Click the Add button.**

   The new IP address appears in a list in the DNS Manager Window.

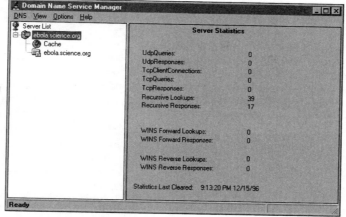

Figure 3-5:
The DNS
Manager
displays
name
server
statistics.

Adding a zone

Two types of zones are possible: *primary* and *secondary*. (Remember that a *zone* is the domain space for which a server is responsible.) If a name server has primary responsibility for a zone, that server is a *primary name server* (or *authoritative name server*).

Each zone also has at least one secondary name server that acts as a backup to the primary server. The secondary name server periodically queries the primary name server for the most current zone information. In the event that other name servers can't reach the primary name server, these servers query the secondary name server, which they expect to have the most current information. Companies running their own primary DNS servers commonly have their ISP provide secondary name service.

To add a zone for your DNS server to manage, follow these steps:

1. **Choose DNS➪New Zone from the menu bar.**

2. **Select either Primary or Secondary, depending on the type of zone you're setting up.**

   If you select Secondary, you need to add both the Zone name and Server domain name. (The following instructions are for setting up a Primary zone.)

3. **Click the Next button.**

4. **Type the name of your new zone in the Zone Name text box (see Figure 3-6).**

   The Zone name is the name of the domain. The name of our domain, for example, is `science.org`.

The future of DNS

Competing technologies to DNS do exist. Competition is good, however, because it drives stagnant systems to change and grow. What some of the competing technologies offer that is currently lacking in DNS are dynamic update capability, the capability for DNS to update itself whenever domains change, and security, where authentication enables DNS servers to be certain from whom they're receiving information.

Currently, Internet drafts are circulating that propose new standards for DNS, including a dynamic update capability. Such capability would enable domain name servers to dynamically insert and delete resource records. Because this capability brings with it a possible security hole, however, another draft proposes a way to make these updates secure by using digital signature technology. Another proposal suggests that the DNS system is an ideal vehicle for managing personal public keys across the Internet.

Note: Pressing the Tab key takes you to the Zone File text box, which the program automatically fills in for you. We recommend that you accept the default value.

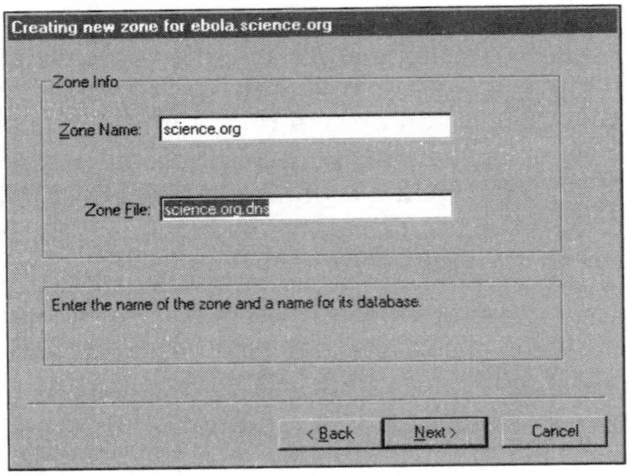

Figure 3-6:
The DNS Manager automatically creates the zone filename from the Zone Name information.

5. **Click the Next button.**

   Another dialog box appears, explaining that you've entered all the zone information.

6. **Click the Finish button.**

The DNS Administrator automatically enters all the basic resource records into the zone database. After finishing the last step in creating a new zone, the basic zone information appears on-screen for you. In Figure 3-7, you can see that three types of resource records are entered: the *start of authority* (SOA), *name server* (NS), and *address* (A) records.

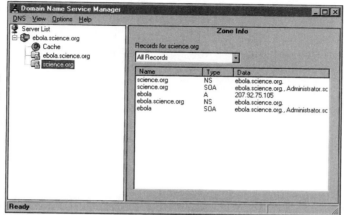

Figure 3-7: The DNS Manager's Zone Info display lists all the resource records.

You can continue updating your zone information by adding new domains, hosts, and records. Choose the corresponding menu command from the DNS menu. Enter any information for which the program prompts you. The DNS Manager tests each of your entries to see whether it's valid. An invalid entry, however, doesn't prevent the DNS Manager from accepting the record. Instead, you receive an error message if the DNS Manager doesn't think you entered a valid value. As you enter new records, the Manager also prompts you for the resource record type. You want to refer to Table 3-3 for these record types whenever you add new records.

Chapter 4

Using Virtual Servers

*Y*ou know that old saying, "You can fool all of the people some of the time, and you can fool some of the people all of the time, but you can't fool all of the people all of the time"? Well, it's just not true with virtual servers. They look and act exactly like dedicated servers all of the time.

That's great, you say, but what under the moons of Mars are dedicated and virtual servers? Aha! You didn't read Chapter 2. And we worked so hard on it, too.

Service, Please!

Dedicated server is just technobabble for the computer that houses Web pages, e-mail boxes, and so forth. A *virtual server* is software that makes it look like a directory on a computer's hard drive is a separate, standalone computer. Because you can have as many directories as a hard drive can hold, the only theoretical limit to how many virtual servers you can fit on a single computer is the size of the hard drive.

An Internet domain name can point to either a dedicated server or a virtual server, so a virtual server provider can have lots of different Web sites on one computer. And that means you can have your own domain name without all the hassle and expense of maintaining a dedicated computer with high-speed lines.

Just to make sure that no one remains unconfused, computer experts also use the word *server* to refer to the software that makes everything work. Therefore, you can have a computer that is called a dedicated server, software for running your Web site that's called a Web server, a program for processing junk mail that's called an e-mail server and, for a few extra bucks and a phone call, a guy who comes to your door who's called a pizza server.

Virtual servers come in two flavors: A full-service provider such as Cove Software, shown in Figure 4-1, will do (nearly) everything for you. Want a new mailbox? Just ask. Want to use FrontPage as your development environment? Just let the provider know. It may take a day (providers are busy people, and the good ones have a lot of clients to deal with), but you don't have to do the grunge work. This is true for most services required to run the server. If you want them to author your Web pages or program CGI add-ons for you, however, that'll cost extra. Almost all virtual server providers do offer such services, by the way. If you need custom artwork or programming, turn to them first.

A do-it-yourself setup such as Iserver (see Figure 4-2), on the other hand, is pretty much an experts-only arrangement. Usually, this means you need to be a UNIX guru. (Most virtual servers are on UNIX boxes, but you can find a few lonely Windows setups if you carefully shop around.) On the dark side,

Figure 4-1: Cove Software is a full-service provider.

if you want a new mailbox, you have to set it up. If you want to install FrontPage extensions, you're on your own. The bright side is that you can do it any time you want, and you don't have to wait for anybody else to get around to it.

Most do-it-yourself providers do everything they can to make your life easier. Iserver, for instance, supplies a Windows program called IManager that allows you to add and delete mailboxes, passwords, and so forth remotely. You can skip the easy part and still telnet in and use UNIX commands to do all this stuff, if you'd rather. Another company, Adgrafix, has an impressive Windows program called Web Site Manager (see Figure 4-3) that lets you do just about anything with point-and-click simplicity.

Make sure the provider runs a backup at least once a day, so the worst that can happen to you is that you lose a day's work. If they want you to pay anything extra for this service, spit in their eye and take your business elsewhere.

If you're not a UNIX guru, but you want to take a crack at it anyway, grab copies of *UNIX For Dummies,* 3rd Edition, and *MORE UNIX For Dummies,* both by John R. Levine and Margaret Levine Young (published by IDG Books Worldwide, Inc.). They tell you everything you'd ever need to know to use a UNIX system.

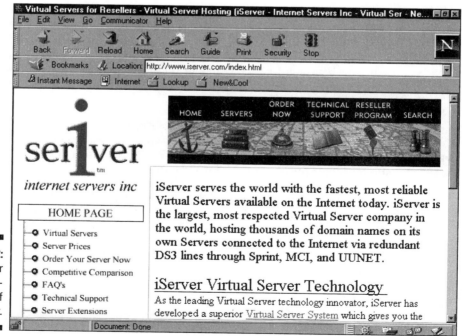

Figure 4-2:
Iserver offers a do-it-yourself arrangement.

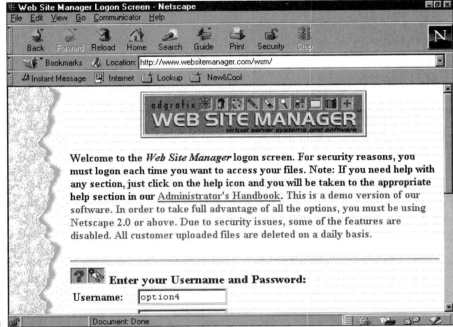

Figure 4-3:
Adgrafix
Web Site
Manager
simplifies
admin-
istration.

Some do-it-yourself providers live a kind of Jekyll-and-Hyde existence. Although it's true that you're responsible for everything after your virtual server is set up, they provide a bunch of popular software all ready to run. Some of that software (such as popular mailing list programs) can be a pain to install. A thoughtful and considerate provider will furnish you with a compressed version that uncompresses into the appropriate directories, saving you lots of headaches.

In any case, you will have to play by the rules of the server supplier. Generally, these aren't too hard to abide by — they're just basic good netiquette such as not *spamming* (sending mass unsolicited junk e-mail), not using the site for illegal purposes like plotting bank robberies or overthrowing the government, and not using the site for libelous purposes. Most suppliers also forbid adult sites, not all of them out of prudishness, but mainly because all those dirty pictures being downloaded by all those people are too great a strain on the system (the computer system, not yours).

Table 4-1 shows the Web addresses of several virtual server suppliers.

Table 4-1	Virtual Server Suppliers
Supplier	*URL*
Accelenet	`http://www.accelenet.net/`
Adgrafix	`http://www.adgrafix.com/`
Cove Software	`http://www.covesoft.com/virtual/`
Delta Net	`http://www.delta.net/services/` `www/www_hosting.html`
Edson Enterprises	`http://www.edsonent.com/`
Esosoft	`http://www.esosoft.com/`
HorseWeb	`http://www/horseweb.com/` `hw_dev.htm`
InfoTech Services	`http://www.itsnet.net/virtual/` `server.html`
Iserver	`http://www.iserver.com/`
NET Limited	`http://www.netlimited.net/Host-` `ing/packages.html`
ProWebSite	`http://www.virtual-server-` `hosting.com/`
Springboard Global Marketing	`http://www.spring-board.com/` `vserver.html`
Vservers	`http://www.vservers.com/`

Some virtual servers use a technique called *virtual hosting.* For most purposes, you can consider virtual hosting as the same as using a virtual server, but virtual hosting is a little different in the way it works. With virtual hosting, although you still have your own separate IP address, e-mail boxes, and so forth, you are sharing the server software with all the other people on the machine. With a true virtual server, you have your own server software as well, and can change it as you see fit.

Jump Right In

The setup and maintenance of the server are handled for you, so it's easy to jump right in and get running. Just follow these steps:

1. **If your provider did not do so for you, register your domain name with InterNIC. (No, that's not Santa's version of the CIA.)**

   You can sometimes talk a provider into lowering your setup fee if you handle the domain name registration yourself. If you don't have a clue how to do it, just pretend you do and turn to Chapter 3.

2. **Upload your files from your computer to your new site using an FTP program.**

   This is assuming you have all the files on your local computer. Although you *can* create the files on your virtual server, it's a good idea to have your own copies of them, in case your provider runs off to Bulgaria with the maid.

   Make sure you put the files in the appropriate directories. That is, you have to put the Web pages in the directory set aside for HTML pages, the downloadable files in the directory set aside for the FTP server, and so on. The exact directory setup may vary between providers, so check with them to be sure you understand where to put the files. If *they* don't know, you're in trouble.

3. **Establish your e-mail addresses.**

   "But I already have an e-mail address from my local ISP," you say, "and I have no need for more than one mailbox." Still, you'll find that people will send mail to your site itself, addressed to "Webmaster" or "Root." If you're crazy enough to want to be able to get this mail, you'll need to do one of two things. You can establish separate mailboxes for every possible address you can think of, which means you'll spend the rest of your natural life checking e-mail. Or you can set up an *alias* e-mail address, which will automatically relay all mail sent to any address at your site to your personal mailbox. In any case, you'll eventually want to send some e-mail with a return address that's the same as your domain name. See Chapter 8 for some creative ways to use mailboxes and aliases (other than to avoid creditors and ex-spouses, that is).

4. **Log on to your site and check to make sure everything's working.**

   If it isn't, call your provider and pretend it's their fault. If it's a long distance call, try to reverse the charges.

Size Isn't Everything

A dedicated server will usually have a hard drive a few gigabytes in size. That's not much if you're planning on putting the collected wisdom of humanity online, but it's a whole lot more than the typical Web site needs, even when you throw in mailboxes, automated newsletters, and the theme song from your favorite movie. One of the greatest appeals of virtual servers is that they come in different sizes. If you want just a few megs to tuck your medium-sized Web site into, you need to pay for only that much. If you want 100 megs to hold a more sophisticated site with all the trimmings, it'll cost a bit more but still not as much as a dedicated server.

If you want to expand later, just rent more disk space. Before you get involved with a provider, make sure you understand exactly what additional space will cost you and what increments it's available in. If you're renting 20 megs, can you go up to 21 or do you have to jump to 50? Always try to expand to unusual amounts, such as 37 megs, just to break the monotony. If it's divisible by 5, it's just no fun.

So how do you decide what size server to get? Unless you want to have tons of mailboxes or lots of 3-D animation with synchronized sound, your best bet is probably to start off small. Get the smallest size server your provider offers that still gives you all the capabilities you need.

Don't Break the Piggy Bank

How much should you spend on your virtual server? As little as possible, of course. Shop around and find a provider who has exactly what you need, and don't pay for any unnecessary extras. If you're going to be using the server only for Web pages, bear in mind that a humongous HTML file will run only about 30 to 50 kilobytes, and a 1K file is not unusual. We once got a virtual server with 75 megs of storage space and found that we actually needed a little under 3 megs worth. We never did figure out what to do with the other 72 megs, although our accountant did suggest some anatomically unlikely solutions.

After you decided who you're going to go with and what you want from them, you'll usually have to fill out an online form to get things started. The nosy people who make these forms want to know all sorts of personal details such as your name, address, and credit card number. In most cases, you can fax or mail the information if you'd prefer.

Make sure that you understand exactly what leasing a virtual server will cost you. In addition to the monthly charges, expect a one-time setup fee. Some providers also charge a fee based on how many hits your site gets; they'll explain that their rates are based on usage but, hey, that's their problem. Plenty of them don't pass the usage charges on. And you'll need to pay InterNIC for the registration. This fee, which you can't negotiate, is currently $50 a year. (When signing up for the first time, you must pay for two years in advance; after that, you pay yearly.) In most cases, you'll have to pay InterNIC separately, but some providers will pay InterNIC for you and then bill you. Watch out that they don't tack an extra fee on for doing that, though.

Speaking of monthly charges, it's not a good idea to get tied into a long-term contract with a provider, unless you're planning on marrying them. Make sure you're able to change providers if you want to. If you ever decide you're not happy with your current provider, it's an easy matter to move the site. All you have to do is contact a new provider, let InterNIC know your new location, and transfer the files. If you're ticked off at your old provider, you don't even have to tell them you're doing it until it's a *fait accompli*. (That's French for "Don't send me any more bills.")

Negotiate! The virtual server business has a lot of competition and most suppliers will be willing to bend a bit. Even if you can't get a break on price, you should be able to get for the same price more services than those offered in the standard package.

Playing Sherlock Holmes

It's a good idea to contact other people who are running virtual servers with the provider. How do you find them? Ask the provider, of course. The problem with this approach is that, like the references on your job resume, they'll list only the ones who'll say nice things about them. Try posting messages on related newsgroups, such as `comp.infosystems.www.authoring.html`, asking about the provider. That way, you're sure to hear from disgruntled former customers. (By the way, did you ever hear of a *gruntled* customer?) Brace yourself, though. You'll receive offers from every virtual server provider on the planet after you post that message.

It also pays to use some of the search services to check for virtual servers. Pop into Excite (`http://www.excite.com/`), AltaVista (`http://altavista.digital.com/`), or Webcrawler (`http://www.webcrawler.com/`) and punch in the search terms **virtual server**. Take the time to read the various descriptions of services, even if you don't intend to use the particular ones you find. Often, the tips and techniques can be useful with the server you finally settle on. If a particular site has great tips but high prices, bookmark them for later reference. You can always use their expertise even if you ultimately sign with someone else who doesn't break your bank account.

Some Web sites compare the different virtual server options. Theblade has such a site at `http://theblade.org/virtserv.htm`. Budget Web (`http://www.budgetweb.com/budgetweb/virtual.sthml`) has a database of virtual server suppliers that you can search. You can even specify that you want only those that offer commercial use, secure servers, Java support, and so on.

If You Can't Beat 'Em . . .

It's possible to build a pretty nice little home-based business reselling virtual servers. It's also possible to lose your shirt. What's reselling? Essentially, you become an agent for the provider, although you're technically an independent contractor. You're responsible for finding clients, making contracts, collecting money, and providing tech support. The provider takes care of everything else.

Actually, the tech support part isn't as scary as it sounds. The provider still handles all the technical problems, but you're the only point of contact for your clients. If they have some problem that's over your head, you just relay the message to the provider, who sends you an answer that you relay to your client. As far as your client is concerned, you're a computer genius.

The reselling phenomenon explains why most of the virtual server providers' Web sites look so much alike. They're actually almost all resellers, using materials supplied by the real providers such as Cove Software and Iserver. (Actually, Iserver is itself a reseller for secure.net, but secure.net doesn't deal with the public.)

The resellers, pretending to be actual providers, sign up their own resellers, who pretend to be actual providers, and so forth. You say that sounds like a fly-by-night multilevel marketing scheme? You win the prize.

To find out whether a supplier is a reseller, just use the InterNIC Whois server at `http://www.rs.internic.net/cgi-bin/whois` and type the name of the supplier. If the servers listed under "Domain servers in listed order" are different from the domain name of the supplier, they're probably a reseller. Copy the domain name listed there into your browser to go to the home page of the real supplier.

Anything you, as a reseller, make over the base price of the virtual server is yours to keep. Of course, with the stiff competition among resellers, the profit margin has become about as thin as Ukrainian soup.

So why does anyone deal with a reseller at all? Well, because of the volume resellers handle, they can usually provide better prices and smaller amounts of disk space than the biggies do.

If you want to get involved in selling virtual servers but don't want to become a reseller, your best option is to lease a dedicated server. Either kind of virtual server supplier — full-service or do-it-yourself — will be happy to lease you a dedicated server instead. A dedicated server is an entire computer that you can use as you please. We've never seen one that isn't a UNIX box, so at the minimum you'll have to be really good at UNIX — as well as an expert on the use of Web servers — to run a dedicated server. This option is not for the casual user.

The big downside of becoming a reseller is that you're responsible for the billing. If you don't get paid, you still have to pay the provider their cut out of your own pocket. And you'll need to decide how you're going to collect the monthly charges. Will you accept checks or do you need to set up a credit card merchant account?

Not only that, but you need pay your provider with a credit card. (Most of them aren't crazy enough to take checks.) That's no big deal if you have only a few clients. But what if you have 200 clients and it costs you $50 a month for each one? You'll need a credit card that will handle a monthly bill of $10,000. Like they say, though, we should all have such problems.

Part II
Publishing Information on the Internet

The 5th Wave   By Rich Tennant

"Hold your horses. It takes time to build a home page for someone your size."

In this part . . .

The World Wide Web is the single best way to publish information on the Internet. The first two chapters in this part give you a firm foundation in Web page creation and layout. And, even if you're an old hand at Web site development, you'll still want to look in on Chapter 7 for details on setting up your own news server.

Chapter 5

Creating Web Pages

● ●

In This Chapter

▶ Building an HTML page

▶ Controlling text

▶ Adding images

▶ Linking to the world

▶ Using page-generation programs

● ●

*T*he heart of the World Wide Web is HTML, which is short for *HyperText Markup Language*. HTML is pretty simple when compared to other computer languages, but it's also remarkably flexible and powerful. You can pick up the basics and start creating Web pages the same day you start looking at HTML. But if you want to really go nuts over HTML, you can also spend eternity exploring all its little nooks and crannies. HTML is constantly undergoing improvement, so there's really no end to it. You could easily make a career out of HTML. Lots of people have.

Although you can create Web pages with programs that can generate HTML pages for you, you'd be cheating yourself if you took that path, at least to begin with. True, such programs take away the need to figure out HTML itself and enable you to concentrate on style and content for each page, but these programs take as much time and effort to master as HTML does. And when you're finished, all you know is how to use one proprietary program. If you put the same amount of effort into working with HTML, you know the Web itself.

All you need to make an HTML page is any old text editor. You can use one of the specialized text editors designed for HTML development (such as HomeSite), which have such niceties as a fancy word processor or colored text to help you differentiate between tags and content. If you use a word processor, however, make sure you save the file as plain text.

Your Web pages have to go on a computer called a *Web server* that is connected to the Internet before anyone aside from you can see them. You can either set up your own HTTP server on your personal computer or subscribe to a World Wide Web publishing service on the Internet, either the Internet service provider (ISP) you use for your own Net access or a virtual server supplier (see Chapter 4). You enjoy no obvious advantage in setting up your own HTTP server on your personal computer, aside from the fact that you avoid paying modest fees to a World Wide Web service provider. Even this advantage will be more than offset, however, by the cost of the dedicated Internet connection that you need if you want your HTTP server to be accessible to other users at all times.

Keep in mind also that the World Wide Web is evolving rapidly; standards are changing, and developers are creating new technologies all the time (to enable you, for example, to conduct true electronic financial transactions by using the World Wide Web). If you set up your own HTTP server, you will need to keep up with these changes and continue to update your HTTP server software or buy add-ons to take advantage of these new technologies. On the other hand, if you're using a Web-publishing service provider, the provider should do all these things for you; if it doesn't, you should change service providers.

Whether you set up your own HTTP server or subscribe to a service provider, you need to create at least one HTML document to publish on the World Wide Web before you consider other options for expanding your presence on the Web. The following sections explain how to create content for your Web site and then send that content to a Web server via the network.

This chapter covers only the basics of HTML. For a more complete experience, seek out *Creating Web Pages For Dummies,* 3rd Edition, by Bud Smith and Arthur Bebak (published by IDG Books Worldwide, Inc.), available at finer bookstores everywhere.

Tag, You're It

An HTML document is pretty much like a plain text document, except it has tags embedded in it that control its appearance. *Tags* are simply commands that tell a Web browser what the page should look like. Most of them are easy to use and intuitive. For instance, if you want text to be italicized, you put it between <I> and </I> tags. If you want text to be in bold print, you put it between <B> and </B> tags. The first tag is called the *start tag* and the second one is called the *end tag.* As you've probably guessed, they tell the Web browser where the effect starts and where it ends. End tags are always the same as the start tag, but have that little slash (/) so that the Web browser can tell the difference. And you'll find plenty more tags where those came from. Tags for laying out the page structure. Tags for adding images and tables and colors. Tags for doing just about anything. We'll go into more detail — including some exceptions — later.

In a rare case of comprehensible technical lingo, tags are said to *contain* the material between them, and that material, you'll be happy to know, is called the *contents*. The various parts of a Web page are often referred to as elements. An *element* is everything from the start tag to the end tag, including the tags themselves.

Everything in a Web page is inside something else, and that means it's between a pair of tags. The first tag you'll run into on a typical Web page is `<HTML>`. That tells the Web browser that it is encountering a Web page. Because this tag has to define where the page begins and ends, there's also an end tag, which is `</HTML>`.

You may notice that some Web pages start with the `<!DOCTYPE>` tag, but it's not necessary, and its use, which is supposed to clarify things, can actually lead to all sorts of problems. It tells the Web browser exactly what version of HTML the page is written in, but the browsers themselves can already handle just about anything without this tag. If you do use it, you must keep very careful track of every detail of your Web page and be sure to change the document type if you decide to use an element that is not included in the version you previously specified. If you really want to delve into the mysteries of document types, check out the World Wide Web Consortium's official documentation at `http://www.w3.org/TR/PR-html40/struct/ global.html`.

Okay, so now you've defined an HTML page, but it has nothing in it. You have to add a head and a body — honest. (Sounds a bit like playing Dr. Frankenstein.) The head contains a bunch of stuff that doesn't ever show up on your Web page when someone views it, and the body is where you put all the material that *does* show up, such as text and images. The head of the document lies between the `<HEAD>` and `</HEAD>` tags, and the body lies between `<BODY>` and `</BODY>`.

The Web page code so far looks like this:

```
<HTML>

<HEAD>
</HEAD>

<BODY>
</BODY>

</HTML>
```

At a minimum, you have to put a title for your page in the head. The title will show up at the top of a Web browser when someone looks at your page, and it's what your Web page will be called when it's picked up by a search engine. The title goes — you have it — between the <TITLE> and </TITLE> tags, as in the following example.

```
<HEAD>

<TITLE>
My Web Page
</TITLE>

</HEAD>
```

The other main thing to include in the head are keywords. *Keywords* are descriptive terms that apply to your Web page. You do this with — brace yourself — metadata. *Metadata* is basically a fancy way to say stuff that isn't really a part of the document but is information *about* the document. The tag for this one is <META> and it's one of those tags that doesn't have a matching end tag. That's because it doesn't have any content to put between two tags; all metadata is included within the start tag. You'll want to list as many descriptive terms as you can think of. The search engines will read this information and classify your Web page accordingly.

In the past, it was a good idea to list the same keyword over and over again so that the search engines will think your Web page has lots of content on a particular subject. This used to work, but search engines are wise to it now, and will not give any weight to multiple occurrences of a term in the keyword listings. They're far more interested in the keywords used than in the number of them.

This is how you put keywords in your Web page:

```
<META name="keywords" content="dachsunds,leopards,clam
          chowder,flying saucers">
```

Put together with the title segment, your head now looks like this:

```
<HEAD>

<TITLE>
My Web Page
</TITLE>

<META name="keywords" content="dachsunds,leopards,clam
          chowder,flying saucers">

</HEAD>
```

Playing traffic cop

You can pull a neat trick with the `<META>` tag. You can make someone go to another Web page automatically, which is very useful if you've changed addresses. To do this, you use the `http-equiv` command, which fools the Web browser into thinking it's received the information from the HTTP (Web) server itself. The following code, for example, will send the visitor to the LinkFinder Web site:

```
<META http-equiv="refresh"
  "content="5"; url="http://
  www.linkfinder.com/">
```

The *content* part tells the browser how many seconds to wait before redirecting itself. In this case, it's five seconds. If you wanted it to be any other number, you'd just put it in instead. The *url* part gives the Web address to switch to. Just replace the example URL with the one you want, and you — or they — are ready to go.

Just in case your visitors are using a Web browser that doesn't support `http-equiv`, you should also provide a regular link that they can click to proceed.

Bodybuilding

The *body* of a Web page is where all the stuff goes that people see. Text, images, tables, forms, you name it: It's in the body. But before we get to all those wonderful elements, you can do some pretty cool things with the `<BODY>` tag itself.

Background color

For starters, you can set the background color of your Web page and the colors of the text, too. You can also change the colors of hypertext links, but we advise against that because people are used to the standard ones.

To set the background color, you use the `bgcolor` attribute. (Attributes are the different settings you can make for the tags.) One factor that will have you tearing out your hair is that colors are specified using hexadecimal notation. Hexadecimal, or hex, notation is base 16, and it counts from 0 through F instead of 0 through 9, believe it or not. (And you'll feel like you've had a hex put on you if you try to understand it.)

Hexadecimal numbers look like #FFD03A. The # is not necessary; it announces that the number is hex, but nothing else looks like a hex number — unless your cat has been walking on your keyboard.

Fortunately, the people who make Web browsers have realized that normal people — not just math wizards — make Web pages too, so the companies have built into the browsers the capability to recognize normal color names in plain English. So you can write bgcolor = "red" instead of bgcolor = "#FF0000".

The colors are RGB triplets. That means that the six "digits" in the hex number break down into three pairs, the first pair for red, the second pair for green, and the third pair for blue. Thus, when you see #FF0000, think FF 00 00. Because F in hexadecimal is the same thing as 15 in decimal notation, FF is the same as $(15 \times 16^1) + (15 \times 16^0)$, which equals $(15 \times 16) + (15 \times 1)$, which equals 255. The reason #FF0000 means red is because it says to use full red, no green, and no blue. If you used #00FF00 instead, you'd be saying to use no red, full green, and no blue. And, finally, #0000FF is no red, no green, full blue. Black is #000000, the total absence of all the colors, and white is #FFFFFF, the full presence of all the colors. By using various combinations of red, green, and blue — remember, you have 256 shades (from 00 through FF) of each to mix — you can create just about any color imaginable.

Microsoft Internet Explorer used to support only 16 named colors, while Netscape Navigator supported a whole lot more. But Microsoft has caught up and the following full set of named colors is now supported by both:

```
aliceblue, antiquewhite, aqua, aquamarine, azure, beige,
bisque, black, blanchedalmond, blue, blueviolet, brown,
burlywood, cadetblue, chartreuse, chocolate, coral,
cornflowerblue, cornsilk, crimson, cyan, darkblue, darkcyan,
darkgoldenrod, darkgray, darkgreen, darkkhaki, darkmagenta,
darkolivegreen, darkorange, darkorchid, darkred, darksalmon,
darkseagreen, darkslateblue, darkslategray, darkturquoise,
darkviolet, deeppink, deepskyblue, dimgray, dodgerblue,
firebrick, floralwhite, forestgreen, fuchsia, gainsboro,
ghostwhite, gold, goldenrod, gray, green, greenyellow, honey-
dew, hotpink, indianred, indigo, ivory, khaki, lavender,
lavenderblush, lawngreen, lemonchiffon, lightblue,
lightcoral, lightcyan, lightgoldenrodyellow, lightgreen,
lightgrey, lightpink, lightsalmon, lightseagreen,
lightskyblue, lightslategray, lightsteelblue, lightyellow,
lime, limegreen, linen, magenta, maroon, mediumaquamarine,
mediumblue, mediumorchid, mediumpurple, mediumseagreen,
mediumslateblue, mediumspringgreen, mediumturquoise,
mediumvioletred, midnightblue, mintcream, mistyrose, mocca-
sin, navajowhite, navy, oldlace, olive, olivedrab, orange,
orangered, orchid, palegoldenrod, palegreen, paleturquoise,
palevioletred, papayawhip, peachpuff, peru, pink, plum,
powderblue, purple, red, rosybrown, royalblue, saddlebrown,
salmon, sandybrown, seagreen, seashell, sienna, silver,
skyblue, slateblue, slategray, snow, springgreen, steelblue,
tan, teal, thistle, tomato, turquoise, violet, wheat, white,
whitesmoke, yellow, yellowgreen
```

Instead of bothering with hex numbers, simply use any of these names —
one is bound to suit you. To set the background color to ivory, for example,
type the following:

```
<BODY bgcolor="ivory">
```

It's usually a good idea to choose a color for your background that contrasts
strongly with the other page elements so that the text doesn't fade into the
background and make your page unreadable.

Background images

If you want to get fancy, you can use a picture instead of a solid color for the
background. You use the `<BODY>` tag, but the attribute this time is `back-`
`ground`. Then you simply indicate what file you want to use for the background image, like this:

```
<BODY background="image.gif">
```

You need to replace the name of the file in the example with the name of the
one you want to use. If the file is not in the same directory as the Web page,
you also need to include the necessary information for locating it. For
instance, if all your images are in a subdirectory named pictures, you write
the code like this:

```
<BODY background="pictures/image.gif">
```

The image will be *tiled,* which means that it will repeat across your page
from border to border. Because it's a background image, everything else on
your page will seem to lie on top of it, as shown in Figure 5-1. You should be
as careful with the background image as with the background color, and for
the same reason: You don't want to end up with a page that's unreadable.

Text color

The color of text on a Web page is black by default, but you can change that
if you want to. Setting the text color works just like the background color,
except you use the `text` attribute. For example, if you want to change the
default text color from black to blue, just set the following in the `<BODY>` tag:

```
<BODY text="blue">
```

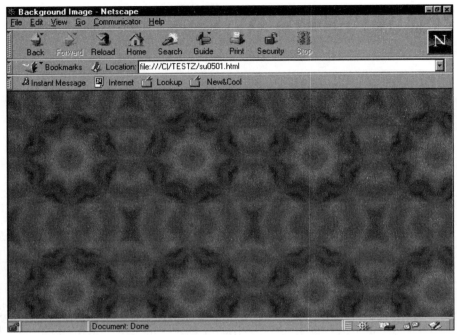

Figure 5-1:
A Web
page with a
background
image.

Laying it on thick

Finally, it's important to realize that you can combine any or all attributes in a single <BODY> tag:

```
<BODY bgcolor="ivory" background="image.gif" text="blue">
```

Getting the word out

With all the emphasis placed on Web graphics these days, you'd think that was all there was to the Web. The vast majority of the material on the Web, however, is text, so it's not too surprising that HTML has a lot of tags for controlling the appearance of text. You can use different levels of text control, depending on what you want to do.

You define paragraphs with the <P> tag and spacing between them with the <BR> tag. Any time you want to start a new paragraph, you need to insert a <P> tag. That tells Web browsers that they're supposed to drop down a line and start fresh. Here's an example; the results are shown in Figure 5-2:

```
<P>This is the first paragraph.
<P>This is the second paragraph.
```

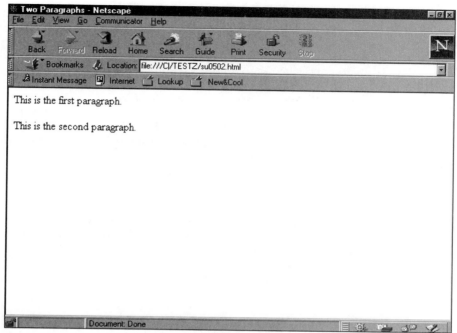

Figure 5-2:
Two
paragraphs.

You probably noticed that there's no `</P>` end tag on the paragraphs. You can insert the end tag if you want to, but it isn't necessary because the beginning of the next paragraph automatically signals the end of the first one.

If you want to put space between the paragraphs, use the `<BR>` tag. You might think that you could do something like the following, but it won't work:

```
<P>This is the first paragraph.
<P>
<P>This is the second paragraph.
```

That's because you aren't allowed to have an empty paragraph. If a paragraph has no content, Web browsers just ignore it. Well, okay, they're all *supposed* to, and you might get away with it for a single blank line if the browser's designers ignored the HTML specification. But the one thing for sure is that you can't stack `<P>` tags for vertical spacing as in the following example:

```
<P>This is the first paragraph.
<P>
<P>
<P>
<P>This is the second paragraph.
```

The correct way to do spacing between paragraphs is like this:

```
<P>This is the first paragraph.
<BR>
<P>This is the second paragraph.
```

Two types of elements are at work in page formatting. Anything that causes a break in the flow of the page contents, such as the <BR> tag, is a *block level* element. Anything that does not affect the flow, such as bold text, is an *inline* element. Technically, you don't need to use a <P> tag following a block level element because the effects are identical, but it's still good form to include it.

Text formatting

We already mentioned the <B> and <I> tags (for changing text to bold or italic form) in the opening to this section, and these tags are probably used most often. Text formatting tags can be sandwiched for multiple effects, too. The following code illustrates using both these tags individually and together; the results are shown in Figure 5-3:

```
<P>This text is <B>bold</B> and this is <I>italic.</I> This
        is <B><I>bold italic.</I></B> This is <I><B>bold
        italic.</B></I> too.
```

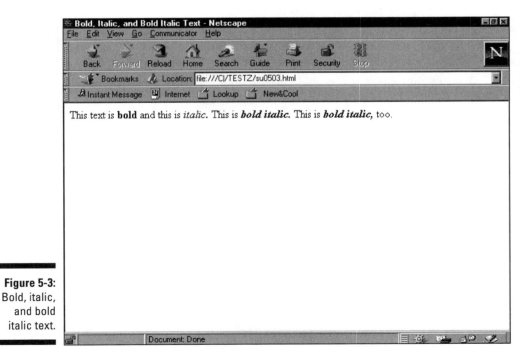

Figure 5-3:
Bold, italic, and bold italic text.

Notice how you sandwich, or nest, the code. As shown in the bold italic text in the example, you can start with <B><I> or <I><B>. Whichever approach you take, however, pay attention to the position of the end tags. Note that the first start tag and the first end tag don't match. The tags are nested, such that the last start tag matches the first end tag. In the first example, the italic part is enclosed within the bold part. In the second one, the bold part is enclosed within the italic part.

You can change the size of fonts, too. Several ways to do so are available, but one of the easiest is to use the <BIG> and <SMALL> tags. These tags respectively increase or decrease the size of the fonts. The following example shows how to use them; the results are shown in Figure 5-4:

```
<P>This text is normal size. <BIG>This is larger.</BIG>
        This is back to normal. <SMALL>This is
        smaller.</SMALL> And now back to normal again.
```

Notice that the effect, just like with bold or italic, is taking place only within the start and end tags. You can nest these tags, too. Of course, using something like <BIG><SMALL> would be silly because they'd cancel each other out. But you can, for example, double the size increase by stacking two <BIG> tags or double the decrease by nesting two <SMALL> tags. Here's how you'd do it; see Figure 5-4 for the results:

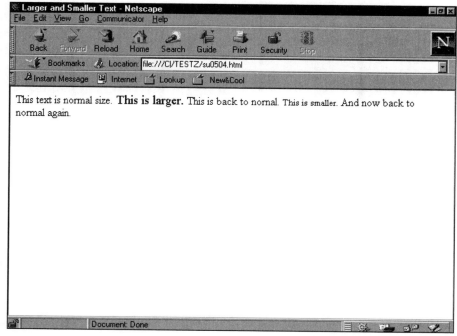

Figure 5-4:
Larger and smaller text.

```
<P>This text is normal size. <BIG><BIG>This is much
     larger.</BIG></BIG> This is back to normal.
     <SMALL><SMALL>This is much smaller. </SMALL></
     SMALL> And now back to normal again.
```

Text color, again

We showed you back in the beginning of this section how to set the color for the text on the entire page. Well, you can also control the text color of a short section of text using the <FONT> tag. A typical use of this tag looks like this:

```
<P>In this sentence, <FONT color="red">these words are in
     red.</FONT>
```

In fact, this tag can allow you to set not only the font color, but also its style and size. You can specify the font face to be used with the face attribute, and the size with — you guessed it again — the size attribute. Let's take a look at the preceding example, but this time with the other attributes added:

```
<P>In this sentence, <FONT face="Arial,Helvetica,Swiss"
     size="5" color="red">these words are in red.</
     FONT>
```

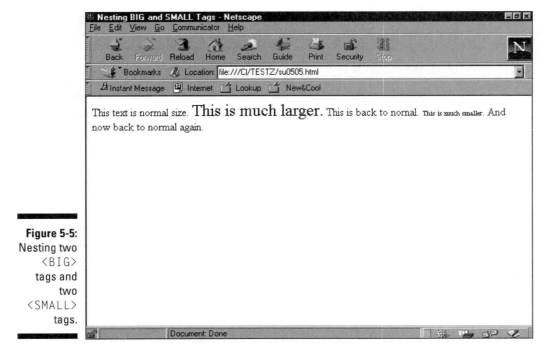

Figure 5-5:
Nesting two
<BIG>
tags and
two
<SMALL>
tags.

The reason we listed three separate font faces is because it's unlikely that everyone would have a particular one on their system. True, most Windows users will have Arial, but Mac users will have a similar font called Helvetica. By listing several different, but essentially identical, font faces, you increase the chances that visitors to your site will see what you intended them to see.

The size, set at 5, is just a bit larger than normal. Font size runs from 1 to 7; 1 is the smallest, 7 is the largest, and 4 is the normal size.

Image Is Everything

Although most of the Web is composed of text, you'll rarely find a Web page without any images. Pictures help inform, enlighten, and brighten the page. Adding an image to a Web page is simple. You just use the <IMG> tag and, like the background image, indicate which file to use, as follows:

```
<IMG src="image.gif">
```

That's all there is to it. Well, mostly all. You should also include the width and height of the image so that the Web browser knows how much space to set aside for it. That way, the text that follows the image can be shown right away rather than after the image is loaded. You can find out how wide and high the image is by loading it into any graphics program, or you can just load it into a Web browser; Navigator, for example, displays the image's size at the top of the screen. After you have the numbers, you add them like this:

```
<IMG src="image.gif" width="100" height="80">
```

The Thigh Bone's Connected to the Knee Bone

Hypertext links are what make the Web a web. They're the strands that connect all the separate parts. To add a link, you use the <A> tag. A typical link looks like this:

```
<A href="http://www.coberlaw.com/">Cohen, Berke, Bernstein,
         Brodie & Kondell</A>
```

The href attribute, an abbreviation for hypertext reference, is the URL of the page you want to link to. (URL, which stands for Uniform Resource Locator, is the Web address of the page.) Everything between the start and end tags will show up on the screen in underlined, blue lettering, as shown in Figure 5-6.

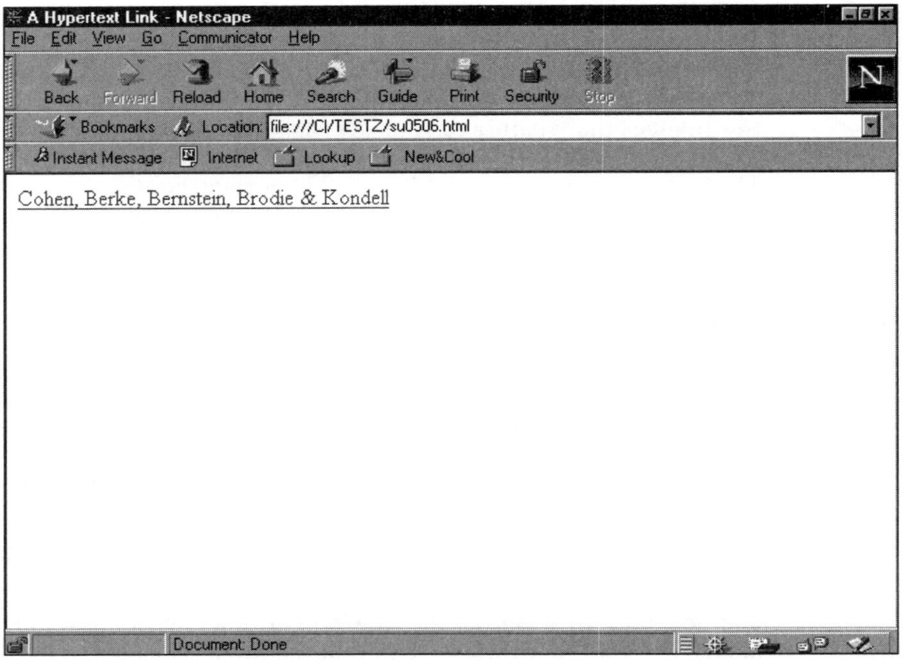

Figure 5-6:
A hypertext
link.

You can link not only to a Web page but also to any Internet resource. You could, for instance, link to an image or a program. The technique is the same: Include the URL of the resource. To link to an image, you simply change the example as follows:

```
<A href="image.gif">This is a picture.</A>
```

When visitors click that link, the image will be displayed in their Web browser.

You can do a lot more with HTML; we've only scratched the surface here. If you want to dig in, grab a copy of *Creating Web Pages For Dummies,* 3rd Edition, by Bud Smith and Arthur Bebak and *HTML 4 For Dummies* by Ed Tittel and Steve James (both published by IDG Books Worldwide, Inc.). In Chapter 6, we take a look at a bit more complex stuff, showing how to use frames, tables, forms, and image maps to help achieve the goals of your site.

Using Page-Generation Programs

If you're not intending to make a career out of site development and don't want to put in the kind of effort it takes to really master HTML, there's an easier way. As we mentioned in the beginning of this chapter, programs can generate a Web page for you. All you have to do is a bit of typing (we still don't have any programs that will do *all* the work), and click a few buttons. Both Netscape and Microsoft include such programs with their Web browsers. Netscape's program is called Composer, and Microsoft's is called FrontPage Express. (The commercial version of FrontPage has more features and retails for $149.)

Using Netscape Composer

Composer is a part of Netscape Communicator, which also includes the famous Netscape Navigator Web browser. The name change from Navigator to Communicator, in case you missed it, happened with version 4.0 of Navigator. (Communicator includes a few other programs, too.) You can download Netscape Communicator from the Netscape Web site at `http://home.netscape.com/download/index.html`.

You can launch Composer from within Netscape Navigator by clicking on the very last icon in the lower-right corner of the screen, as shown in Figure 5-7. Alternatively, you can select Communicator⇨Page Composer from the menu.

Figure 5-7:
The Netscape Composer icon in Netscape Navigator.

Composer icon

Either way, you end up in Composer as shown in Figure 5-8. The Web page is obviously blank, but it is not empty. Composer has already created the basic HTML coding of a Web page for you. To see this, choose <u>V</u>iew⇨Page So<u>u</u>rce. The results will look like Figure 5-9, except you will be listed as the author of your Web page.

As you add text, images, and other elements in Composer, the HTML code will continue to be automatically generated, enabling you to quickly create Web pages in a WYSIWYG (what you see is what you get) environment without having to perform any programming. If you've ever used a word processor, you'll be right at home with Composer.

To create the Web page shown in Figure 5-10, follow these steps:

1. **On the first line, type** This is a heading. **and press the Enter key to move down to the next line.**

2. **On the second line, type** This is some text. **and press the Enter key to move down to the next line.**

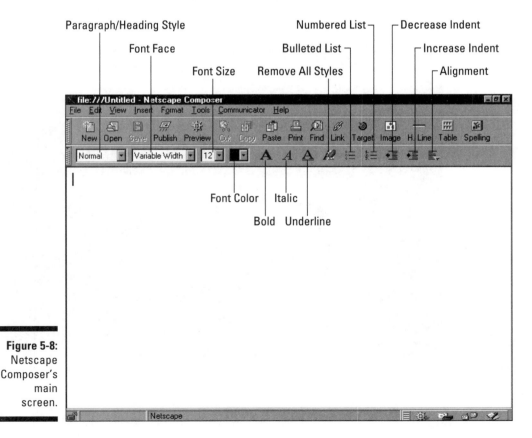

Figure 5-8:
Netscape
Composer's
main
screen.

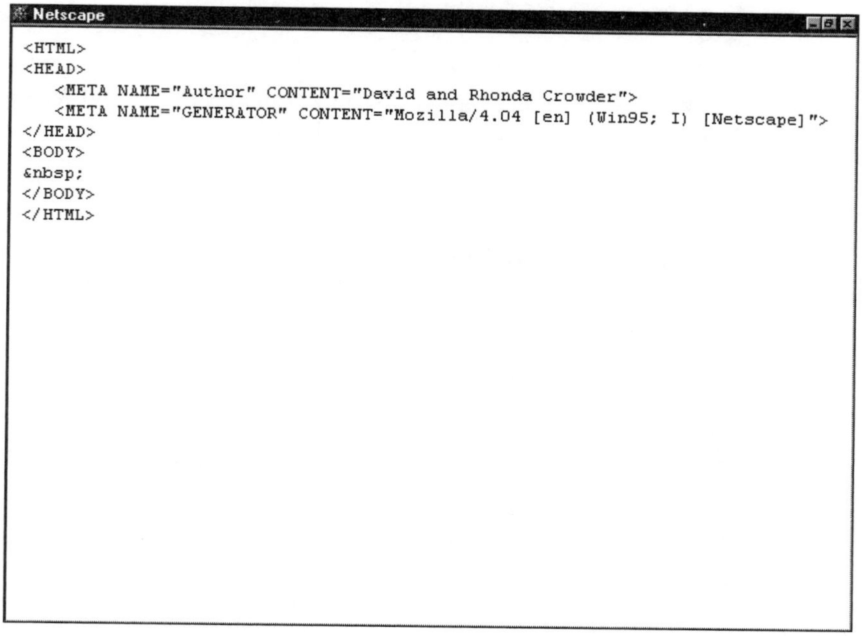

```
Netscape                                                          _ □ ×
<HTML>
<HEAD>
    <META NAME="Author" CONTENT="David and Rhonda Crowder">
    <META NAME="GENERATOR" CONTENT="Mozilla/4.04 [en] (Win95; I) [Netscape]">
</HEAD>
<BODY>
 
</BODY>
</HTML>
```

Figure 5-9:
HTML
source of
the blank
page.

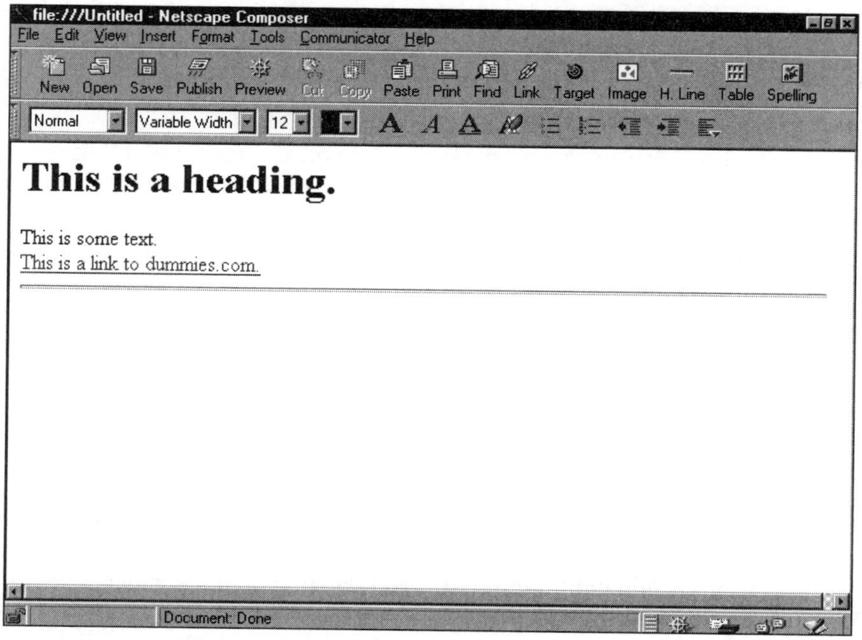

```
file:///Untitled - Netscape Composer                              _ □ ×
File  Edit  View  Insert  Format  Tools  Communicator  Help

  New  Open  Save  Publish  Preview  Cut  Copy  Paste  Print  Find  Link  Target  Image  H. Line  Table  Spelling

 Normal ▾  Variable Width ▾  12 ▾  ■ ▾   A  A  A  ♪  ≣  ≣  ◂≣  ▸≣  ≣.

This is a heading.

This is some text.
This is a link to dummies.com.
─────────────────────────────────────────────────────────

                                                          
Document: Done
```

Figure 5-10:
Example
Web page.

3. **Click the Link button in the toolbar.**

   The dialog box shown in Figure 5-11 appears.

4. **Enter the text just like you see in Figure 5-10 (or feel free to substitute your own), and then click the OK button.**

   The link appears just as you typed it.

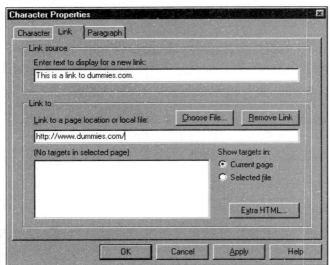

Figure 5-11:
Link dialog
box.

5. **Click anywhere within the text on the first line, click the Paragraph/ Heading Style drop-down list (labeled in Figure 5-8), and then select Heading 1 from the list.**

6. **If you want to save the results, click the Save button and give the file a name.**

7. **Click the OK button to finish.**

In the space of a minute or two, you've created a fully functional Web page complete with heading, text, hyperlink, and horizontal line. And it's just as easy to add other elements such as images or tables.

If you don't even want to be bothered with that much work, Netscape makes it even easier with *templates* and *wizards*. These are handy little software assistants that automatically create a complete Web site or a specialized Web section within your site. To take advantage of them, just click the New button, and then click either the From Template button or the From Page Wizard button on the pop-up menu shown in Figure 5-12. You will be automatically connected to Netscape on the Web, where the wizards reside. All you have to do is follow the instructions. Figure 5-13 shows a typical wizard.

Figure 5-12:
The Create
New Page
menu.

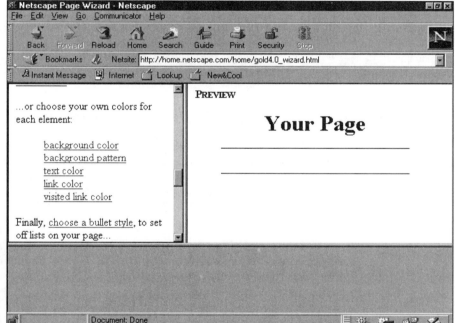

Figure 5-13:
An online
page
creation
wizard.

To publish your Web page, simply click Composer's Publish button to display the Publish dialog box, as shown in Figure 5-14. The page title and HTML filename are already filled in for you, but you can change them if you want. Type the Web address where you want to publish the page, fill in the User Name and Password text boxes, and click the OK button.

You must have access rights on the Web site where you are publishing the page. Unless you have a valid username and password, you cannot publish your page.

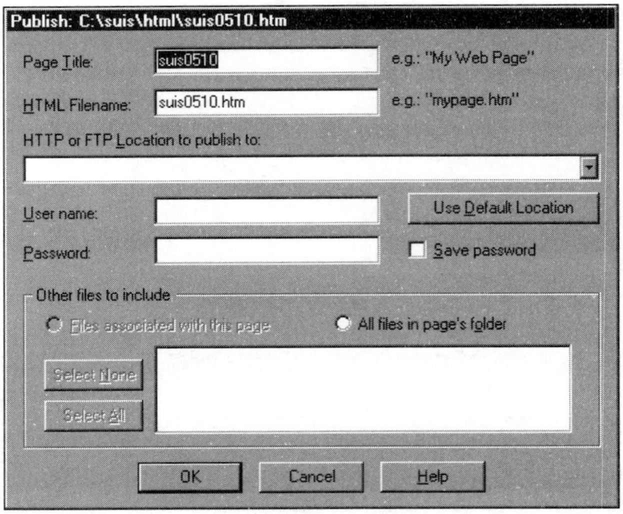

Figure 5-14:
The Publish
dialog box.

Using Microsoft FrontPage Express

Microsoft FrontPage Express, shown in Figure 5-15, works in much the same
way as Netscape Composer. FrontPage Express really shines in its form
creation capability and its *Webbots,* or *bots* (software robots that eliminate
the need for Web programming). The following example combines these two
features to show how easy it is to create the interactive form shown in
Figure 5-16 with FrontPage Express.

1. **To create the first line of the form, type** First Name:, **type a space, and
   then click the One Line Text Box button (labeled in Figure 5-15).
   Press Enter to move to the next line.**

2. **To create the second line of the form, type** Last Name:, **type a space,
   and then click the One Line Text Box button. Press Enter.**

3. **To create the third line of the form, click the Check Box button, type
   a space, and then type** Check here if you want a subscription. **Press
   Enter.**

4. **To create the fourth and final line of the form, click the Push Button
   button.**

5. **Right-click anywhere within the form.**

   The pop-up menu in Figure 5-17 appears.

6. **Click Form Properties.**

   The Form Properties dialog box appears, as shown in Figure 5-18.

One Line Text Box

Check Box   Push Button

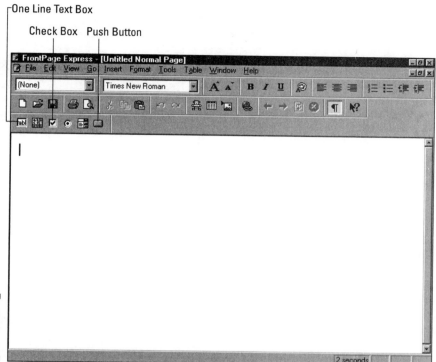

Figure 5-15:
FrontPage
Express.

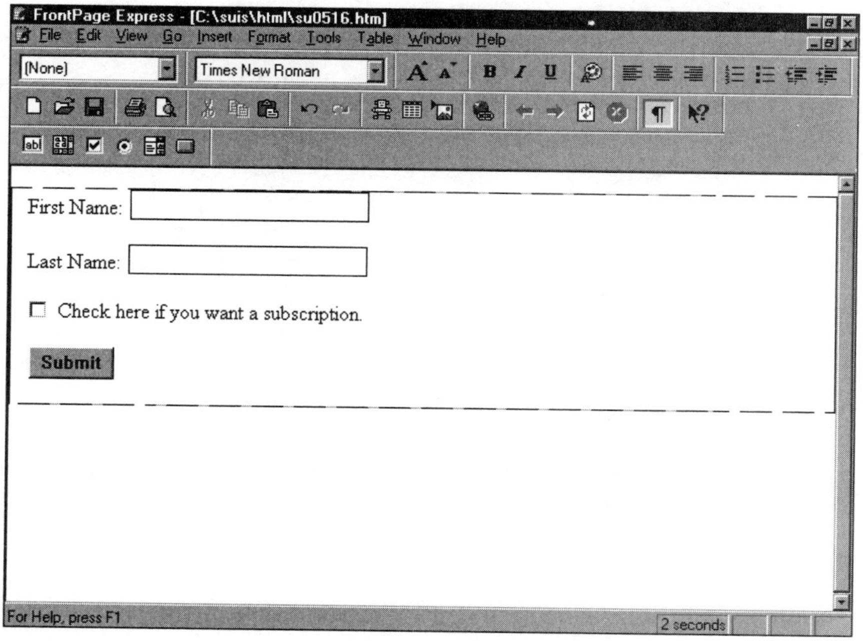

Figure 5-16:
An
interactive
form.

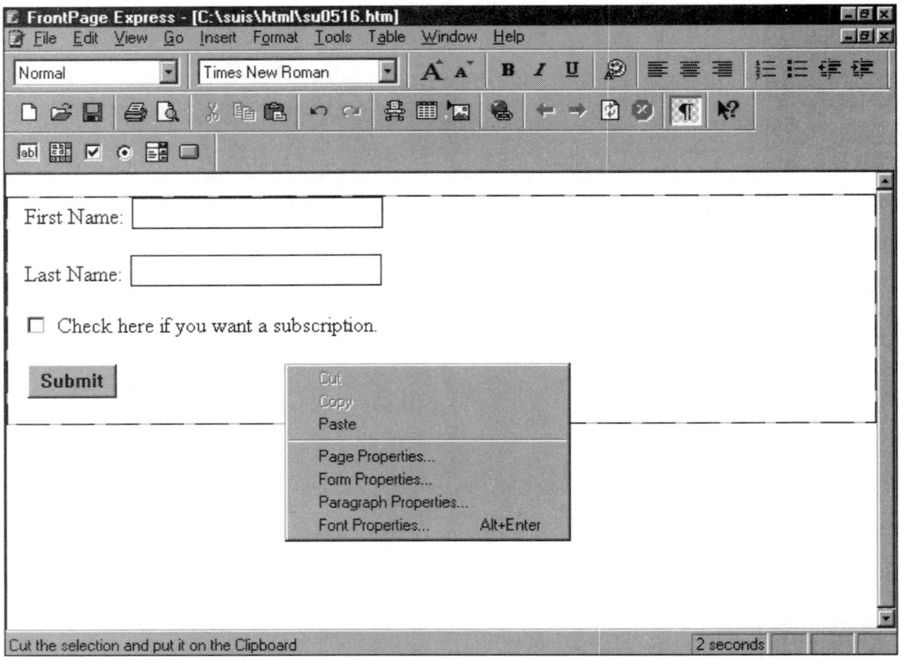

Figure 5-17:
The form
pop-up
menu.

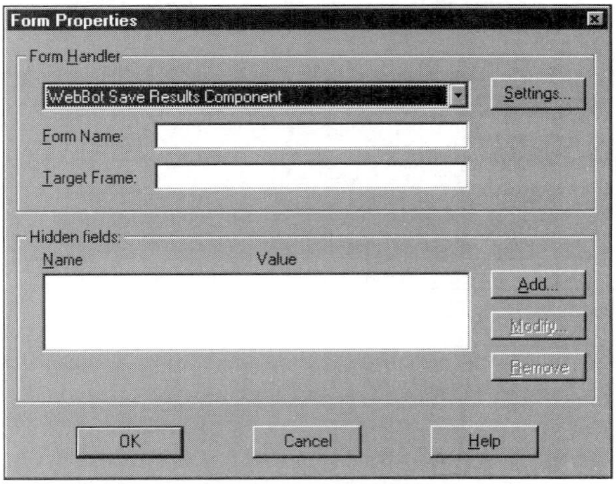

Figure 5-18:
The Form
Properties
dialog box.

7. Click the drop-down list box under Form <u>H</u>andler and scroll down
   until you find *Webbot Save Results Component.* Click it to select it.

8. In the <u>F</u>orm Name text box, type a name for the form.

9. Click the Settings button.

The Settings for Saving Results of Form dialog box appears, as shown in Figure 5-19.

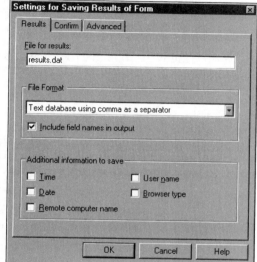

Figure 5-19:
The Settings for Saving Results of Form dialog box.

10. In the File for Results text box, type the name of the file in which you want to record users' responses.

In this example, we called it *results.dat.*

11. Click the drop-down list box under File Format and scroll down until you find *Text Database Using Comma As A Separator.* Click it to select it, and then click the OK button.

You return to the Form Properties dialog box.

12. Click the OK button to complete the creation of the form.

There! In twelve easy steps, you've created an interactive form. Publish it to a Web server that supports FrontPage extensions and you're ready to go.

FrontPage has a major drawback. Many of its features are designed to work only with the Microsoft Internet Explorer Web browser, so approximately 70 percent of the people on the Web *won't be able to use your site.* Think long and hard before you commit to eliminating that many people from your audience.

Many, but not all, Web servers work with FrontPage server extensions. If you use an Internet service provider to host your Web site, you must ask the provider whether its Web server supports the Microsoft FrontPage server extensions before you begin. If you run your own Web server, check with Microsoft to find out whether FrontPage server extensions work with your server. Of course, FrontPage is designed to work with the Microsoft Personal Web Server that is included with it.

Unfortunately, FrontPage Express does not have Composer's capability to publish your work on the World Wide Web. You have to use another program such as an FTP client to do that. (The commercial version does have a Publish button.) See the section called "Publishing Files on Your Web Site."

The next step is to try to view your pages in a browser. The only way to know for certain that your Web site is accessible to Internet users is to try to contact it yourself by using a browser. If your Web site appears as you expect, other Web users probably can see everything, too. Don't assume, however, that everything works just because it works for you. Ask somebody else to try your site and report back to you.

Make sure to check your Web site using both Netscape's browser and Microsoft's browser, to see whether you inadvertently added any browser-specific elements.

Publishing Files on Your Web Site

After you finish creating the pages for your Web site, you must send the pages to the Web server so that other people can access your pages through a Web browser. You can send content to a Web server in several ways. Depending on the services that your Web-publishing service provider offers or the features that your Web server software provides, you may have a different set of options for getting your Web pages onto your Web server.

The simplest way to send content to your Web server is to copy the files to a folder on your computer's hard drive in a directory that your Web server is configured to look for HTML files. This method works only if you run your own Web server software on your computer. If you use a Macintosh and run the Personal WebSTAR server, you could also drag and drop files on the WebSTAR program icon to publish them. If you don't run a Web server program on your computer, you must send Web pages to a Web server over the network.

Putting files in your server's Web-page folder

We can't emphasize enough the importance of a clear understanding of this last step in publishing content through your Web site. For privacy reasons, other people on the Internet normally can't access the files on your computer's hard drive, but if you're running your own Web server, you must bear in mind that a Web server does give other people access to files on your computer's hard drive. The Web server doesn't give other people unlimited access to every file on your computer, however, because that arrangement would be insecure and would compromise your privacy. Instead, Web servers enable users to access only files in certain folders. If you want other people to be able to access a particular file through your Web server, you must place that file in one of the folders that your Web server enables users to access.

You could, for example, configure a Web server to use the following directory as the default (or *root*) Web-content folder:

```
C:\INETPUB\WWWROOT\
```

Any file or folder in the WWWROOT folder is now accessible to other people through the Web server. To publish a new Web-page HTML file through your Web server, you save the file and any associated graphics or other items in the WWWROOT folder or one of its subfolders. You could, for example, save a new Web-page HTML file in a folder named SAMPLES that's a subfolder in WWWROOT.

From your Web server, your new Web page is then available to anyone who uses a URL similar to that of the following example:

```
http://your.computer/samples/newpage.html
```

Note: Because the WWWROOT folder is your Web-publishing home directory, it is considered the root (or \) of your Web-publishing directory hierarchy and therefore is not included in the URL of your Web page.

If you decide not to run your own Web server software, you must rent space on a Web server maintained by an Internet service provider. To publish your Web-site content through your rented Web server, you still must put files in a special folder. Your service provider's Web server operates exactly the same way as the Web server software that the chapter describes. Your service provider's Web server looks in a particular folder for all your Web-page content, as does the Web server software that you can run on your own computer. The following section explains the issues involved in using a Web-publishing service provider.

Using a Web-publishing service provider

Rather than run your own server, you can subscribe to a Web-publishing service, meaning that your Web pages reside on someone else's computer. That computer attaches to the Internet full time and runs a Web server program. This arrangement ensures that your documents are available through the Web all the time, normally through a fast Internet connection.

Most World Wide Web service providers charge by the number of bytes you publish, or the amount of network traffic that your publishing generates, or both. More people reading your World Wide Web material means more work for your service provider, so the provider passes on the cost to you. You may reach a point at which setting up your own HTTP server is more cost-effective than paying a World Wide Web publisher. You must balance your needs against your resources to decide on the best approach.

After you subscribe to a World Wide Web publishing service, your service provider gives you at least the following:

- User ID
- Password
- Directory in which to place your files so that they're available at your Web site

Your service provider also gives you instructions for logging on using your user ID and password and for sending files to your World Wide Web directory. To publish your HTML documents and other Web files, simply follow your service provider's instructions to send the files to your Web directory.

The most common way to send files to your Web directory on your service provider's server is to use an FTP (File Transfer Protocol) client program. WS_FTP, an FTP client program, is one of the most popular FTP programs for Windows; Fetch is a similar FTP client for the Macintosh. (Macintosh programs always have friendlier names than Windows programs.)

The first thing you do in using your FTP client program to send files to your Web directory is to tell your FTP client program which FTP server to contact. Your Internet service provider tells you the domain name of the FTP server to which you need to send Web files. Figure 5-20 shows how WS_FTP asks you which FTP server to contact (in this case, ftp.science.org). The Macintosh FTP client (Fetch) and other Windows FTP clients have a different way of asking you to enter the name of the FTP server to contact.

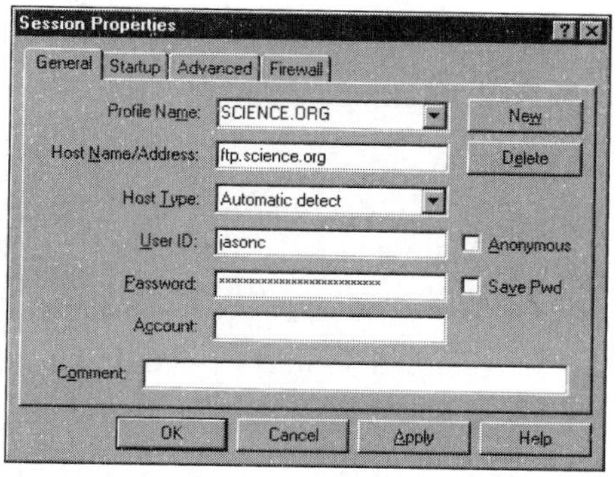

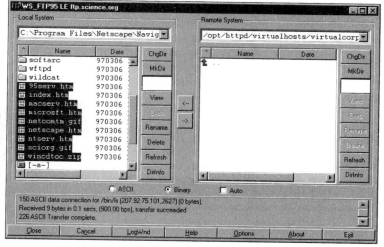

Figure 5-20:
Contact
your ISP's
FTP server
by using an
FTP client.

After your FTP client program successfully connects to the FTP server, you must locate your remote Web directory and tell the FTP client program to send your Web files to that directory. Every FTP client program works differently; Figure 5-21 shows how WS_FTP works. The WS_FTP ChgDir button on the Remote System side (the right side) of the WS_FTP window enables you to specify the full name of your Web directory.

Figure 5-21:
Locate your
remote Web
directory by
using your
FTP client
program.

In the sample screen shown in Figure 5-21, the full name of the sample remote Web directory is as follows:

```
/opt/httpd/virtualhosts/virtualcorp
```

This directory is the one in which you must put Web files if the files are to become accessible to visitors to your Web site. Save any files you want publicly accessible to Web site visitors in this directory. Be aware that the full name of your remote Web directory will be something different.

You also want to locate on your local system the directory in which you save all the files for your Web site. You must send these files to your remote Web directory so that the files are published on your Web site. At this point, all the files have successfully transferred from the local system directory to the remote Web directory. Now these files should be accessible to your Web-site visitors.

You definitely want to check to make sure that the files you just sent to your remote Web directory are available through your Web site. Start a Web browser and point the browser at the URL of your site to make sure that the files are accessible. If everything is in order, you can exit your FTP client program. In WS_FTP, you exit the program by clicking the Exit button.

Chapter 6
Web Page Layout

*T*his chapter is a follow-up to Chapter 5. If you haven't read Chapter 5 yet, you'll probably get a bit lost, so flip back and get the basics down first. If you already know the basics of Web page creation, hop right in! We'll be digging into the elements beyond basic content that go into making up a Web page.

What's on the Menu?

Hypertext links, which we cover in Chapter 5, are the way people get from place to place on the World Wide Web. But they have another use. Hypertext links can link within the page as well as outside it.

Links connect to other pages via the URL, or Internet address, of the other page but cannot connect to a specific part of a Web page. Well, a special kind of URL called a *fragment URL* is not in the official specs but works just fine for this purpose. You can use it to build a menu that lets people jump to any place you want in a Web page instead of having to start at the top and scroll down screen by screen, looking for what they want.

The way to use a fragment URL is to establish a *named anchor*. You can put a named anchor anywhere you want to in an HTML document, but you should make sure to choose a good spot where it would make sense for someone to jump to, such as a heading that starts a section of the page. How do you make a named anchor? You just use *id* (as in *identification*). Here's an example of how to make a named anchor with a secondary heading element:

```
<H2 id="level2">This is Level Two</H2>
```

Now that you have a named anchor, all you have to do is put in a link to it. You do that the same way you'd add a normal link, but you use the id of the element you want to jump to instead of the Web address of a different page. You have to add a hash mark (#) in front of it, as in the following example:

```
<A href="#level2">Go to Level Two</A>
```

You can set up a series of named anchors, one for each different place in the HTML document that people might want to go. Suppose you have a document that lists different kinds of animals, each with its own heading. You could set up the headings like this:

```
<H2 id="lions">King of the Beasts</H2>
<H2 id="tigers">Very Large Housecat</H2>
<H2 id="bears">Smokey Strikes Again</H2>
```

In between the headings, of course, you'd have all your material on lions and tigers and bears (oh, my!).

The next thing you'd do would be to set up a menu of links at the top of the page, like this:

```
<A href="#lions">Lions</A>
<A href="#tigers">Tigers</A>
<A href="#bears">Bears</A>
```

The result would look like Figure 6-1.

You can use fragment URLs also by appending them to normal URLs. That lets you reference a point in a separate HTML document from the one you put the link in. To access the section on bears from a different Web page, for example, you'd need to use a link like the following:

```
<A href="http://www.threeanimals.org/
        animallist.html#bears">Link to Bears on the
        Other Page</A>.
```

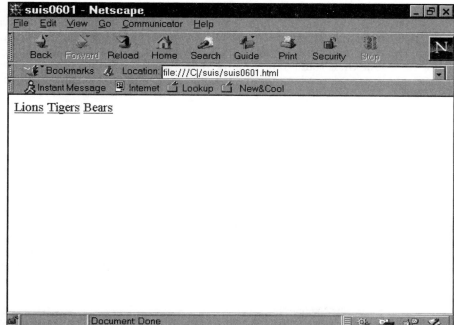

Figure 6-1:
A hypertext
menu.

A Thousand Words

In Chapter 5, you discover that you put an image into a Web page using the
following code:

```
<IMG src="image.gif">
```

Well, you can make an image into a hyperlink. Just use the same code and put
it in the middle of an anchor where you would normally put text, like this:

```
<A href="http://www.linkfinder.com/"><IMG
          src="image.gif"></A>
```

When you do this, you end up with a picture that people can use the same
way they can a regular hypertext link — just click it and you're off across the
World Wide Web. The image is surrounded with a blue border and the
cursor changes to a pointing hand when placed over the image.

But what if you want to put in lots of links? You'd need a whole bunch of
pictures, each with its own separate hypertext link coded. Or you can use an
image map.

Image maps are special images designed to accommodate multiple hypertext links. Although there's no theoretical limit to how many links you can put into one image, practicality limits it to whatever number your users can be expected to comprehend. Cram 5,000 links into a small image and you'll have something that nobody wants to use. Make an image large enough to comfortably hold that many, and it will require a year and a half to download.

We'll keep it simple and do our lions and tigers and bears menu with an image map. Just three links, only this time we'll give each beast its own Web page. Here's the first thing we need:

```
<IMG src="threeanimals.gif" usemap="#beastmap">
```

It's just like a normal image tag, but with an extra attribute: usemap. The usemap attribute tells us — and the Web browser — that the image is not a normal image, but an image map. The preceding code says to get the coordinates for the links from a map called beastmap. So where's beastmap? It's somewhere else in the body of the same HTML document. Maps, appropriately enough, start with a MAP tag. The following code and Figure 6-2 illustrate the lions and tigers and bears image map.

```
<MAP NAME="beastmap">
<AREA SHAPE=RECT COORDS="0,0,232,157" HREF="http://
          www.threeanimals.org/lions.html">
<AREA SHAPE=CIRCLE COORDS="256,267,106" HREF="http://
          www.threeanimals.org/tigers.html">
<AREA SHAPE=POLY COORDS="446,560,530,545,549,476,546,460,435,
          392,386,392,313,423,295,454,292,543,431,563,453,
          559,446,560" HREF="http://www.threeanimals.org/
          bears.html">
<AREA SHAPE=default HREF="http://www.threeanimals.org/
          index.html">
</MAP>
```

Notice that the maps have both start (<MAP>) and end (</MAP>) tags. The AREA tag is self-contained and has no end tag. So what in the world is an AREA tag? And what's with all the numbers and stuff? Image maps respond as hypertext links when you click on part of the image. The information in the AREA tag tells the image map what to do with each part of the image.

The first part, SHAPE, indicates which of the three possible shapes (rectangle, circle, or polygon) is around the portion of the image the link is associated with. The next part, COORDS (short for *coordinates*), tells how big the shape is. The final part, HREF, is just a good old hypertext link.

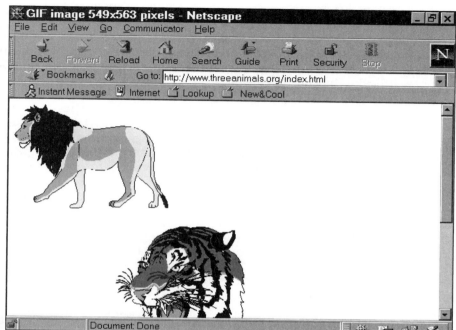

Figure 6-2:
An image
map.

The last entry, SHAPE=default, is for when users click outside the defined areas. In that case, they go to the home page of the site rather than to one of the animal pages.

So how in the world do you get all those numbers? Well, if you don't mind going nutty, you can load the image you're using for the image map into just about any graphics program and move the mouse pointer around the edges, jotting down the coordinates. Then you can take your handwritten notes and type the numbers into your HTML page, hoping you don't get any of them wrong.

If you'd rather hang on to your sanity and have a little bit of time to do things like eat and sleep, you take the easy way out and use an image map generation program. They're easy to use — you just draw the shapes around the image areas and tell the program to make you an image map. Chapter 18 tells you where to find image map generation programs.

Divide and Conquer

Horizontal rules are used to divide one section of an HTML page from another. Basically, they're lines that run across the page and look as though they're embedded in the page.

Many people replace them with GIF images of fancy lines and never use them at all. You can, however, do many things with horizontal rules. You can set them to different widths and thicknesses. You can align them to the left, right, or middle of the page. You can set them so that they appear not embedded, but as a flat line drawn across the page. And you can set them to different colors.

The basic tag for horizontal rules is `<HR>`. There is no end tag. You modify horizontal rules by adding different attributes within the tag. To change the width to 100 pixels, for example, you use `<HR width="100">`. Because you don't know what screen resolution visitors to your site will be using, however, you might not want to set an absolute width. In that case, you can set a width that is a percentage of the page width. For a line half as wide as the page, you would use `<HR width="50%">`.

The thickness of the horizontal rule is set in much the same way, but you use the `size` attribute and you can't set a percentage, because a Web browser has no way of knowing how high the page is. Therefore, you set an absolute pixel value for thickness, such as `<HR size="10">`.

To align a horizontal rule, you use the `align` attribute, like this: `<HR align="center">`. You can align to left, center, or right. It means nothing to align a horizontal rule that does not have its width set to less than the page width, though, because it will stretch from side to side regardless.

To set a horizontal rule so that it doesn't seem to sink into the page, you use `<HR noshade>`. And to set the color, you use — surprise! — the `color` attribute, like this `<HR color="#FF00FF">`. You can use the color names listed in Chapter 5 instead of a hex value if you prefer.

Setting the Table

Tables are either very boring or very useful, depending on how you apply them. In their most basic usage, they're nothing more than columns and rows that form boxes called *cells,* probably filled with boring numbers. But cells can also hold images, text, and hypertext links — anything an HTML page itself can contain.

Lots of people use tables to structure entire Web pages. Many table elements, such as captions, headers, and footers, are not involved in page layout, so we don't deal with them here. For more information on them, please see *Creating Web Pages For Dummies,* 3rd Edition, by Bud Smith and Arthur Bebak and *HTML For Dummies* by Ed Tittel and Steve James (both published by IDG Books Worldwide, Inc.).

The basic table coding is as follows:

```
<TABLE>
<TR>
<TD>
Table data goes here.
</TD>
</TR>
</TABLE>
```

The <TABLE> and </TABLE> tags define the beginning and end of the table. The <TR> and </TR> tags define the beginning and end of a row. The <TD> and </TD> tags define the beginning and end of a particular cell within the row.

Although tables can have visible borders and dividing lines called *rules* between the cells, these are not useful for layout purposes. Thus, you should set the border attribute to 0, as in the following example:

```
<TABLE border="0">
<TR>
<TD>
Table data goes here.
</TD>
</TR>
</TABLE>
```

Fill Out the Form, Please

Forms are an important part of Web pages because you use them to get input from visitors to your site. That input is then either sent to you or processed by a program (see Chapter 16). Forms are built out of elements called *controls* that enable people to give them information. Forms have both start and end tags (<FORM> and </FORM>).

The first thing you see in a form is the action attribute; the second is the method. The action is what the form does; the method is how the form passes information along. The most common method is post, and the other method is get. The post method allows more information to be passed more easily.

The value of the method is normally one of two things. It's either the URL of a program that processes the data from user input or it's a mailto URL that tells the form to send the data to you through e-mail. The URL approach typically looks like this:

```
<FORM action="http://www.dosomething.com/cgi-bin/
              takeaction.pl" method="post">
(form contents go here)
</FORM>
```

The mailto method looks like this:

```
<FORM action="mailto:me@myaddress.com" method="post">
(form contents go here)
</FORM>
```

The controls that go in between the start and end tags are most commonly composed of variations on the input element. This element is the most important one for form development because it includes so many different input controls, such as check boxes, radio buttons, text boxes, and the submit and reset buttons.

Check boxes are squares that display a check mark when a user clicks them. Like all controls, you must give them a name and a value. The name of the control and the value it contains comprise the information sent to a program or an e-mail message.

A check box has only two states: checked or unchecked. If you simply declare its existence, it is unchecked, as in the following example:

```
<INPUT type="checkbox" name="box1" value="ralph">
```

You can also declare the check box to be selected when the form is created, like this:

```
<INPUT type="checkbox" name="box1" value="ralph" checked>
```

Another type of input is a radio button, which looks like a circle. Radio buttons are like check boxes except for one important difference. In a grouping of several check boxes, you can check more than one check box, but in a grouping of several radio buttons, you can check only one radio button. So, if someone might make several nonexclusive choices, use check boxes. Where there's only one possible choice that can be made from several possibilities, use a group of radio buttons. You declare them the same way you declare check boxes, except you use `radio` instead of `checkbox`:

```
<INPUT type="radio" name="button1" value="ralph">
```

As with check boxes, you can set a radio button to be selected without any input from the user:

```
<INPUT type="radio" name="button1" value="ralph" checked>
```

Each radio button must have a different name. If you wanted to set up an array of radio buttons, you'd have to have something like the following:

```
<INPUT type="radio" name="button1" value="ralph" checked>
<INPUT type="radio" name="button2" value="george">
<INPUT type="radio" name="button3" value="sandra">
```

The `text` type sets up a small box in which a single line of text can be typed:

```
<INPUT type="text" name="myname">
```

If you need to have a larger amount of text, you use the `TEXTAREA` element instead of the `INPUT` element. It looks like Figure 6-3, and a typical coding looks like this:

```
<TEXTAREA name="typehere" cols="50" rows="20">
</TEXTAREA>
```

Selection lists are an important part of form design. Although you can use a group of radio buttons to offer choices among options, if you have more than about four options to offer, a selection list is the best way to go. A selection list is much more compact than a very large group of radio buttons because it creates a drop-down list of choices. To make a selection list, you use the `SELECT` tag and include several `OPTION` elements, as in the following code:

```
<SELECT name="chooseit">
<OPTION> Alternative 1</OPTION>
<OPTION> Alternative 2</OPTION>
<OPTION> Alternative 3</OPTION>
</SELECT>
```

See Figure 6-4 for a form that uses all the elements discussed in this section.

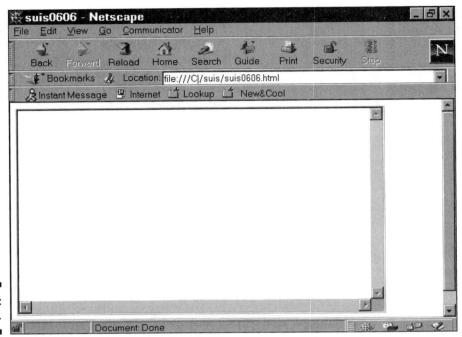

Figure 6-3:
A text area.

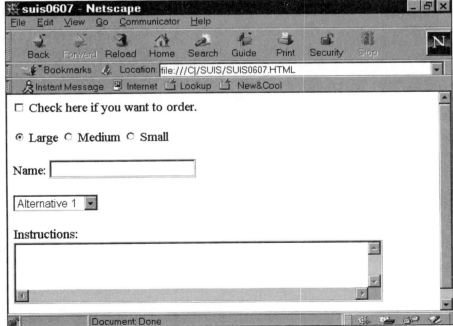

Figure 6-4:
A form
with many
elements.

Marshall, I Wuz Framed!

Frames are great for laying out Web pages because you can use them to set up areas on a single page that react differently. The LinkFinder site (`http://www.linkfinder.com/`), for example, is built on frames. (A frameless version can be selected also in case someone is using an antiquated browser or just plain doesn't like frames.) As shown in Figure 6-5, the top frame shows the LinkFinder logo, the left one shows the list of categories in the site, and the main one on the lower right is where different Web pages are displayed.

Frames, which are built on the `FRAMESET` element, are an alternative to normal HTML design, which uses the `BODY` element. Framesets are used to divide pages into separate functional elements. Unlike the `BODY` element, more than one `FRAMESET` element can be contained in an HTML page. The following code illustrates how you can have frames contained within other frames:

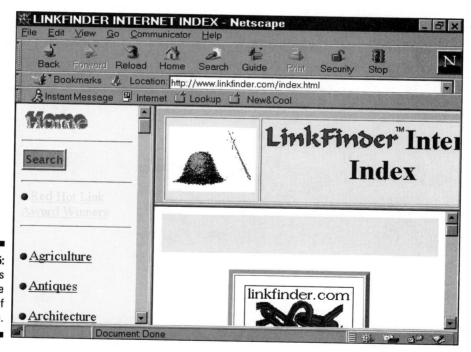

Figure 6-5:
Frames
define the
structure of
a Web site.

```
<FRAMESET cols="100,*">
    <FRAME name="Sharon" src="her.html" scrolling="auto">
<FRAMESET rows="220,*">
    <FRAME name="Susan" src="her2.html" scrolling="no">
    <FRAME name="Myra" src="her3.html" scrolling="auto">
</FRAMESET>
</FRAMESET>
```

The first frameset is a vertical one, which is why it is defined in terms of cols (columns). The second frameset, which is contained within the first one, is defined in terms of rows. This leads to one column on the left that is 100 pixels wide. The * means to leave the rest of the space for the second frameset. That frameset is horizontal instead of vertical (composed of rows instead of columns), and takes the first 220 pixels from the top of the page for the frame named Susan and leaves the rest of the page for the frame named Myra.

The src part specifies the source of the frame (in other words, the URL). And, finally, the scrolling part defines whether or not scrollbars are in the frame. You can do lots more with frames. See *Creating Web Pages For Dummies* and *HTML For Dummies* for details.

Chapter 7

Setting Up an Internet News Server

● ●

In This Chapter

▶ Getting a handle on Internet News

▶ Creating local newsgroups

▶ Setting up your own news server

● ●

*I*nternet news, commonly referred to as *Usenet news,* is a simple resource that enables people around the world to carry on conversations and exchange information. The term *news* implies a professional, journalistic source of information, but Usenet news rarely resembles anything professional. The reason for this lack of professionalism is that the vast majority of the global Usenet is uncontrolled, so anyone can post a message about anything. As a result, having a real conversation about a particular topic is difficult; even more difficult at times is keeping the conversation focused on the original topic.

Nonetheless, Usenet news remains a valuable resource for global topical conversation and information and is an aspect of using the Internet that some people find the most rewarding. The uncontrolled nature of Usenet is part of the reason for its popularity. People can (and do) discuss anything — anything at all — in Usenet newsgroups.

Using Internet News

Internet News is a software system that enables people to read and post messages in topic-specific message areas called *newsgroups.* Some newsgroups, such as alt.alien.visitors or alt.destroy.the.internet, are strange or useless. Many other newsgroups are serious interactive tools that provide indispensable resources for technical and scientific professionals.

To understand the difference between a local newsgroup and a global one that is part of Usenet, you need to know a little about how people read newsgroups, how you distribute news messages through the Internet, and how the news system operates.

Internet News is a client/server system, with the News server managing the newsgroups. Participants use client software, called a *newsreader,* to read and post messages to the groups. Until recently, people used News almost exclusively as a distributed, global Internet system known as *Usenet.* Each News server within the Usenet system forwarded new message postings to other News servers until the messages propagated to every News server in the world that participated in Usenet.

More recently, people with Internet sites have provided public access to local newsgroups published from their own News servers rather than start new newsgroups within the global Usenet system. Providing public access to your own News server is simpler and more flexible than participating in Usenet. The process of starting a new group within the Usenet system is cumbersome and political, and you shouldn't attempt to do so unless you have both a strong tolerance for lunacy and a real love of political infighting.

This chapter describes the technical function of Internet News in an easy and simple-to-understand manner. The chapter also explores ways in which you or your company can establish a presence on Internet News and integrate this valuable interactive resource into your Internet site. Although creating a new global Usenet newsgroup is possible, we recommend that you instead set up your own Internet News server at your Internet site, or use one of the simpler discussion group programs described in Chapter 10.

Looking at Both Sides of the News

News servers use protocols, and protocols usually have weird acronyms. The Internet News protocol, for example, is *NNTP,* or *Network News Transport Protocol.* In this chapter, we show you how to configure your own NNTP News server, set up newsgroups, and configure your local News server to either contribute to the global Usenet News system or keep newsgroup postings to itself so that users must come to your site to read and post to your newsgroups. Setting up an Internet News server, however, is only half the story. As a News server provider, you need to know about the software that people are likely to use to read and post messages in your newsgroups.

Both Netscape and Microsoft provide easy-to-use newsreaders. Netscape provides a newsreader as a component of Communicator, and Microsoft provides one called Outlook Express as part of Internet Explorer 4. A number of standalone newsreaders are available, such as Agent (and a scaled-down version called Free Agent that is, as the name implies, free).

Configuring and using newsreaders — the Netscape or Microsoft products, or some other brand — is a fairly standard process. You

✔ Configure the newsreader to contact a News server that enables you to connect to it.

✔ Download the list of newsgroups offered by the News server and choose which ones to view.

The first configuration step — telling a newsreader which News server to connect to — is an aspect about newsreaders that has changed recently. Normally, a user needs to configure a newsreader just once for use with his or her Internet service provider's Usenet News server. The user then has access to all the Usenet newsgroups provided by the ISP. However, many companies or people who provide newsgroups that you don't find in Usenet run their own News servers. Many of these News servers provide newsgroups on product-specific topics or topics that complement the offerings of an Internet site. Other servers provide newsgroups with particular topic categories. The science.org News server, for example, provides publicly accessible science- and technology-related newsgroups. To access these newsgroups, a user simply uses a Web browser to access the following URL:

```
news:news.science.org/
```

The user's Web browser launches a newsreader program whenever the browser encounters a URL that begins with the news: prefix, such as the one in the preceding example. (If you are not familiar with URL syntax by now, this prefix may be news to you.) We discuss the news: URL syntax in more detail later, when we show you how to include a link to your Internet News resource on your World Wide Web site.

More and more people are abandoning the Usenet groups, which tend to fill with ads that less-considerate people leave in unrelated newsgroups. You also find much of the pornographic content on the Internet in these newsgroups. Parents who are concerned about explicit content are especially concerned about their children having access to Usenet newsgroups.

The news: URL prefix has a special meaning to many Web browsers. Some older browsers don't understand the news: URL and give the user an error message, but the majority of Web browsers in use today do understand the news: URL. You can type a news: URL just as you can type an http: URL or can click a hyperlink in a Web page. If you enter news: all by itself in a Web browser, a newsreader program usually appears on-screen. To access a particular newsgroup automatically after the newsreader appears, you can type the name of the newsgroup that you want to access immediately after the news: prefix. The following URL for example, accesses the global newsgroup news.answers shown in Figure 7-1:

```
news:news.answers
```

Now comes the tricky part. The URL shown in the preceding example is a valid URL for the news.answers newsgroup, but unlike the URL for your Web site, the news:news.answers URL doesn't specify a unique resource on the Internet. Remember that the URL of your Web site is a unique address; whenever anyone on the Internet accesses your Web site, that person sees the same Web page that everyone else sees. With the news:news.answers URL, however, each person sees something different and accesses a different News server. (Remember that a *News server* is a program that maintains newsgroups and news messages and communicates with newsreaders.) The newsgroup news.answers is an example of a global Usenet newsgroup that each user accesses on his or her local News server.

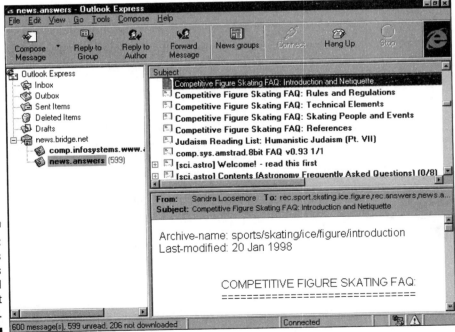

Figure 7-1:
Newreaders
can access
global
Usenet
newsgroups.

After a user posts a message to a global newsgroup, that message enters the global news stream, beginning with the News server that the user's Internet service provider (ISP) maintains. Then the message is distributed automatically to other News servers on the Internet. Not every message that you post to a global newsgroup makes its way to every News server, so people who read a global newsgroup can't necessarily access every message that people post to the newsgroup.

For most newsgroups, this situation isn't a big deal. The kinds of conversations that occur in global newsgroups don't require 100 percent reliability. But the unreliable nature of global newsgroups does preclude your company from offering customer support or other important business electronic conferencing through a global newsgroup. The answer to this problem is to create a local newsgroup instead.

A *local newsgroup* is one that exists only on a single News server. Because a local newsgroup isn't distributed globally, anyone on the Internet who accesses a local newsgroup sees precisely the same messages that every other person sees. This situation enables you to use local newsgroups to conduct important discussions in which every participant must access every message, as is the case in a customer-support group.

To access a local newsgroup, you use the familiar URL format of a prefix followed by a colon and two forward slashes (as in news:), followed by the domain name or IP address of the server. The URL, for example, points to the Internet News server at science.org. You can also specify a specific newsgroup on news.science.org, as in the following URL, which points to a newsgroup for genetics students:

```
news:news.science.org/science.org.genetics.student
```

Figure 7-2 shows the Microsoft newsreader program after the program contacts the news.science.org News server and accesses the science.org.genetics.student newsgroup. This newsgroup is a local newsgroup that you can access globally.

Thousands upon thousands of Usenet newsgroups are available on the Internet, and you may wonder how they all got there, especially if you want to create one yourself. The following section answers this question; later sections show you how to create a Usenet newsgroup, how to set up your own News server program, and how to create your own local newsgroups.

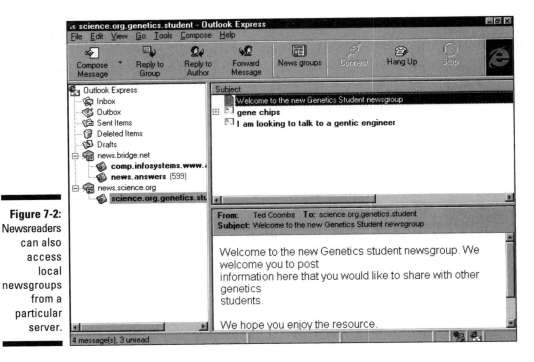

Figure 7-2:
Newsreaders
can also
access
local
newsgroups
from a
particular
server.

Where do little newsgroups come from?

You may have seen some of the Usenet newsgroups, such as those mentioned earlier in this chapter, and wondered how people came up with those
odd names. And what's with all those dots in the names? Newsgroup creators organize their newsgroups, whether those newsgroups are part of the
Usenet system or available only on your local News server, in a *newsgroup
hierarchy.* The people who wrote the first News-server software decided to
organize newsgroups in categories. The categories were given short sym-
bolic names, such as news, comp, and sci. This naming convention forms
the newsgroup hierarchy. A newsgroup with a name that begins with one of
those category names is part of that newsgroup hierarchy. Following are a
few samples of different newsgroup hierarchies:

- ✔ news.answers
- ✔ comp.forsale
- ✔ sci.energy

Each newsgroup category serves a particular purpose. Table 7-1 shows the
seven major categories that make up the core of the global Usenet newsgroup
hierarchy.

Table 7-1	The Seven Major Global Usenet Newsgroup Categories
Hierarchy	**Purpose**
news	Groups that pertain to the Internet News system itself
sci	Scientific newsgroups for serious discussions
rec	Newsgroups for discussion of recreational activities
comp	Computer-related newsgroups
misc	Miscellaneous discussion groups (no focus)
soc	Groups for socializing or talking about social issues
talk	Debates about controversial topics

Organizations that run News servers create local newsgroups. Most universities, for example, have News servers and provide local newsgroups for discussion of campus-specific issues. Internet access providers have local newsgroups to provide technical support or to give their customers a place to talk among themselves.

The names of local newsgroups don't need to adhere to the global Usenet News naming convention. The Internet access provider Netcom, Inc. (at http://www.netcom.com/), for example, provides several local newsgroups with names that begin with netcom., such as netcom.support.

Organizations create and name global newsgroups in two ways, depending on the type of group involved in the process. Official Usenet newsgroup categories are very strict about new group names. The official global Usenet newsgroup categories listed in Table 7-1 rely on a voting process. During this voting process, participants select — or possibly even vote on — the exact name for the group. The unofficial Usenet newsgroup categories, such as alt., rely on anarchy for group creation. These unofficial Usenet News categories don't impose any naming restrictions, so these groups can use just about any name imaginable.

Move over, Larry King and Art Bell: Moderated groups

Most newsgroups allow anyone to post anything. The quality of the people who participate by posting messages determines the quality of the messages in a newsgroup. Inappropriate postings often become the norm for that newsgroup. A special type of newsgroup solves this problem by enabling someone to approve or reject articles before a user can post an article in the newsgroup. This type of newsgroup is known as a *moderated newsgroup*.

One person — usually the creator of the newsgroup — becomes the moderator for that group. Articles that people post to the newsgroup go directly to the moderator instead of to the group. The moderator reads each message and then approves or rejects the article.

Moderating a newsgroup is an excellent way to maintain a question-and-answer format or to establish a level of editorial quality. This arrangement is also effective for newsgroups that function as one-way news and information sources. In these newsgroups, the moderator is the sole supplier of information to the newsgroup; all other postings, he or she can reject.

The following section shows you how to create both moderated and unmoderated global and local newsgroups. The information in this section (and earlier sections of this chapter) should enable you to decide which type of newsgroup is most appropriate for your needs.

Note: Global newsgroups are essentially public property. You don't own that group, even if the group was your idea in the first place, and you can't control the group, even if you moderate it.

Forming a Local Newsgroup

The organizations that control News servers create local newsgroups. Because an organization has total control of the groups that exist on its News server, that organization can create any group instantly. Contact your Internet service provider to find out whether it can create a local newsgroup for you and, if so, whether users elsewhere on the Internet can access the local newsgroup.

If you're searching for a host for your local newsgroup, keep the following two points in mind:

✔ The entire local-newsgroup concept is somewhat new on the Internet. Don't be surprised if your local ISP has never received such a request.

✔ The name of your local newsgroup shouldn't conflict with the name of a global newsgroup. Identical names may cause serious technical problems. The news administrator is likely to resolve this conflict by dropping your group in favor of the global one. This resolution keeps the News server software from getting confused.

Until recently, most people used local newsgroups for only local discussions. These included universities, Internet access providers, and ISPs that provide news servers with local newsgroups, such as tech support newsgroups solely for the use of their customers. Outsiders were prevented from accessing the local newsgroups or simply never tried to access them, because gaining access wasn't easy. Now that most Web browsers support the `news:hostname/groupname` URL syntax, however, you can host a local newsgroup that people can access globally.

Still, creating a local newsgroup isn't common yet. Be patient and be persistent if you encounter a confused response to your request to create a local newsgroup. (If all else fails, buy the news administrator a copy of this book.)

Any idea for a newsgroup is valid. Some Usenet newsgroups have become famous. The `rec.food` newsgroups, for example, are renowned as a rich source of recipes. Other groups have loyal followings. Companies such as Microsoft and Netscape provide local News servers to which thousands post daily, discussing their products. What makes these newsgroups popular is the involvement and feeling of community that surrounds the group. Creating a newsgroup on a topic that interests not only you but also many other people can be an excellent way to make friends or meet colleagues.

Running Your Own News Server

Running a News server on your Internet site can be one of the most rewarding aspects of maintaining an Internet site. If you work with Web servers and list servers, you find that people come and go from your site, sometimes leaving little more than log entries. A great number of people who use your News server may post information there, however, thus participating in your Internet resource. As mentioned elsewhere in this book, taking part in providing information on the Internet is important. Newsgroups often provide more important information than Web pages. People use these resources when, for example, they need to share important technical information with one another.

Instead of burdening yourself by creating static content, as you do in a Web page, you generally find that the moment you fire up your News server and start a newsgroup, you have an important, vital Internet resource at your fingertips.

If you want other people to participate in your newsgroups, you and other people in your organization must actively participate in the newsgroup. Seed the newsgroup initially with topics of interest, demonstrating the type of information you hope to see in the newsgroup. High-quality postings beget more high-quality postings. Set your standards early. Changing later — or, more importantly, regaining disillusioned visitors to your News server — is almost impossible.

News servers have the following two primary capabilities:

✔ **To give users access to all Usenet newsgroups (or to a subset of newsgroups).** This capability is one that you may want to provide, whether or not you choose to start your own newsgroups. To give your users access to Usenet newsgroups, you need someone who's running a News server that provides Usenet newsgroups to agree to forward the newsgroup messages to your server on a regular basis. Getting your newsgroup messages in this manner is known as *having a feed*. The other provider feeds messages to your News server regularly.

✔ **To provide local newsgroups.** You create these newsgroups locally, and they aren't considered to be part of the Usenet news hierarchy. After you create local newsgroups, you must decide whether to enable visitors from the Internet to view your local newsgroups or restrict access to these groups, enabling only users on your local intranet to view your newsgroups. (Remember that an intranet is a local area network that runs network applications, such as News and the World Wide Web.)

The Windows 95/NT News server that we discuss in the following section has an additional capability: sucking newsgroup messages from a News server (much as a newsreader program does). Newsreaders download message headers from a News server and normally leave the full text of the message on the server until the newsreader requests the text. The News server that we discuss requests from another News server the full text of every message in each newsgroup. All you need to provide your users with newsgroups in this manner is normal read access to a News server.

Getting started

To serve up your own newsgroup, you first need to install a News server. We chose DNews for Windows 95/NT and Macintosh as the News server to demonstrate in this book (versions are also available for various flavors of UNIX). This News server is simple to install and maintain; has a full list of features; and has the sucking capability described in the preceding section, which enables you to provide Usenet newsgroups without a feed. (DNews is shareware, so remember to send in your license fee if you intend to keep using it.)

You can download DNews from the following URL:

```
http://netwinsite.com/dnews.htm
```

You perform most of the work involved in setting up your DNews News server during installation. We walk you through each step of the installation in detail in this section. Just follow these steps:

1. **Start the setup program on your PC or Macintosh.**

   After specifying where to install the files, the first dialog box that appears requests your fully qualified IP name or number. (Refer to Chapter 3 for a complete description of fully qualified domain names and IP numbers.) Figure 7-3 shows the dialog box with a `science.org` machine name, which you must replace with your computer's fully qualified domain name. This dialog box usually appears with this text box already filled in for you.

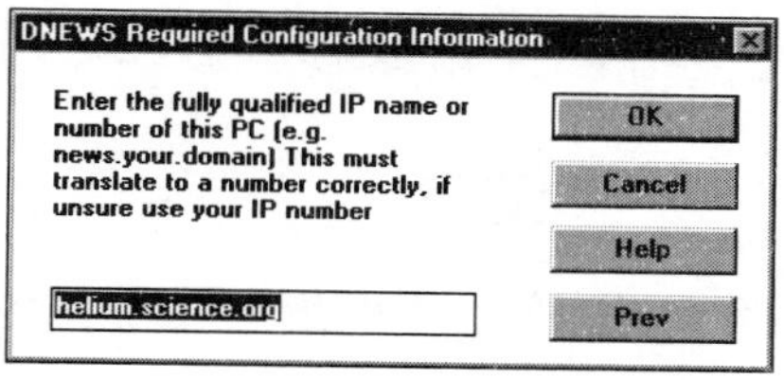

Figure 7-3:
Enter
your fully
qualified
domain
name.

2. **Correct the entry in the dialog box, if necessary, and then click OK.**

   The next dialog box asks whether you have a feed or whether your News server is going to suck its News messages from a News server. By default, the Yes I'm going to Suck News check box is selected, as shown in Figure 7-4.

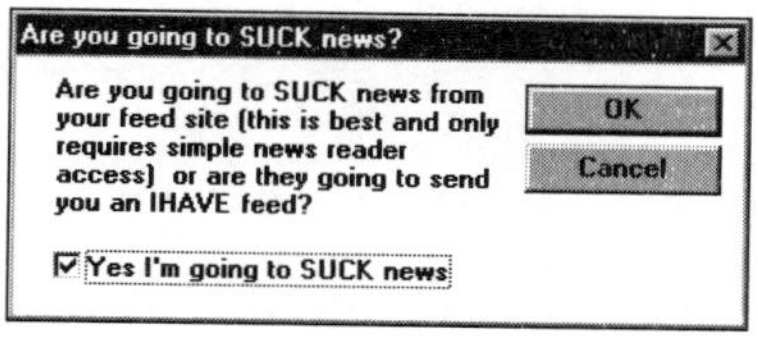

Figure 7-4:
Decide
whether
your News
server will
suck news.

3. **If you don't have a feed, leave the check box in Figure 7-4 checked, and then click OK.**

4. **If you have a feed, do the following:**

   a. **Click to clear the check box in Figure 7-4, and then click OK.**

   b. **Enter the fully qualified domain name of the News server that DNews needs to contact to request news, and then click OK.**

   Replace the default sample shown in Figure 7-5 with the correct domain name.

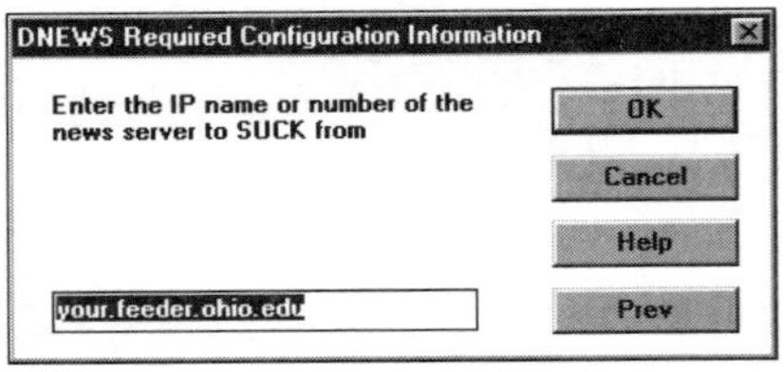

Figure 7-5:
Enter the domain name of the server from which DNews will suck.

DNEWS Required Configuration Information	☒
Enter the IP name or number of the news server to SUCK from	OK
	Cancel
	Help
your.feeder.ohio.edu	Prev

5. **Supply the domain name of your e-mail gateway, and then click OK (see Figure 7-6).**

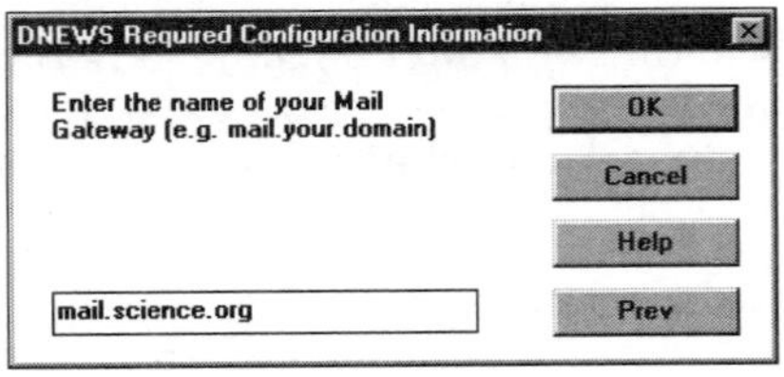

Figure 7-6:
Enter the fully qualified domain name of your e-mail gateway.

DNEWS Required Configuration Information	☒
Enter the name of your Mail Gateway (e.g. mail.your.domain)	OK
	Cancel
	Help
mail.science.org	Prev

News works closely with your e-mail system. You can find the information you need to complete this dialog box in the properties of your e-mail client program; alternatively, ask your network administrator. You must supply this information so that the News server can send reports to the news administrator and also send postings to moderators of moderated newsgroups for approval. Your e-mail client program has a menu choice for setting and viewing properties. Start your e-mail client at this time and view the properties to retrieve this information.

In the following step, you get to designate who will receive reports and complaints from the DNews server program.

6. **Enter the e-mail address of the News administrator in this dialog box, and then click OK (see Figure 7-7).**

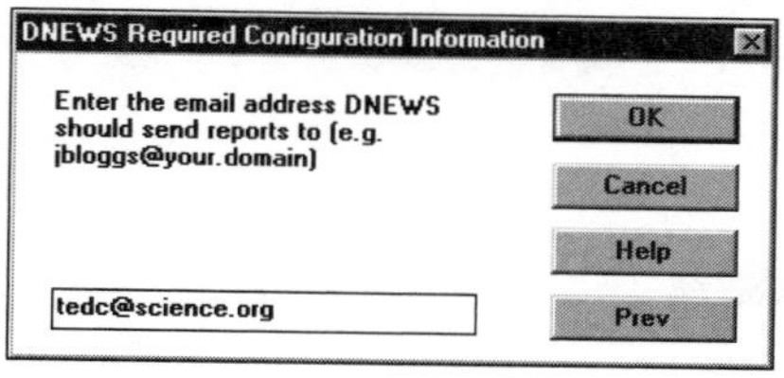

Figure 7-7:
Designate
a News
administrator
and enter
the admin-
istrator's
e-mail
address
here.

Note: Please don't enter tedc@science.org, as shown in Figure 7-7. Ted doesn't want to receive messages from your News server. He likes e-mail, but not *that* much.

7. **Enter the number of megabytes you want to allocate to the News server for storage in the text box, and then click OK.**

The default value is 100 (see Figure 7-8). You may need to adjust this number later.

Note: Specifying too much can leave you without room for other programs; specifying too little can leave you with inadequate space to store newsgroup information.

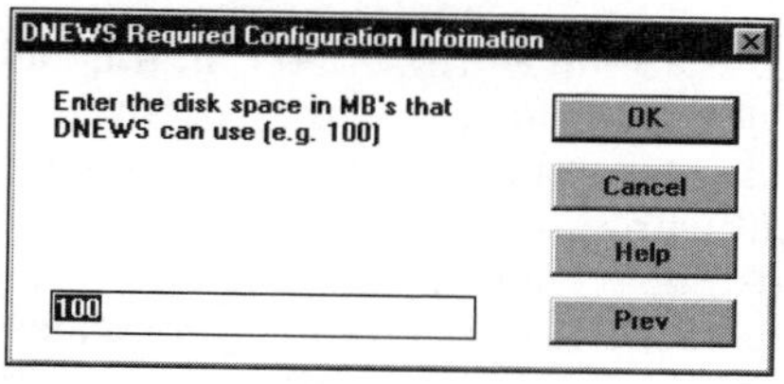

Figure 7-8:
Allocate
hard-disk
space to
store
newsgroup
information.

Some Usenet newsgroups, especially the `alt.binary` hierarchy, can use a considerable amount of hard disk space. Make sure that you have the processing power, bandwidth, and hard disk space to support the storage and transfer (to and from the server) of large binary files. Not heeding this warning could overload your computer to the point where it can't function until you reboot. Be warned, too, that many Usenet `alt.binary` files contain graphically explicit material that may not be suitable for children.

8. **In the next dialog box, enter the domain to which DNews needs to send e-mail confirmations, and then click OK (see Figure 7-9).**

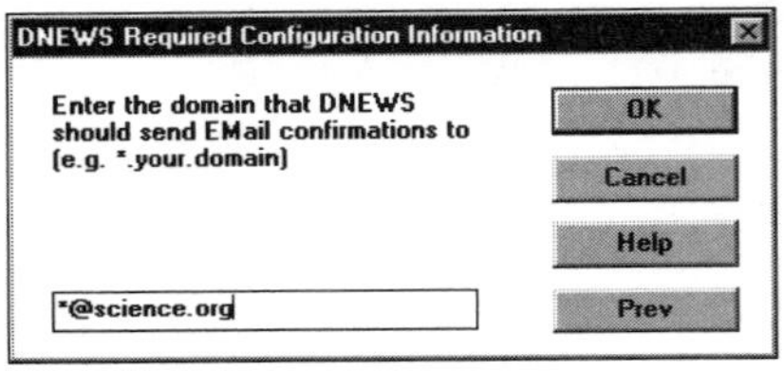

Figure 7-9:
Specify local users so they can receive confirmations of their posting.

> **DNEWS Required Configuration Information**
>
> Enter the domain that DNEWS should send EMail confirmations to (e.g. *.your.domain)
>
> *@science.org
>
> OK
> Cancel
> Help
> Prev

Note: This dialog box is a little tricky to fill out, so take care in doing so.

The information you enter in this dialog box gives DNews an idea of who the local users are so that the program can send e-mail confirmations to them. These confirmations tell the users that their postings were successfully sent to a nonlocal newsgroup.

9. **If you want to restrict your newsgroups to users in your intranet, enter the IP address of your domain with an asterisk (*) in the last (host) portion of the IP address in this dialog box, and then click OK.**

You could enter, for example, **207.92.75.***.

If you want to provide access to the world, enter * in this field, as shown in Figure 7-10. Providing world access may be your choice if you're providing only local newsgroups and want everyone to be able to access these groups. But whoa — think hard. Do you *really* want to provide news to the world? Believe me, if you provide it, seekers *will* come! Access to a majority of the Usenet hierarchy appeals to many people who enjoy having free access to newsgroups. (Several free Usenet servers already exist on the Internet. Providing Usenet for free may be nice but it isn't necessary.)

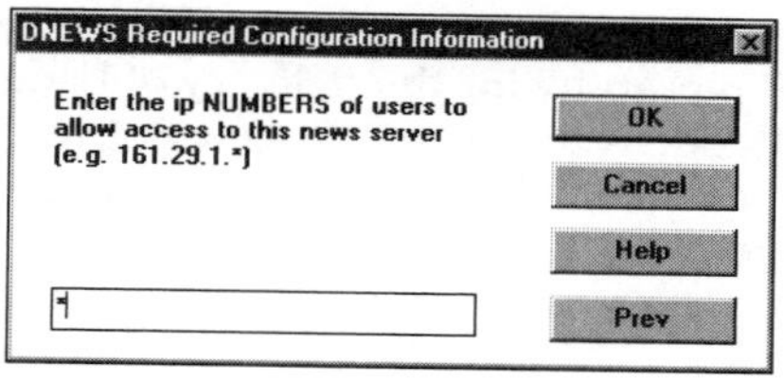

Figure 7-10:
Enter the IP
address of
users who
can access
your News
server.

DNEWS Required Configuration Information

Enter the ip NUMBERS of users to
allow access to this news server
(e.g. 161.29.1.*)

OK

Cancel

Help

Prev

10. **Enter the domain names of users to whom you want to give access to your News server, and then click OK.**

   This step is similar to Step 9. Figure 7-11 shows an example in which you allow only computers within the `science.org` domain to access the DNews server. Using a domain name may be more inclusive when the domain incorporates several blocks of IP addresses.

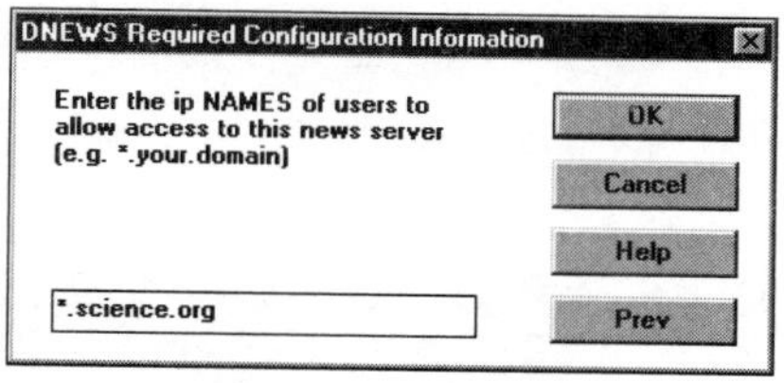

Figure 7-11:
Enter the
domain
name of
users who
can access
your News
server.

DNEWS Required Configuration Information

Enter the ip NAMES of users to
allow access to this news server
(e.g. *.your.domain)

OK

Cancel

Help

*.science.org

Prev

You've completed your setup. The main DNews Manager dialog box appears, as shown in Figure 7-12. Should you ever want to set up these parameters again, you can click the Setup Wizard button in the DNews Manager dialog box. The Setup wizard takes you through the same steps you went through during installation. You can always choose to administer your News server by running the DNews Manager.

Setting up an incoming feed

A *feed* is the traditional way that a News server receives Usenet news. This setup is known as operating an *IHAVE* feed. News servers that have an IHAVE feed passively listen for the *upstream,* or *provider,* News server to send News messages to them, which is the way Usenet is primarily set up. (The upstream

News server is the program that provides news to your server.) Each News server that participates in Usenet has a feed from some other News server; no central server or structured hierarchy for the delivery of Usenet news exists. If you were to diagram the delivery of news this way, the diagram might appear to be similar to a cotton ball under a microscope — a great cloud of fiber, strung every which way.

Getting active

Each News server that operates with an IHAVE feed must have a list of the active newsgroups on the upstream News server. You store this list of newsgroups in a file with a name such as ACTIVE or ACTIVE_FILE. Before you can begin receiving your feed, you need to load this file onto your local machine.

You can FTP (that is, use the File Transfer Protocol program) to transfer the ACTIVE file from the upstream machine and save the file on your local hard drive. You can get instructions from the news administrator of the upstream server for downloading a copy of the ACTIVE file. Save the file to the following path and filename:

```
\DNEWS\SPOOL\ACTIVE.DAT
```

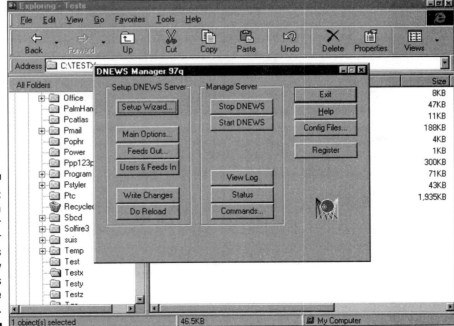

Figure 7-12:
You can administer your DNews server by using this administrative tool.

If you can't get an ACTIVE file from the upstream machine, you can load one from the following FTP site. (***Note:*** The file may have a slightly different name, with the word *active* in the filename.)

```
ftp.std.com
```

You can also find a FAQ (frequently asked questions) document for DNews at the preceding FTP site. Look in the /FTP/VENDORS/NETWIN/DNEWS directory.

Sending an outgoing feed

DNews has a feature called Live Links that automatically sends messages that you receive on your site on to a recipient machine downstream. (A downstream machine is any computer to which you send news. This designation, of course, makes your computer the upstream machine.) This setup operates differently — and more efficiently — than the setups of other News servers. Instead of reading the messages from the hard disk and then sending them downstream, DNews forwards the messages immediately, even before storing them on your hard drive. This setup enables you to support multiple machines downstream, with little effect on your Internet site.

Set up your NEWSFEEDS.CONF file with the following entry for each downstream machine you want to support:

```
site qualified.domain.name
type live
groups *
```

Edit the NEWSFEEDS.CONF file by using any text editor, such as Notepad. You can find the NEWSFEEDS.CONF file in the \DNEWS directory. The `qualified.domain.name` is the fully qualified domain name of the downstream machine. As you become more familiar with DNews, you can add parameters to further customize your outgoing feed.

Sending local posts upstream

Because DNews can provide a News server without having an IHAVE feed, you can post messages back to upstream machines by using a workaround. We call this a *posting feed*. To enable you to send messages this way, DNews pretends to be a newsreader. Messages you post to the upstream machine go out looking as though they were sent by a newsreader.

The important step in preparing DNews to post messages in this manner is setting the `exclude` parameter in the NEWSFEEDS.CONF file to exclude your provider. Use a text editor to add the following lines to the NEWSFEEDS. CONF file:

```
site me
Groups *
site $nntp_feeder
type built in
posting
groups *
exclude news.provider.net
```

Posting with an IHAVE feed

The IHAVE feed is the normal way to send articles upstream. To convert a posting feed to an IHAVE feed, simply remove the word `posting` from your NEWSFEEDS.CONF file. Removing this word sets up DNews to post messages in a more conventional manner.

Controlling the News Server

You control the DNews News server by sending it commands. Clicking the Commands button in the DNews Manager dialog box displays a complete list of commands along with short descriptions. (***Note:*** Before its designers created this Windows interface, DNews had a command-line interface called Tellnews, which is why the commands in DNews are still known in its documentation as Tellnews commands.) Select the command you want to execute by double-clicking the command name in this list. If the command requires parameters, a dialog box appears, asking you to fill in the required parameters. To ease any possible confusion, the dialog box includes a description of each parameter.

One of the commands in the list that appears after you click the Commands button is `EXPIRE`. If you issue the `EXPIRE` command, DNews begins deleting all expired newsgroup messages. Other important commands include the following:

- `EXIT` shuts down the DNews server.
- `GETGROUPS` retrieves newsgroups in a sucking DNews configuration.

> ✔ KEY is used to enter your license key, which is given to you when you register the program. (Remember that DNews is shareware, and you should license the program as soon as possible.)
>
> ✔ KILLGROUP removes a group from the active file.

If you want a longer description of each command and its use, the DNews documentation includes a full list of commands in the COMMANDS.HTM file, located in the \DNEWS\MANUAL\ directory.

Now that your News server is set up and running, the next step is to create some local newsgroups.

Creating Local Newsgroups

Earlier in this chapter, we discuss setting up DNews to provide Usenet news. A much more exciting use for a News server is setting up local newsgroups. A good idea is to plan your local newsgroup hierarchy *before* you begin creating newsgroups. You don't need to follow the Usenet hierarchy if you never intend for other News servers to host your local newsgroups.

Creating your own hierarchy of newsgroups is easy: Think about a broad topic heading, and make this heading the first hierarchical level. *Support,* for example, may serve as a topic heading for newsgroups that support your company's products. The next level of the hierarchy might use the name of your products. If your company makes saw blades, a newsgroup that you may decide to create is support.saw_blades.

To set up local newsgroups on your News server, follow these steps:

1. **Start the DNews Manager by launching it from the Windows 95 Start menu, and then click the Commands button in the DNews Manager dialog box.**

   A list of commands appears.

2. **Double-click the Newsgroup command.**

   The Command Parameters dialog box appears.

3. **In the Group text box, fill in the name of the newsgroup.**

4. **If your newsgroup is moderated, enter m in the next parameter text box; otherwise, for unmoderated groups (normal groups), enter y.**

5. **Enter your name as the creator of the newsgroup in the field provided for that purpose.**

6. In the Description text box, enter a short description of the newsgroup, and then click OK.

This description appears in the ACTIVE.NAMES file.

This process is all you need to do to get going. Completely administrating a News server is beyond the scope of this chapter. Refer to the DNews manual for details.

Internet News and the World Wide Web

The newsgroups that exist around the world today — whether they are global and part of Usenet or local and provided by a single organization — offer an incredible amount of information and serve as a forum for dialogue on just about any topic. Until recently, however, using Internet News at all was difficult for most people, and accessing the local newsgroups provided by an organization's News server was impossible. The newest Web browser and newsreader programs, however, are easier than earlier programs for people to use to participate in News as part of their Internet experience. Current Web browsers even support embedded `news:` URL hyperlinks in Web pages, so that users need only click a link to read a newsgroup on your News server.

Administering a DNews server

A DNews server is simple to set up and run compared with many other News servers. As you dig into the meat of administering your News servers, keep in mind some of the security issues involved in this task, such as the following:

✔ Whether you want to enable visitors to your News server to create their own newsgroups

✔ Whether you want to require user IDs and passwords for logging on

Running a News server can be fun and extremely rewarding. As you become familiar with the intricacies of setting up and running a News server, you find new, creative ways to interface your News server with other network programs, such as your list server.

Not every News server, however, has the capability to interface with other programs. Some advanced commercial News servers work seamlessly with list servers. The list server automatically forwards messages to the News server as though they were sent to a newsgroup.

Check out the `science.org` Internet site to see how newsgroups and mailing lists can tie together. You can also check out the "Setting Up an Internet Site" page at `science.org` for updated information on other News servers. The address is as follows:

`http://computers.science.org/internet/site/setup/`

In constructing a Web page, you can place a newsgroup reference as a hypertext link in an HTML document by using the following code:

```
<A href="news:alt.surfing">alt.surfing</A>
```

This HTML syntax provides a hyperlink that a user can click to launch a newsreader program and go right to the `alt.surfing` Usenet newsgroup. If you use a visual HTML editor program such as Netscape Composer or Microsoft FrontPage, you need not even concern yourself with the HTML code. Instead, you can just create a link to the following URL:

```
news:alt.surfing
```

Another method enables you to designate a specific News server with a hypertext link. The following HTML code takes the user right to the News server at `science.org`:

```
<A href="news:news.science.org">news:news.science.org</A>
```

Again, instead of using HTML code, you can just create a link to the following URL in Netscape Composer or Microsoft FrontPage:

```
news:news.science.org
```

Taking this technique one step further, you can create a link to a specific News server and newsgroup by using the following HTML code:

```
<A href="news:news.science.org/science.org.general">
general</A>
```

Linking directly to your News server and newsgroup is particularly advantageous if you have a local newsgroup for customer support or product feedback. Putting such a link right in your Web page makes your news resource a significant part of your Web presence. Consider printing the `news:` URL for your news resource, along with your `http://` URL for your Web site, in company brochures or on business cards.

Usenet news is one of the most valuable interactive information resources on the Internet. People enjoy and benefit from the discussions that occur in newsgroups. Starting a new global Usenet newsgroup or running your own local News server is a superb extension to your existing Web site. The potential of newsgroups to serve as simple, powerful, global business tools is finally being realized, now that Web browsers support the integration of Internet News into the World Wide Web. Setting up your own Internet News server is also one of the best ways to move beyond the World Wide Web in the construction of a multifaceted Internet site.

Part III
Setting Up Basic Internet Services

The 5th Wave   By Rich Tennant

"IT'S ANOTHER DEEP SPACE PROBE FROM EARTH,
SEEKING CONTACT FROM EXTRATERRESTRIALS.
I WISH THEY'D JUST INCLUDE AN E-MAIL ADDRESS."

In this part . . .

The best thing about the Internet is that it's an unlimited communications resource. Software designed to work on the Internet can be made to do just about anything that you can imagine a computer doing. This part introduces several more Internet software packages that add functionality and appeal to your Internet site.

The key to turning your Internet site into a competitive advantage, a functional virtual workplace, or a useful public relations tool is to add enabling server software. To communicate with others automatically through e-mail, set up an automated e-mail server. To exchange files easily and securely with others, set up your own FTP server. To form a cohesive community surrounding a special interest (even if that special interest is you), create a new automated electronic mailing list.

Chapter 8

Using E-Mail Autoresponders and Mailboxes

• •

In This Chapter

▶ Creating your own electronic mailboxes

▶ Responding to e-mail automatically

▶ Providing information through an e-mail information service

▶ Setting up an e-mail information server on your PC or Mac

▶ Creating a mailing list for your Internet site

▶ Using an Internet service provider to run a mailing list

▶ Turning your mailing list into an interactive information resource

• •

*M*ore people use electronic mail (also known as *e-mail*) than any other Internet utility. Current estimates place the number of e-mail users in the tens of millions. All commercial online services — such as CompuServe, America Online, and Prodigy — provide Internet e-mail service to their customers. Furthermore, organizations of all sizes are creating links between their internal e-mail systems and the Internet.

Reasons for Using E-Mail

E-mail is a practical and useful way to distribute information, especially if your site appeals to Net surfers who can't support the additional bandwidth demands of the Web.

Consider international visitors to your site. In some countries, the Web is barely usable because the communications network can't handle the flow of graphics through the system. On recent trips to India and Indonesia, we found that using the World Wide Web in those countries was tedious, with many interruptions because of connection loss and slow Internet connections. The Internet backbone in many countries is slower than the average ISDN connection. Yet you must make allowances for delivery of information to such locations even if the Web is not appropriate for the task.

Knowing that the Web is not available to everyone on the Internet makes e-mail an even more interesting tool for the Internet site developer. Keep in mind that although e-mail is not as glamorous as the World Wide Web, e-mail is the single most widely used tool on the Internet. On the Net, new users and old-timers alike know and understand e-mail, and they use it every day.

Many forward-thinking companies realize the important role that e-mail plays in communicating with other Internet users. A telecommunications engineering company called Qualcomm, for example, uses e-mail to distribute information about job opportunities. Anyone who wants information about Qualcomm jobs can send e-mail to jobs@qualcomm.com. This special e-mail address illustrates several advantages of e-mail compared with other Internet information resources. Internet e-mail addresses, properly used, are

- ✔ Easy to remember.
- ✔ Simple to advertise.
- ✔ Accessible to every person who has e-mail access.
- ✔ Less complicated to use than Gopher, FTP, and the Web.

Another common use for e-mail is providing contact information and a basic introduction to Internet users who want to know more about an organization. Companies often use a special e-mail address for this purpose, such as info@science.org. The info and jobs e-mail addresses are excellent examples of the power and importance of e-mail for every Internet site.

By providing information through special e-mail addresses, you can target a specific audience for a specific purpose. Other information resources, such as the World Wide Web, are like your storefront and large-scale advertising efforts, whereas communicating with people through e-mail is like having a conversation on the telephone or giving someone your business card.

If you have plenty of time on your hands, the only thing you need to provide information through e-mail is an e-mail account of your own. You can respond to each piece of incoming e-mail manually and return whatever information the sender requires. But this approach is unwieldy, especially if you receive a large number of e-mail messages. One of the primary reasons to provide information through e-mail is to automate the process of communicating directly with people via the Internet. Without automation, providing information through e-mail is little better than using the telephone to speak with each caller personally.

Providing information through your existing e-mail account

E-mail accounts are like opinions: Everyone has one, and they're all different. Because e-mail accounts vary so greatly, your existing account with MCI, CompuServe, America Online, or your local ISP — or even your corporate e-mail account — probably doesn't enable you to respond to incoming e-mail automatically. This limitation doesn't mean that you should ignore the possibility, however; it means that giving detailed instructions for non-Internet e-mail systems is beyond the scope of this book.

Regardless, you don't need to give up your existing e-mail account. If you're like most people, you've already added your e-mail address to business cards and stationery. You can obtain a new e-mail service to provide information on the Internet but keep your existing account for your personal e-mail.

The idea that manually replying to each e-mail request provides a bit of class and a human touch is a tempting one. Initially, to anyone who is new to business on the Internet, taking such a course does seem to be classy. What this strategy really says, however, is that you're not using your resources effectively. You probably have better things to do than to send your electronic brochure to every person who asks for it. So automate your responses to repetitive e-mail requests.

Getting the Most Out of E-Mail

The first step in using e-mail as part of your Internet site is establishing electronic mailboxes, either by setting up your own e-mail server program or by using an Internet service provider or virtual server supplier. After you create electronic mailboxes, you can provide information through e-mail in either of the following ways:

- ✔ Reply automatically, with a predefined message, to incoming e-mail
- ✔ Use an Internet e-mail information service to fulfill specific information requests

Of these two options, replying to e-mail automatically may be the more useful. This method is simple, yet powerful, and you can set up the system quickly. The following section shows you how to reply to e-mail automatically, and a later section of this chapter, "Using Your Personal Computer as a Mail Server," shows you how to set up an electronic mail server for your

Internet site. If you're not going to run your own e-mail server program, you don't need to concern yourself about how to construct electronic mailboxes. As you read the following sections, however, assume that you've decided to use an Internet service provider for your electronic mailboxes.

Replying Automatically to Incoming E-Mail

If you ever sent e-mail that never reached its destination or that wasn't replied to for weeks, you know how useful an automatic reply is. An *automatic reply* tells people who send e-mail that their mail was received. The reply can also contain references to other information sources or tell people how to contact you in other ways.

An automatic reply is especially useful as a way to communicate with customers. If you run a store with walk-in business, for example, you can use an e-mail address that sends an automatic reply as a way to tell people what your hours of operation are and to give directions to your store. You always want to add your automatic-reply e-mail address to your advertising, especially to your ad in the phone book.

You can create an automatic-reply e-mail address in any of the following ways:

  ✔ Subscribe to an automatic-reply e-mail service on the Internet
  ✔ Use a mail client program that has new-mail filtering capability
  ✔ Set up a UNIX shell account with an Internet service provider

Responding automatically through a service provider

If you subscribe to an automatic-reply e-mail service, follow these steps to create an automatic reply:

1. **Create a text file containing the message you want to send as the automatic reply.**

   You can use any text editor or word-processing program to create this document, as long as you save the message as a text-only file.

2. Send the text file to your service provider.

Your provider gives you instructions for this process. All providers are different. Some accept the message through e-mail; others enable you to fax the message to them and then they retype the text for you.

3. Give out the e-mail address that the provider assigns to you.

This e-mail address is different than the one you normally use to receive e-mail. If people contact this e-mail address, they automatically receive your automatic reply.

If you have access to e-mail, test the automatic reply by sending a message to the e-mail address yourself.

 Your service provider should ask whether to save the e-mail that's sent to your automatic-reply account. If you choose not to save the e-mail, make sure that you mention in your reply message that no human being reads the sender's e-mail. Otherwise, people may assume, even after receiving an automatic reply, that a human eventually reads their messages and replies personally.

If you decide to save the e-mail that's sent to your reply account, find out from your service provider exactly where the service saves incoming e-mail. If you have another e-mail account, most service providers can forward e-mail messages to that account. If you prefer, you can ask your provider to keep the messages in a separate mailbox. Your provider can tell you how to access those messages. Many e-mail client programs, such as Microsoft Outlook, enable you to specify multiple mailboxes from which to retrieve mail. Such a feature simplifies retrieval of e-mail from several places.

Whether you save or discard the e-mail sent to your automatic-reply account ultimately depends on how you use the service. If you create a simple text file that contains your store's hours of operation and gives directions to your customers, you can safely discard every message sent to the automatic-reply account. If, on the other hand, you use your automatic-reply account as a first contact for potential clients, you want to save the e-mail that's sent to the automatic-reply account so that you can follow up later with a more involved e-mail message. Your detailed reply can answer any questions posed in the original message and take your marketing efforts even further.

Do-it-yourself automatic reply using a mail client

This section and the one that follows describe two options for creating your own automatic-reply e-mail account. Here, we describe how to use a mail client program that has new-mail filtering capability. In the next section, we describe how to use a UNIX shell account.

New-mail filtering is the capability to have your e-mail client program figure out what to do with your incoming mail, based on your instructions. Not all e-mail client programs have this capability. A popular e-mail client program for Windows that has new-mail-filtering capability is called Pegasus (see the following sections). A version of Pegasus is available for the Macintosh as well.

In addition, the popular e-mail program Eudora supports new-mail filtering in its commercial version. You may want to read the following sections on Pegasus anyway, however, because they give you a good idea of what to look for in an e-mail client program.

You can always find the most up-to-date information on Pegasus at `http://www.pegasus.usa.com` and on Eudora at `http://www.eudora.com/`.

Replying automatically by using a large, winged horse

Pegasus, a mail client written by David Harris, is a popular full-featured Windows e-mail client program. After you define mail-filtering rules, Pegasus can filter and respond to new mail as the messages arrive in your mailbox. A *rule,* in this context, is a directive you give to your computer, just as you give an instruction to an assistant. You may tell someone, "If Bob calls, tell him I went golfing." A mail-filtering rule is similar: "If you get mail from George, file it under New Business." You don't get to type the rule in plain English, but constructing rules for handling your e-mail is simple in Pegasus.

Setting e-mail rules in Pegasus

You create rules to control what Pegasus responds to and what it does as a response. To set e-mail-handling rules in Pegasus, follow these steps:

1. **In the Pegasus program, choose Tools➪Mail filtering rules➪Edit new mail filtering rules.**

2. **Choose between the Rules Applied When Folder Is Opened and the Rules Applied When Folder Is Closed options.**

   Selecting the Opened option preprocesses your e-mail. Selecting the Closed option processes rules after you finish reading your e-mail.

   The Rules For New Mail window appears, as shown in Figure 8-1.

3. **To create a new rule, click the Add Rule button.**

   The Edit Rule dialog box appears, enabling you to define or change rules. Your rule can tell Pegasus to look for text in either the header or the body of the mail message.

4. **Click either the In These Headers option or the As an Expression option (see Figure 8-2).**

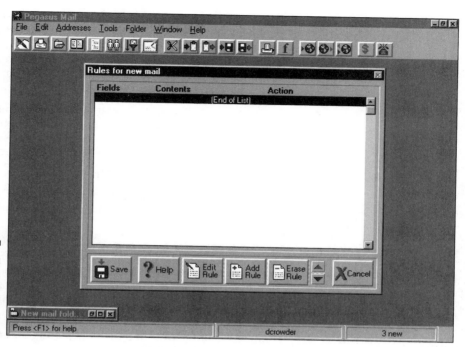

Figure 8-1:
The Rules
For New
Mail
window.

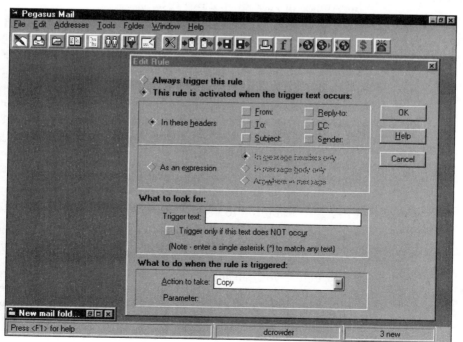

Figure 8-2:
Create rules
by using
this easy-
to-use
dialog box.

By selecting the In These Headers option, you tell Pegasus to look for key words in the selected parts of the e-mail message. After receiving mail, Pegasus automatically looks for the words you specify in From, To, Subject, Reply-to, CC, or Sender. You can select more than one check box to have Pegasus look for the text you identify in any of the areas you indicate.

If you select the As an Expression option, you give Pegasus permission to look for information in a more global manner. Depending on what option you then select, Pegasus looks for information In Message Headers Only, In Message Body Only, or Anywhere in the Message.

5. **In the Trigger Text box, enter the text that triggers the rule.**

   This text can be someone's name, a product name, or some keyword or command that's unique enough for your computer to answer appropriately.

   Try to choose words that you're sure are going to appear only in the messages in which you expect them to appear. Avoid words that are too generic or that have multiple meanings. If you tell your computer to send love letters whenever it sees the word *Sue* in the body of the message, for example, you may get an interesting reaction from an unfriendly lawyer.

6. **Now tell the computer what action to take by selecting an action from the Action to Take drop-down list.**

   Pegasus can do many things with the incoming e-mail, including move messages to a particular folder, delete messages automatically, and reply to messages automatically. To create an automatic-reply filter, select either Send Text File or Send Binary File.

   After you select a send option from the Action to Take list, the Select a File dialog box appears, enabling you to select the file that you want to send automatically in response to the incoming e-mail message.

7. **Choose a file in the Select a File dialog box by clicking the filename, and then click the OK button.**

   You return to the Edit Rule dialog box, where the full path of the file now appears below the Action to Take drop-down list.

8. **Click the OK button to accept your new automatic-reply rule.**

   Now the selected file goes out automatically in response to messages that contain the specified trigger text.

Obviously, before you can select a file to send via this automatic-response method, you need to create this file. To do so, you need to use a text editor such as Notepad and type the information that you want to deliver automatically. If you use a word-processing program instead, be sure to save the file as text because word processors insert formatting codes that you don't want included in your file. Most word processors offer the capability to save a document as text. You normally see a list of file types from which to choose. Select Text, which saves the file and may add a TXT extension to the filename.

Pegasus is not a full e-mail information server, but the program has valuable features that enable you to use your personal e-mail account more effectively. Pegasus is simple to use and is also a great e-mail client program.

Do-it-yourself automatic reply using a UNIX shell account

If you're a do-it-yourself type, you can create your own automatic-reply e-mail account by obtaining a UNIX shell account from a service provider. A UNIX shell account comes with its own e-mail address, and you can use a special UNIX utility, called the `vacation` program, to reply to incoming e-mail automatically.

To use the `vacation` program to reply to incoming e-mail automatically, you need a UNIX shell account from an Internet service provider. Your ISP must give you access to the `vacation` program, so make sure that you ask ahead of time whether a `vacation` program is available.

To use the `vacation` program to reply to incoming e-mail automatically, follow these steps:

1. **Before doing anything else, verify that your UNIX shell account has access to the** `vacation` **program by logging on to your UNIX shell account.**

   You normally use the telnet client included with most operating systems. If you're using Windows 95 or Windows NT, start telnet by choosing Start⇨Run. In the Open text box that appears, type **telnet** and then click OK. The telnet program starts running. Select Connect to Remote Host from the telnet menu, and enter the IP address of your ISP. After clicking OK, a logon prompt should appear. Enter your logon ID and password after you're prompted for that information. If you successfully logged on to your UNIX shell account, you most likely see a UNIX command prompt (%).

2. **Type the following command at the command prompt:**

   ```
   which vacation
   ```

This command tells your UNIX shell account to search for the `vacation` program. If the account locates the program, you see something like the following line:

```
/usr/ucb/vacation
```

If your UNIX shell account can't find the `vacation` program, you see something like the following line instead:

```
no vacation in /usr/local/bin /usr/ucb /usr/bin
```

If your UNIX shell account responds with a suggestion such as `Caribbean Cruise` or `Hawaii`, or with `which:Commandnotfound`, the program probably misunderstood your request. Ask your ISP for help.

3. **After you're sure that your UNIX shell account can locate the `vacation` program, type the following command at the command prompt:**

```
touch .vacation.msg
```

This command creates a new file called .VACATION.MSG, which contains the automatic-reply message for the `vacation` program to use. Because editing a file in a UNIX shell account is easier said than done, we show you a way to create your reply message without editing a file. (This method isn't the only one — just the easiest.)

4. **Type the following command at the command prompt:**

```
cat >> .vacation.msg
```

After you type this command, your UNIX shell account doesn't display anything; it just sits there, waiting for you to type some text.

5. **Type the message you want to send as your reply to incoming e-mail.**

Make sure that you press Enter at the end of each line. To leave a space between paragraphs, simply press Enter twice. To include a subject in the e-mail reply, type the subject in the first line. Following is an example that a company called Virtual Corporation might use as its reply message:

```
Subject: Automatic reply from Virtual Corporation
Thank you for sending e-mail to Virtual Corporation.
Because of the volume of e-mail we receive, it
may take a few days for a human being to read
your message. If you need to contact us immediately,
you can call (800) 555-1212 to reach any of the
following departments:
```

```
Sales: ext. 216; Marketing: ext. 840
Public Relations: ext. 408; Human Resources: ext. 600

Be sure to check out our other Internet information
resources at:

WWW: http://www.virtualcorporation.com/
Gopher: gopher://gopher.virtualcorporation.com/
FTP: ftp://ftp.virtualcorporation.com/

Thank you for your interest in Virtual Corporation.
```

6. **After you finish typing your reply message, press Ctrl+D.**

   This action saves your reply message to the .VACATION.MSG file and returns you to the command prompt.

If you make a mistake while typing your message, press Ctrl+D to save the incorrect message. Next, erase the .VACATION.MSG file by using the following command:

```
rm .vacation.msg
```

Then repeat the preceding instructions, beginning with the command `touch.vacation.msg`.

Creating your reply locally

If you prefer, you can create your reply message on your personal computer and then send the message to your UNIX shell account. (Contact your service provider for help on sending a file to your UNIX shell account.) Follow these steps:

1. **Perform the steps in the preceding section.**

2. **After you send the text file, rename the file by using the following command (because you can't create filenames on PCs and Macs by using a period as the first character):**

   ```
   mv TextFile .vacation.msg
   ```

3. **Replace *TextFile* in this command with the name of your file.**

4. **Type the following command to activate the `vacation` program:**

   ```
   vacation
   ```

After typing this command, you should see something like the following:

```
This program can be used to answer your mail
automatically when you go away on vacation.
You have a message file in .vacation.msg. Would you
like to see it?
```

If you don't see a similar response after typing the vacation command, contact your UNIX-shell-account service provider for assistance.

The last line asks whether you want to see your reply message.

5. **Type** y **and press Enter to view your message.**

   After displaying your message, vacation asks whether you want to edit the message.

6. **Unless you know how to edit a file in your UNIX shell account, type** n **and press Enter.**

   Next, vacation asks whether you want to enable the vacation feature by creating a .FORWARD file.

7. **Type** y **and press Enter.**

   The vacation program creates the special .FORWARD file to activate the vacation feature and then displays the following message:

```
Vacation feature ENABLED. Please remember to turn it
off when you get back from vacation. Bon voyage.
```

   Now your vacation program is ready. Anyone who sends e-mail to your UNIX shell account receives an automatic reply from the program.

To turn off the vacation program, type the following command to remove the .FORWARD file:

```
rm .forward
```

The vacation program is one way to create your own automatic-reply e-mail account. If you already have a UNIX shell account on the Internet, using the vacation program doesn't cost you a penny or require a new account with an Internet service provider.

Modifying the vacation program

One last thing you need to know is that, by default, the vacation program sends the reply message only once per week to a given e-mail address. If the same person sends e-mail to your UNIX shell account twice in one week, that person gets a reply only the first time. To change this situation, you must modify the .FORWARD file. If you know how to modify files in your UNIX shell account, make the change that we describe in the following section; otherwise, keep reading for a simpler way to modify the .FORWARD file.

Changing the .FORWARD file in UNIX

To modify the .FORWARD file in your UNIX shell account, look at the original file. The original version of the .FORWARD file should have a line that looks something like the following example:

```
\youruserid, "|/usr/ucb/vacation youruserid"
```

The change you need to make is small. Immediately following `vacation`, insert the following segment:

```
-t2s
```

Your new .FORWARD file should look something like the following example:

```
\youruserid, "|/usr/ucb/vacation -t2s youruserid"
```

This change tells the `vacation` program to wait two seconds, instead of one week, before sending the reply message to the same e-mail address. This way, the program responds to every message it receives, even if a particular user has already received a reply within the past week.

Creating a new .FORWARD file

If modifying the .FORWARD file in your UNIX shell account proves to be too difficult, you can erase the file and create a new one by following these steps:

1. **View the current .FORWARD file by typing the following at the command prompt:**

   ```
   cat .forward
   ```

2. **At the command prompt, remove the current .FORWARD file by typing the following:**

   ```
   rm .forward
   ```

3. **Now type the following command to create a new .FORWARD file:**

   ```
   cat > .forward
   ```

   After you type this command, your UNIX shell account waits for you to type the text for the new version of the file.

4. **Type the following:**

```
\youruserid, "|/path/vacation -t2s youruserid"
```

Make sure that you replace *youruserid* with your UNIX shell account logon ID and */path/vacation* with whatever was there before in the old .FORWARD file.

5. **Press Ctrl+D to save the new .FORWARD file.**

Starting Your Own E-Mail Information Service

Automatic-reply e-mail accounts are great if you have only one message to send to people on the Internet. If you want to distribute many messages and files through e-mail, however, you need an *e-mail information server* — a program that reads incoming e-mail and responds to special commands within the message.

One command that most e-mail information servers respond to is the following request for help:

```
help
```

If an Internet user sends a message that contains the command help to an e-mail information server, the server replies with a message that contains instructions. Following is another command to which most e-mail information servers respond:

```
get filename
```

Sometimes, users type the send command instead of the get command, as follows:

```
send filename
```

After an e-mail information server receives a message that contains a command of this sort, the server checks to see whether a file named *filename* exists in its file archive. If *filename* does exist, the server replies to the e-mail message by sending a copy of the file. If *filename* doesn't exist in the archive, the server replies with an error message.

Many e-mail information servers are smart enough to send help if the incoming message doesn't contain a valid command.

You can provide information through an e-mail information server in two ways:

✔ Subscribe to an e-mail information service on the Internet

✔ Set up your own e-mail server on your personal computer

The next few sections describe these two options.

Using an Internet e-mail information service provider

E-mail information service providers vary greatly in terms of the services they offer and in the ways in which their services operate. The two commands mentioned in the preceding section — help and get (or send) — have become informal standards for e-mail information servers on the Internet. If the service offered by your provider doesn't support these commands, or at least the help command, your e-mail information service may be difficult for people to use. Before you subscribe to an e-mail information service on the Internet, ask for a demonstration, and make sure that the service supports the help command.

The basic idea behind subscribing to an e-mail information service offered by a service provider is that you rent space for your files on the provider's computer. The provider gives you a new e-mail address, and anyone who wants to receive one of your files by e-mail sends a command to that e-mail address. The procedure is a bit like that for FTP, but instead of an FTP client program, the service uses e-mail messages to transfer files. (See Chapter 9 for more information on the File Transfer Protocol.)

Providing files through e-mail has one major advantage over traditional FTP: Internet users can receive copies of your files through e-mail rather than directly from your FTP server. Because you don't need direct Internet access to receive e-mail, people still can access your files. If you use only FTP to transfer files to interested visitors to your site, you may eliminate a large number of potential visitors who can't access FTP.

To subscribe to an e-mail information service on the Internet, ask a service provider for a demonstration of its e-mail service. This demonstration typically involves sending an e-mail message to a demonstration server, so you need access to an e-mail account of your own. If you like the way in which the provider's server responds to your message, sign up!

Your service provider gives you the following items after you subscribe:

- ✔ The e-mail address of your new e-mail information server
- ✔ Instructions on adding files to your e-mail information server

One file that you want to add to your server is a text file called INDEX, which normally contains a list of all files available from your e-mail information server. This file enables users of your e-mail information server to retrieve a list of available files by sending the following command to your e-mail information server:

```
get index
```

Depending on the service provider, you also may need to create or modify the file that goes to users after they ask for help. After you do that, your e-mail information server is ready to respond to messages and send files through e-mail to anyone on the Internet.

Making money using your e-mail information server

E-mail information servers are similar to FTP, World Wide Web, and Gopher servers in that anyone on the Internet can obtain information from them. You normally can't charge for access to your files, but you can charge for the use of your files.

Some e-mail information service providers offer a special type of e-mail information service that does enable you to charge for access to your files. By using this service, you create user accounts and passwords for each person who accesses your e-mail information server. To retrieve a file from your e-mail information server, a user must include a password in the e-mail message, along with the file request. If the password is valid, the server sends the file and bills the user's account accordingly.

Setting Up mailto Links

You can use a special type of hyperlink in the World Wide Web to create a link to an e-mail address. This special type of hyperlink is called a mailto link. Here's an example:

```
mailto:info@whatever.com
```

To turn a `mailto` link into a World Wide Web hyperlink, create an anchor by using the `mailto` syntax. The following HTML line creates such an anchor:

```
<A HREF="mailto:info@whatever.com">Send us
e-mail</A>
```

You can also have the `mailto` link provide the subject of the e-mail message automatically. The syntax for that is `mailto:address?subject`. Here's how it looks with a subject line added:

```
<A HREF="mailto:info@whatever.com?Want Information">Send us
e-mail</A>
```

The message would arrive in your e-mail box with the subject line already saying "Want Information," and you could easily have all messages with that subject separated into their own folder.

Most people put `mailto` links at the bottom of each Web page, and they normally use the same address for all of them. If you use a different address for the `mailto` link on each of your Web pages, you'll be able to tell which page generated the e-mail message. It's a good idea to make sure that all these different addresses go to only one of your e-mail boxes, though, unless you have a lot of spare time. That's a simple thing to do. See the section called "Alias accounts" later in this chapter for details.

There is a proposal to add more capabilities to the `mailto` link, such as the subject line specification. Sometime soon, you will probably also be able to specify the body of the message; this would be accomplished using the syntax `mailto:address?body`. Another possibility is the capability to carbon copy the message to another e-mail address; this would be accomplished by using the syntax `mailto:address?cc=secondaddress`.

The `mailto` syntax doesn't serve any purpose outside the World Wide Web. Adding a `mailto` link to your stationery or to your business card, for example, wouldn't make sense. Simply give people your e-mail address so that they can request more information about your site by using the `help` command.

Using Your Personal Computer as a Mail Server

If your computer has a direct connection to the Internet, you can set up your own e-mail server. An *e-mail server* is a program that receives e-mail from other computers and then routes the mail to its destination. By using an e-mail server of your own, you can create both automatic-reply e-mail accounts and e-mail information servers without paying extra to your Internet service provider. You don't need to worry, therefore, about breaking open the piggy bank if you want to provide many types of information through several automatic-reply e-mail accounts.

Best of all, because your computer acts as an Internet e-mail server, you can create as many normal e-mail accounts as you need at no extra charge. If you run a small or medium-size business, this method is the best way to give your employees Internet e-mail accounts of their own.

All e-mail servers on the Internet speak the same language: *Simple Mail Transfer Protocol,* or *SMTP* (pronounced *ess-em-tee-pee*). Don't confuse an *e-mail server,* which actually speaks SMTP, with an e-mail *information server,* which simply reads incoming e-mail and responds to commands within the message. Because an e-mail server speaks SMTP, that type of server can receive e-mail directly from other e-mail servers. E-mail information servers, which can't speak SMTP, must rely on an e-mail server to function. An e-mail server is like the postman who delivers the mail. You, the receiver of the mail, are more like an e-mail information server, responding to the mail the postman delivers.

To run your own SMTP-based e-mail server on your personal computer, your computer must have a direct connection to the Internet. You need a domain name of your own (as explained in Chapter 3), and your Internet access provider must provide domain-name service for your domain to enable people on the Internet to send mail to your e-mail server.

Besides communicating with other Internet e-mail servers by using SMTP, an e-mail server provides normal e-mail accounts to individual users. While delivering e-mail to individual users, an e-mail server acts a little like an electronic post office. E-mail messages arrive at the post office and then go out to each person's electronic mailbox. To pick up their e-mail, users must request their e-mail from the e-mail server by using the *Post Office Protocol (POP).*

E-mail servers that speak Post Office Protocol are known as *POP servers. POP* is an important term to remember, because the people who have e-mail accounts on your server must use a program known as a *POP client* to retrieve e-mail from their electronic mailboxes. The most common POP client is a program called Eudora, although many POP clients exist for every type of computer. For the most part, no difference exists between a POP client and a normal e-mail client, because most e-mail clients use the Post Office Protocol.

Setting up an e-mail server without a direct Internet connection

SMTP e-mail servers on the Internet deliver mail directly to their intended recipients. These servers have a motto similar to that of their physical counterparts: "Neither line noise, nor network congestion, nor power outages shall keep an e-mail server from its appointed tasks." If your e-mail server isn't available when another e-mail server wants to deliver a message, however, your e-mail could end up in Larry's closet in Argentina or who knows where else on the planet.

SMTP is meant for use in delivering mail between e-mail servers that reside on the Internet. If your e-mail server is available on the Internet for only a few minutes each day because you don't have a dedicated Internet connection, other SMTP servers may have trouble delivering your e-mail. A few Internet access providers have special e-mail services that eliminate this problem, but this new type of SMTP e-mail service isn't common yet. You need to talk with your access provider about the implications of running your own SMTP e-mail server without dedicated Internet access before you ever attempt to do so.

If you don't have a direct Internet connection, SMTP isn't the best way to receive e-mail from your service provider. UNIX to UNIX Copy (UUCP) — a communications protocol that exchanges files between two computers automatically — is a much better option for receiving Internet e-mail if you're going to connect to the Internet only occasionally. UUCP is designed to do what SMTP has trouble with: deliver e-mail to computers that don't have a direct connection to the Internet.

At least one UUCP software package is available for MS-DOS and the Macintosh, but it's complicated, and we don't like using it. Other UUCP packages for Windows and the Macintosh should be available soon; these packages should enable you to do everything described in this chapter without a direct Internet connection. More important, Internet access providers everywhere should soon be offering SMTP e-mail service that's reliable even if your connection to the Internet isn't.

Are you blown away by all these abbreviations — SMTP, POP, UUCP? If so, the following list should help clear things up for you:

- ✔ An e-mail server is a program that receives e-mail from other computers and then routes the mail to its destination.

- ✔ Post Office Protocol (POP) is the protocol that sorts and delivers mail on an SMTP server to the appropriate user's mailbox.

- ✔ Simple Mail Transfer Protocol (SMTP) is the language that all e-mail servers on the Internet speak.

- ✔ An e-mail information server is a program that reads incoming e-mail and responds to special commands within the message.

✔ The vacation program is a UNIX utility that you use to reply automatically to incoming e-mail.

✔ An automatic-reply e-mail account is a service that you set up to send mail to interested parties who request information. You can use your Internet service provider or your own system to set up this account.

✔ Larry's closet is the place where your e-mail goes if the electronic post office misplaces it.

Setting Up a Windows E-Mail Server

One of the software packages that inspired this book is SLmail, written by Jack De Winter and now owned by Seattle Lab. SLmail, which is included on the *Setting Up An Internet Site For Dummies* CD-ROM, is a complete Windows SMTP server that supports both automatic-reply and e-mail information server e-mail accounts. The server also is a functional POP server, which you can use to set up as many e-mail accounts as you want.

To run SLmail, you need Windows 95 or Windows NT and TCP/IP access to the Internet. Make sure that you communicate extensively with your Internet access provider as you set up your e-mail service so that the provider fully understands what you're doing. This communication helps your provider configure its computers to work correctly with your SLmail server and keeps your e-mail from getting lost. The SLmail main window appears after you install and run the SLmail program on your computer.

After you start SLmail for the first time, the program uses the settings in your existing Internet software to configure itself; the main window shows you some of the settings that the program chooses. Even if SLmail gets everything right, checking the detailed configuration, just to make sure that everything is okay, is a good idea.

Configuring SLmail

To configure SLmail, follow these steps to verify and correct the SLmail system configuration:

1. **Choose System⇨Configure.**

   The configuration dialog box appears.

2. **Click the System tab, shown in Figure 8-3.**

   For SLmail to work, you must set up the three areas of the System tab correctly.

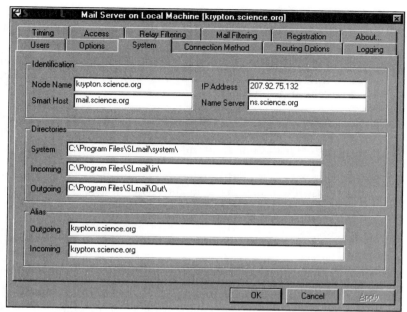

Figure 8-3:
Configure
SLmail.

3. **In the Node Name text box, verify or enter the fully-qualified domain name of the computer on which you're running SLmail.**

   In the example shown in Figure 8-3, the computer's name is `krypton.science.org`. Make sure that the Node Name text box contains the full domain name of your computer.

4. **In the IP Address text box, enter your computer's IP address.**

5. **In the Smart Host text box, enter the full name or the IP address of your Internet access provider's e-mail server.**

   This host is the computer to which the program directs outgoing e-mail, if SLmail decides to have another e-mail server help deliver certain messages.

6. **Make certain that each directory listed in the Directories area of the dialog box is valid.**

   System is the directory in which you install SLmail. The Incoming and Outgoing directories determine where SLmail stores e-mail as the program processes it. The same directory can appear in all three boxes.

7. **If you entered something other than your registered domain name in the Node Name text box, enter your registered domain name in both the Incoming and the Outgoing text boxes in the Alias area of the System tab.**

Entering your registered domain name in both text boxes tells SLmail that sending and receiving mail by using your real domain name, instead of the name that you enter in the Node Name field, is okay.

8. **If you made any changes in the settings in the System tab, click OK to save the changes and exit, and then restart SLmail so that your changes can take effect.**

Note that you can launch the configuration dialog box not only from the SLmail program, but also from the Start menu (by choosing Start⇨Programs⇨ SL Products⇨SLmail Configuration).

A few other configuration dialog boxes may be important if you have a complex network or an unusual mail-transfer mechanism. You can access these dialog boxes through the SLmail Configuration menu. If you're setting up a standard system, however, you can move on to the best part: creating user e-mail accounts.

Creating user accounts

Click the Users tab, shown in Figure 8-4. Every time you see this tab, think about all the people in the world who pay unreasonable rates for a single e-mail account through an online service. This tab releases you from the prison of online-service e-mail by enabling you to create your own Internet e-mail accounts on your SLmail e-mail server.

The Users tab enables you to create five types of e-mail accounts. By creating different types of accounts, you can do more with your SLmail server than simply receive e-mail. The five account types are

 ✔ User.
 ✔ Alias.
 ✔ Responder.
 ✔ Forward.
 ✔ List.

In the following sections, we cover each of these account types except the List type, which we cover in Chapter 10. You may want to set up some or all these account types for your Internet site.

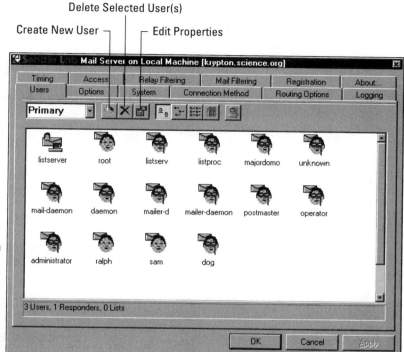

Delete Selected User(s)

Create New User ⌐   ⌐ Edit Properties

Figure 8-4:
Create
e-mail
accounts
with the
Users tab.

User accounts

User accounts are the normal e-mail accounts through which people send and receive mail. Each person who has a User account on your SLmail server can use a POP client, such as Eudora, to access his or her mailbox.

To create a User account, follow these steps:

1. **On the Users tab, click the Create New User button (labeled in Figure 8-4).**

   The menu shown in Figure 8-5 appears.

2. **Select User.**

   A new icon labeled `new_user` is created, as shown in Figure 8-6.

3. **Simply type over the phrase *new_user,* replacing it with the user ID for the new account.**

   Note: The user ID should not contain spaces.

4. **Click the Edit Properties button (labeled in Figure 8-4).**

   The Edit User dialog box appears, as shown in Figure 8-7.

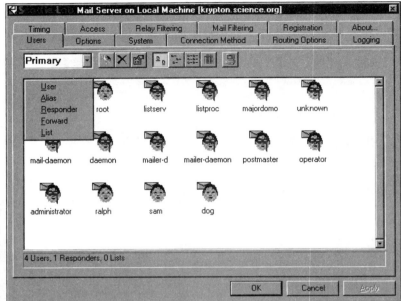

Figure 8-5:
Choose the
user type
from the
menu.

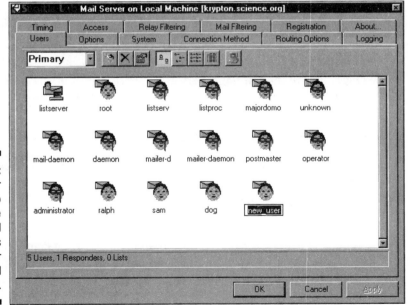

Figure 8-6:
Add user
accounts to
create
individual
mailboxes
for your
e-mail
users.

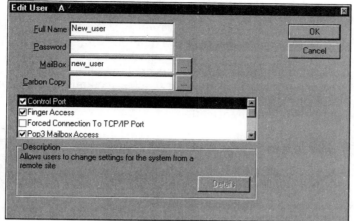

Figure 8-7:
The Edit
User dialog
box.

5. **In the Full Name text box, type the user's full name (or any other descriptive text).**

6. **In the Password text box, type a password for the account.**

   The user must supply this password to access the account on your SLmail server. As you type the password, each character appears as an asterisk (*), so enter the password carefully.

7. **Verify that the MailBox text box contains an acceptable filename.**

   The mailbox file usually has a name similar to the user ID. This file is where the program stores e-mail for this user.

8. **In the Carbon Copy text box, type an e-mail address if you want to send a copy of the messages this user receives to another e-mail address.**

   If you're the boss in your company, please don't enter your own e-mail address in the Carbon Copy field so that you can read all your employees' e-mail. We consider e-mail to be private communication if it's addressed to an individual. If you feel that keeping tabs on all business communication is important, assign a separate e-mail address that is clearly of a business nature (such as `webmaster`, `jobs`, or `accounting`), and enable one or more of your employees to receive business-related e-mail at that address instead of at a private one. Recognize and respect the privacy rights of your workers.

9. **Click the OK button to accept the new user.**

Alias accounts

Alias accounts, which are the simplest type, provide other names by which particular users can receive e-mail at a different address than their usual one. This means any e-mail sent to the alias account actually goes to another account. In SLmail, alias accounts are limited to local users. SLmail uses the term *forward account* to refer to alias accounts that forward mail to e-mail addresses in other domains. See the "Forward accounts" section later in this chapter for more information.

You can create as many alias accounts as you need by following these steps:

1. **In the Users tab, click the Create New User button (labeled in Figure 8-4).**

2. **Select Alias from the menu.**

   A new icon labeled `new_alias` is created.

3. **Simply type over the phrase *new_alias,* replacing it with the user ID for the new account.**

   Note: The user ID should not contain spaces.

   Alias icons are exactly like New User icons, except they have a bandit's mask over the face.

4. **Click the Edit Properties button (labeled in Figure 8-4).**

   The Add Alias dialog box appears, as shown in Figure 8-8.

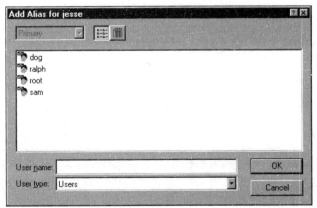

Figure 8-8:
The Add Alias dialog box.

5. **Select one of the listed users by clicking the name.**

   The name appears in the User Name box at the bottom of the screen.

6. **Click the OK button.**

   The Edit Alias dialog box appears, as shown in Figure 8-9.

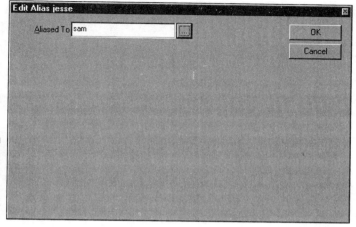

Figure 8-9:
The Edit
Alias dialog
box.

7. **If you are satisfied with your choice, simply click the OK button to complete the task.**

8. **If you have chosen the wrong name, click the ellipse (...) button to return to the Add Alias dialog box, and continue with Step 5.**

Alias accounts are a great way to make your small company look much larger than it actually is. You can set up a series of aliases along the lines of accounting@whatever.com, admin@whatever.com, personnel@whatever.com, and so forth, all of which actually send messages to your own e-mail account.

Responder accounts

Responder accounts enable you to set up an automatic-reply e-mail account or a full e-mail information server by using SLmail. This account always responds to e-mail automatically. Don't use this account as a regular e-mail account unless you always want the computer to respond for you. The Responder account is managed by an auto responder. (You're likely to see this term written as both *auto responder* and *autoresponder*. Both versions mean the same thing.)

To create a new Responder account, follow these steps:

1. **In the Users tab, click the Create New User button (labeled in Figure 8-4).**

2. **Select <u>R</u>esponder from the menu.**

   A new icon labeled new_responder is created, as shown in Figure 8-10.

Figure 8-10:
Adding
a new
responder.

3. **Simply type over the phrase** *new_responder,* **replacing it with the user ID for the new account.**

   Note: The user ID should not contain spaces.

4. **Click the Edit Properties button (labeled in Figure 8-4).**

   The Edit Responder dialog box appears, as shown in Figure 8-11. The Name field, by default, contains the name that you entered when you created the account. If you want, however, you can enter another name, which will be shown in all the messages the account sends out. Leave Link To alone.

5. **To use this Responder account as an e-mail information server, scroll down in the list to select the Send Files Only on User's Request check box.**

   This option tells the Responder account not to respond with a file unless the incoming e-mail contains a valid file request. Otherwise, deselect this check box so that the responder account replies to any incoming e-mail by sending the file or files you specify.

6. **Change the other settings in the list box to meet your needs:**

   - If you want the autoresponder to send files as attachments instead of as normal e-mail messages, for example, select the Send Files as Attachments check box.

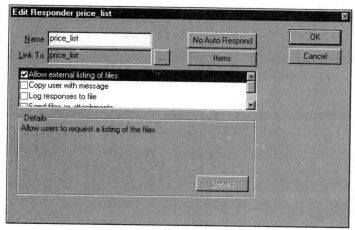

Figure 8-11:
The Edit
Responder
dialog box.

- To send a copy of incoming e-mail messages to another e-mail address, select the Copy User with Message check box and then select the user who is to receive the copy from the dialog box shown in Figure 8-12, which pops up when you select this option.

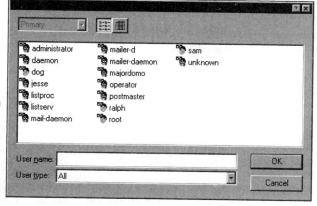

Figure 8-12:
Select the
user who is
to receive
the copy.

- To log responses to a file, select the Log Responses to File check box and then select a file from the Choose a Log File dialog box, shown in Figure 8-13.

7. In the Edit Responder dialog box, click the Items button.

The Edit Responder Items dialog box appears, as shown in Figure 8-14. You use this dialog box to tell the autoresponder which files to send. If you selected the Send Files Only on User's Request check box in the

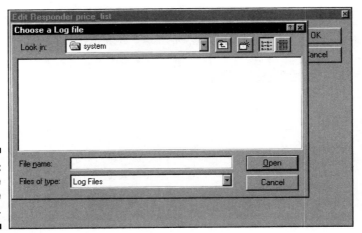

Figure 8-13:
The Choose
a Log File
dialog box.

Choose a Log File dialog box, the autoresponder sends a file only if it receives an e-mail message containing a command such as the following, in which *filename* appears in the dialog box's file list:

```
send filename
```

Figure 8-14:
The Edit
Responder
Items dialog
box.

8. To add an item to the file list, press the Insert key (or right-click and select Insert from the menu), and then type the name of the file.

If you don't know the name of the file, click the Browse button (...), which appears when you press the Insert key, to select the file from the Open dialog box that appears.

9. After you finish adding files to the file list, click the OK button.

10. **If you want to avoid accepting autoresponder requests from particular domains or from e-mail accounts with a particular content, do the following:**

    a. **Click the No Auto Respond button.**

    The Edit Responder No Response List dialog box appears, as shown in Figure 8-15.

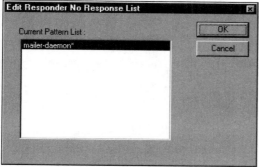

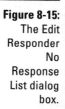

Figure 8-15:
The Edit
Responder
No
Response
List dialog
box.

b. **Press the Insert key (or right-click and select Insert from the pop-up menu), and then type the pattern you want to deny autoresponse to.**

    SLmail comes with one default denial in place: `mailer-daemon@*`. This means the autoresponder won't send messages back to another e-mail server program — thus avoiding a situation that could easily result in the two programs endlessly sending each other messages. You can use this denial faculty to shut off all requests from a particular domain (by, for instance, adding *badcompany.com* to the list).

c. **When you're finished, click the OK button.**

11. **In the Configure Autoresponder dialog box, click the OK button to accept your changes and return to the Users tab.**

Forward accounts

Sometimes, you need to forward mail for a particular user to a new e-mail address. If an employee named John leaves your company and goes to work for another company, for example, you may want to forward his mail to his new e-mail address (depending, of course, on how much you like John and on his reason for leaving your company).

To forward mail to another e-mail address, you create a *Forward account*. To create a Forward account with the same name as an old User account (as in the case of your ex-employee, John), you first must delete the old User account. In the Users tab, select the User account from the list, click the Delete button, and then follow these steps to add a new Forward account:

1. **On the Users tab, click the Create New User button (labeled in Figure 8-4).**

2. **Select Forward from the menu.**

   A new icon labeled `new_forward` is created, as shown in Figure 8-16.

Figure 8-16:
Add
Forward
accounts
to create
e-mail
relays.

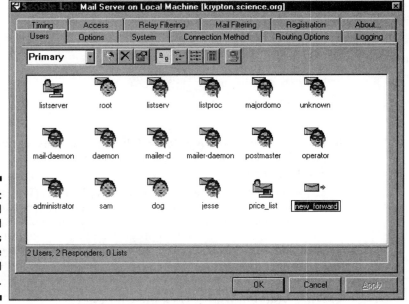

3. **Simply type over the phrase *new_forward*, replacing it with the user ID for the new account.**

   Note: The user ID should not contain spaces.

4. **Click the Edit Properties button (labeled in Figure 8-4).**

   The Forward To dialog box appears, as shown in Figure 8-17.

5. **In the User Name text box, type the e-mail address you want messages forwarded to and then click the OK button.**

   The Edit Forward dialog box appears, as shown in Figure 8-18.

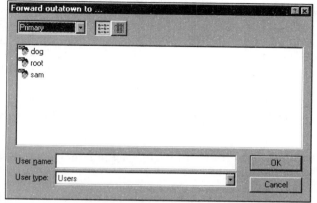

Figure 8-17:
The
Forward To
dialog box.

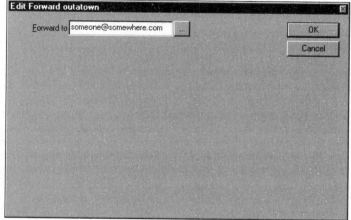

Figure 8-18:
The Edit
Forward
dialog box.

6. If the e-mail address you entered is correct, click the OK button to return to the Users tab.

7. If the e-mail address you entered is not correct, click the ellipse (...) button to return to the Forward To dialog box, and continue with Step 5.

Wrapping up

After you finish adding accounts, click the OK button. This action returns you to the main application window. Administering an e-mail server isn't difficult. You can add any of these account types whenever you need them.

Enabling POP in SLmail

Finally, to enable the capability for e-mail client programs to use the Post Office Protocol (POP) to contact the SLmail server and retrieve the contents of electronic mailboxes, click the Access tab, shown in Figure 8-19. Verify that Pop3 Mailbox Access is enabled. As long as the plug next to it doesn't have a red circle around it, POP is enabled. If it isn't, right-click it to access the pop-up menu shown in Figure 8-20, select Toggle, and the red circle will go away.

Don't mess with the Edit Properties part of the pop-up menu unless you really know what you're doing.

You've probably used Internet e-mail yourself in the past without understanding completely what your Internet service provider needs to do for you to use your electronic mailbox. Well, after you set up your own Internet e-mail server and configure mailboxes, you'll know exactly what an ISP does for every one of its customers who has an Internet e-mail address.

Using Your E-Mail Information Server

Immediately upon setting up an e-mail information server, you can begin doing several creative things. Whether or not you do what this section describes, you should at least incorporate your e-mail information resource into your World Wide Web page by using a `mailto` link. Adding an e-mail information server to your home page makes your Internet presence more interactive and also sets your company apart from those that believe the World Wide Web is the only thing on the Internet that matters.

Send binary files through e-mail

To send binary files through e-mail, you first must encode the file using a utility such as BinHex or UUEncode. If you encode a binary file (most programs are binary files), you convert that file to a text-only format. You can then send this text-only file through e-mail, and all that the recipient needs to do is decode the message to end up with a binary file again. Many e-mail readers decode the message automatically, enabling people to receive and use your binary files easily.

Several programs are available on the Internet to enable you to encode and decode files. You can obtain more information about UUEncode and

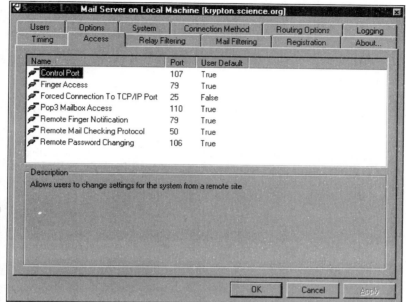

Figure 8-19:
Enable POP
access to
the SLmail
server.

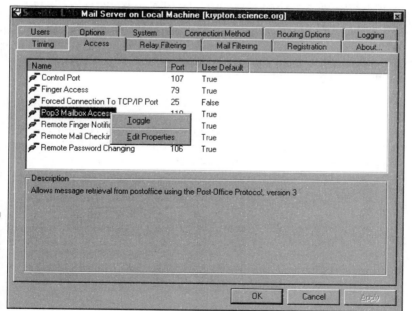

Figure 8-20:
Select
Toggle from
the pop-up
menu.

UUDecode online. The Setting Up An Internet Site home page can also help you. You can reach this page at the following URL:

```
http://computers.science.org/internet/site/setup/
```

The entire process of sending a binary file via e-mail sometimes confuses the receiver. With so many people just coming on to the Internet, one more step in receiving and sending files may be too much for many people to handle.

For documents that do not rely on specific formatting and for those documents that don't include graphics, consider sending them in text format. This procedure eliminates the need for you to UUEncode or BinHex-encode the file — and, more importantly, relieves the recipient of the responsibility of knowing how to deal with the strange-looking file you sent.

Provide World Wide Web documents

One of the most clever things you can do with your e-mail information server is to provide World Wide Web documents. After Internet users retrieve one of your Web documents through e-mail, they can save that document on their personal computers and then view the file by using their Web browsers. If the users have TCP/IP connections to the Internet, they can click any hyperlink in your document; their Web browsers respond exactly as they would had they contacted your HTTP server to retrieve the document. This method is a creative way to provide World Wide Web documents without running an HTTP server or paying a Web publishing service to host your Web pages.

Thus, an e-mail information server is just as important to your Internet site as a World Wide Web home page. You can find no better way to distribute information than via e-mail, because e-mail enables you to reach more people cheaper and faster than other methods. In addition, e-mail enables you to find out exactly who contacts you. E-mail is true two-way communication — something that any psychologist or business professional knows is an essential part of any relationship (even an electronic one).

Chapter 9

Exchanging Files on the Internet

In This Chapter

▶ Understanding how FTP works

▶ Providing files to others on the Internet

▶ Receiving files from others by using FTP

▶ Setting up a permanent FTP site

*T*he Internet is the ultimate in diverse computing environments. After you connect to the Internet, you join a computer network that integrates everything from Cray supercomputers to computerized pop machines. This diversity works because all the computers speak the same set of languages to transfer and store executable and data files.

Transferring files is an important function of the Internet. If your computer can't transfer files, you can't get the latest software programs or send files to your associates. An important aspect of almost any program that runs on the Internet is the way in which this transfer occurs.

Programs transfer files in several ways. Some programs use simple network communications to transfer files; others use a *protocol* (that is, a set of commands) known as *File Transfer Protocol*, or *FTP*.

Understanding How FTP Works

By setting up your own FTP server, you can send files to and receive files from other people on the Internet or on a local area network. Anyone who uses a World Wide Web browser, such as Netscape Navigator, can send and receive files through your FTP server.

FTP is a protocol that enables computers to transfer files across the Internet. An *FTP client program* (also known as an *FTP client*) sends a request to an *FTP server program* (also called an *FTP server*), asking to exchange information and transfer files. The server then verifies that the user is authorized to send or receive files and responds to the request accordingly. World Wide Web browsers that support FTP can support both file uploading and downloading or, in some older browsers, file downloading (retrieval) only.

One desirable feature of FTP is the fact that the protocol maintains the original formatting of the file it transfers. Unlike other file-transfer techniques, such as those you use to attach a file to an e-mail message, FTP doesn't require users to decode received files before they can use those files. (You must convert files that you transfer through e-mail to text-only formats. Several programs can perform this conversion; the most common is *UUEncode*. To decode a file that someone UUEncodes, you must configure the e-mail client receiving the e-mail that contains the encoded file to use the UUDecode program.)

Using the FTP client

Many graphical FTP client software programs are available as freeware or shareware. One of our favorite FTP clients available on the Internet is WS_FTP (available for Windows 3.1, Windows 95, and Windows NT). You can find this program on the *Setting Up An Internet Site For Dummies* CD-ROM.

The top of the window shown in Figure 9-1 has a text box for the *profile name,* which simply is a name you give this connection setup so that you can use the same setup again without reconfiguration. You can use anything for the profile name; the name is solely for your benefit and doesn't affect the way that WS_FTP operates. For the sake of simplicity, you can enter as the profile name the name of the host to which you're connecting.

The host name can be either a registered Internet domain name or the IP (Internet Protocol) address of an FTP server. In Figure 9-1, the host name of the FTP server is `ftp1.ipswitch.com`.

Enter the appropriate user ID and password (or select the Anonymous Login check box to have the program fill in these spaces automatically). Then click OK to establish the connection to the server.

Using anonymous FTP

Can you imagine handing out a password to every single person who wants access to your FTP site? You probably don't know most of the people who send or receive files through your FTP server, and you certainly don't have time to give them all personal accounts with passwords.

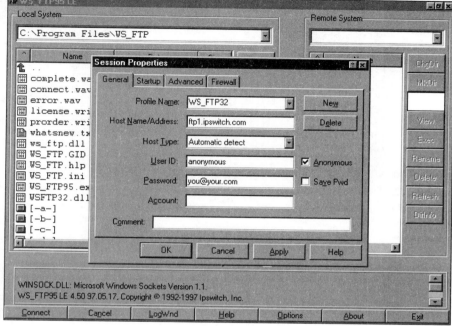

Figure 9-1:
Connecting
to an FTP
server by
using the
WS_FTP
client
program.

Many FTP server programs use a special logon account called *anonymous FTP* to enable anyone on the Internet to log on and transfer files. Users can enter the word **anonymous** as the user ID and then enter their e-mail address or the word **guest** as the password. (Many FTP sites require the e-mail address, so it's the preferable choice for your password.) But does this setup mean that the Internal Revenue Service can access financial records on your computer to see how accurate your tax return is? No. You can set up FTP server software so that the public can access only those files that don't compromise your computer or your private information. (Whew!)

After a successful connection to the desired FTP server, the file transfer dialog box shown in Figure 9-2 should appear. This dialog box shows the local file system (the one running the FTP client) and the remote file system (the one running the FTP server). In Figure 9-2, you see the local file system in the list on the left side of the dialog box and the remote file system displaying directories in the list on the right side of the dialog box.

The next step before you use WS_FTP to transfer files is selecting the files you want to transfer. To download files from the FTP server to your local machine, highlight the files you want to transfer by clicking their names in the Remote System column (right column) of the file transfer dialog box. To navigate the directories, you can either double-click a directory name that

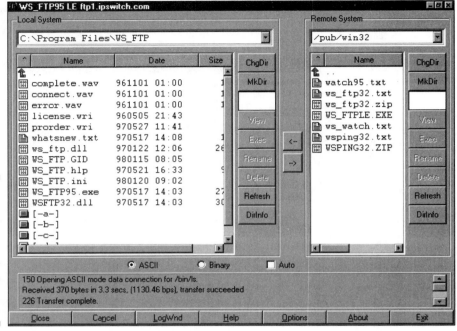

Figure 9-2:
Select files
to send or
receive and
click the
arrow
buttons to
begin the
transfer.

appears as a file folder (refer to Figure 9-2), or click the ChgDir button and
then type the full path of the directory you want to access in the text box in
the Change Directory dialog box that appears. Clicking the OK button
changes the directory and closes the Change Directory dialog box.

Often, directories have hundreds of files, and searching for the files you
want to transfer can become tedious. The small text box below the MkDir
button is for entering a *template*. This template consists of a wildcard (*)
and a file extension. If you want to view only files with a .WAV extension, for
example, enter ***.WAV** in the text box. The display of files adjusts to show
only files that have the .WAV extension.

Two arrows appear between the local file system column and the remote file
system column. You use these arrows to send selected files between the two
file systems. Highlighting a file on the local file system and clicking the
arrow that points toward the remote file system initiates a file transfer
between the file systems.

To download files to your local system, highlight the files you want downloaded in the remote file system column and then click the arrow between
the two lists that points from the remote system list to the local file system

list (the arrow on top). To upload files to the server, you follow the same procedure, except you need to highlight the files to upload in the local file system and then click the arrow that's pointing toward the remote system, or server, list (the bottom arrow). To select multiple files for transfer, hold down the Ctrl key (to select noncontiguous files) or the Shift key (to select contiguous files) while selecting with the mouse.

An important selection in WS_FTP — and even more important in using a text-based FTP client — is the type of file transfer to use. WS_FTP offers two radio buttons and a check box for file-type selection: ASCII, Binary, and Auto. Choose between ASCII (for text files) and Binary (for most word-processing files, graphics, executable programs, and sound files). Text files that you transfer as ASCII remain text, although binary files that you transfer as ASCII are no longer usable. In using a text-based FTP client, either from the DOS or UNIX prompt, you can select binary mode by entering the letter **I** at the FTP prompt. Text-based FTP clients start in ASCII mode by default.

A dialog box then appears if you're using WS_FTP as you transfer files. If you have a sound card in your computer, a sound tells you that the file is being transferred. WS_FTP makes an "uh-oh!" sound if an error occurs. After the file finishes transferring, you hear a strange sound and the dialog box goes away. If an error occurs, you may need to restart the file transfer.

Deciding whether FTP is right for you

Some of the options for transferring files on the Internet are as follows:

- ✔ FTP
- ✔ World Wide Web
- ✔ E-mail file attachments
- ✔ Socket communications

FTP is a great way to exchange files with someone on a regular basis. You can run your own FTP server or purchase FTP services from your Internet service provider. You can provide password-protected user accounts for accessing your files instead of providing public access to them.

One of the simplest ways to transfer files is to provide them from your World Wide Web site. Placing a file in the publicly accessible Web publishing directory and then sending someone a URL for accessing the file provides a simple way to retrieve files by using a Web browser. Unfortunately, anyone can access publicly accessible files.

You can, however, create a private Web directory in which to store files. You limit access to the directory — and the files — by establishing a list of valid user names and their associated passwords. Anyone who clicks the link to that directory will be asked to supply both those pieces of information. Those who can't don't get in. The procedure varies a bit among different Web servers. The one we're detailing here is for the Apache/NCSA family, which is the most popular on the Web.

First, you need to create a password file. Just sing along with the following:

1. **If your Web server is in your home or office, sit down at the keyboard and log on.**

   If your Web server is remote, such as an ISP or a virtual server, you have to use a telnet program to log on (see Chapter 3).

2. **Change to the directory in which you want to set up the password-protected files.**

   If necessary, create the directory first. If you need help with basic UNIX commands, grab a copy of *UNIX For Dummies,* 3rd Edition, by John R. Levine and Margaret Levine Young (published by IDG Books Worldwide, Inc.).

3. **Type** htpasswd -c *pathname username.*

   Replace *pathname* with the name of the password file. You might want to be creative and call the file something other than password or pw — perhaps Songs_of_the_Serengeti. Replace *username* with the name the user will use. When you press the Enter key, the program responds that it is adding the user.

   Don't type the -c after the first time. It's used to create the file, and if you type it again with the same filename, you'll overwrite the original file. Just type **htpasswd *pathname username*.** It's a really, really good idea to keep a backup copy of the password file just in case.

4. **When asked, type the password you want the user to supply.**

   As with most passwords, it won't show while you type it, so be careful to spell it correctly.

5. **Because htpasswd is a suspicious little devil, it'll make you type it again, just to be sure.**

   If you type it incorrectly either time, you'll get a pleasant little error message that says, "They don't match, sorry." If they do match, the new user and password are added to the file.

If you want to change an existing user's password, go through the same procedure as you did when you added the user originally. The only difference is that the program will indicate that it is changing the password instead of adding the user.

You'll also need to create an access configuration file (known to its friends as ACF). Limber up your fingers and hit the keyboard again. Using your favorite text editor, type the following:

```
AuthType Basic
AuthUserFile pathname
AuthName realm
<Limit GET>
require valid-user
</Limit>
```

You have to replace *pathname* with the full path, including the filename, to the file containing the user names and passwords. You can replace *realm* with whatever you want to; it's just a name you give the protected directory so it won't feel antisocial. Save this ACF file as .htaccess in the same directory as the password file.

A *global ACF* (usually called *access.conf*) controls how and whether individual directories can use their own ACFs. If your ACF doesn't work, have your Web server administrator check to see whether the AllowOverride directive is set to None or whether other restrictions are interfering with your local ACF. It's also possible that the default ACF filename of *.htaccess* has been changed in the *srm.conf* file using the AccessFileName directive. If that's the case, simply change your filename to match the one your Web server administrator has chosen.

People now use e-mail file attachments a great deal to transfer files. This method is the easiest way to transfer files, but many e-mail servers place restrictions on the maximum size of a file you can transfer through e-mail.

Programmers can actually build robust file-transfer technologies by using socket communications. The priority to build this type of technology is low, however, because most people are satisfied with FTP as a mechanism for transferring files over the Internet.

Providing Files by Using FTP

The potential uses of FTP are limitless. Some companies use an FTP server to provide customer support; other companies use FTP for communicating with employees at remote sites. A construction company, for example, can use FTP to transfer construction drawings back and forth from remote construction sites. If the foreman in Montana requests a drawing change, he or she can use FTP to transfer the file to the home-office FTP site. The home office then makes the change and places the corrected drawing on its FTP site for the remote employee to download.

You can easily fulfill numerous needs by providing files to the general public or to specific people using FTP. The applications of FTP file transfer are endless.

Using an Internet FTP service provider

The simplest, quickest, and least painful way to provide files through FTP involves using an existing FTP service provider. FTP service providers come in all shapes and sizes. Nonetheless, all providers have a few things in common, as described in the following list:

- ✔ Their Internet connections are probably faster than yours.

- ✔ They enable you to provide files on the Internet through their FTP servers, so you don't need to set up and maintain your own server.

- ✔ They like being paid.

Using an FTP service provider should enable you to bypass many initial hassles and set up a good FTP site immediately. This method is the suggested strategy if you currently have limited resources, such as a low-bandwidth Internet connection, or if you aren't connected to the Internet with a dedicated connection running 24 hours a day, 7 days a week.

Companies that are concerned about security can opt to have their FTP sites provided by an FTP service provider. This course reduces the need for a protective firewall by increasing the security of corporate machines and also reduces the manpower necessary to administer an FTP server, as well as the hardware and bandwidth necessary to provide this service. Companies should conduct a serious cost-benefit analysis to see whether using an FTP service provider is more cost-effective than running their own sites.

The company that you use to connect to the Internet may also offer FTP service. If not, you can always subscribe to an FTP service provided by another organization. Some service providers even give you a graphical interface to make setting up and maintaining your FTP service easy (although having a graphical interface certainly isn't essential).

Your FTP service provider tells you the following two important things when you set up FTP service:

- ✔ Which directory to store files in so that users can access those files through anonymous FTP called, appropriately enough, your *anonymous FTP directory*

- ✔ How to put files in your anonymous FTP directory

The pathway to your anonymous FTP directory should look something like the one in the following example:

```
/PUB/YOURUSERID
```

The PUB directory (short for public directory) is a standard directory set up by FTP administrators as part of anonymous FTP sites. The next directory establishes where you can find files associated with your account; service providers typically name this directory with your user ID. This directory is where you place publicly accessible files and subdirectories. Files in this directory are publicly accessible through the Internet, meaning that anyone who can access this directory can download files.

Getting a UNIX shell account

If you request FTP service from an Internet service provider, you can also request a UNIX shell account that any computer with a telnet client can access. *Telnet* is a network application that enables you to log on remotely to a UNIX machine. After you log on, you can work as though you were sitting in front of the UNIX machine. The UNIX shell account makes maintaining the files in your FTP directory simpler, assuming that you're familiar with UNIX. A UNIX shell account is also useful for many of the other services that this book discusses. If you aren't familiar with UNIX, you can pick up a copy of *UNIX For Dummies,* 3rd Edition (IDG Books Worldwide, Inc.) — an excellent resource.

Putting files in your FTP directory

You generally have two ways to put a file in your anonymous FTP directory:

✔ Beg and plead with your FTP service provider to do the job for you. (Remember, however, to have the provider show you how.) Then send in a disk with the files on it.

✔ Send the file by using FTP. To do so, log on to the FTP server from your local computer by using your user ID and password; then send the file to your anonymous FTP directory.

If your FTP service provider set everything up correctly, you can transfer files into and out of your FTP directory. You can have special security set up, enabling you alone to upload files to your FTP directory and enabling other users to only download files. The next few sections explain how to accomplish these tasks. We also describe how to create directories and set the security permissions for special upload-only or download-only directories.

Removing files from your anonymous FTP site

To remove a file from your anonymous FTP site, simply delete the file by using one of the following options:

- ✔ Using WS_FTP, highlight the file you want to remove by clicking the filename in the server-side list; then click the Delete button. (Refer to the section "Using the FTP client," earlier in this chapter.)

- ✔ Using a UNIX text-based FTP client, type the following command at the FTP prompt:

  delete *filename*

- ✔ From a UNIX shell account, remove files from the anonymous FTP directory by typing the following rm command at the UNIX prompt:

  rm *filename*

Receiving files from others

Your FTP service provider probably also gives you a special subdirectory called INCOMING. The full path name of the directory usually looks something like the following example:

```
/PUB/YOURUSERID/INCOMING
```

FTP users can send files to the incoming directory but can't download files from this directory. This arrangement gives you a secure way to receive files from other users through FTP. One of our service providers (CTSNet, at http://www.cts.com/) calls this directory an *FTP drop-box;* some providers also refer to this subdirectory as your *incoming directory* or your *FTP inbox.* (For Windows 95 users, directories are folders.)

Checking the security of your incoming directory

Some FTP server programs enable people to get files out of an incoming directory if they know the exact names of the files. This setup is not very secure, however, because anyone who guesses the name of a file in your incoming directory can download a copy of that file. To find out whether your incoming directory behaves this way, follow these steps:

1. **Use your FTP client program to connect to your FTP server.**

   (If you're using WS_FTP, refer to the section "Using the FTP client" earlier in this chapter.)

2. **Log on as** anonymous.

3. **Send a file to your incoming directory.**

4. **Try to get the file out of the incoming directory by using its filename.**

If you can get the file, anyone else on the Internet can also get the file as long as that person knows (or can guess) the filename. Your incoming directory has a minor security hole, although it may be one you can live with.

If the incoming directory in your FTP service comes with the security hole we describe in this section, you can use that hole to your advantage. If you need to give files to a particular person, you can place the files in your incoming directory and then tell the other person the specific names of the files, so that the person can retrieve those files from your incoming directory. To anyone who doesn't know the filename, the incoming directory appears to be empty.

If possible, you can create an incoming directory and name that directory OUTGOING. This approach keeps the names of the files in your outgoing directory from appearing. Again, anyone who knows the name of a file in the outgoing directory can retrieve that file. This approach is one of the simplest ways to control access to files in directories that an FTP service provider provides. The alternative is to give a user ID and password to each person who wants secure access to your service.

Telling others how to access your anonymous FTP directory

You can tell other people how to access your FTP directory in one of the following ways:

✔ Use a Uniform Resource Locator (URL) so that others can access your site by using a Web browser.

✔ Give other users long, drawn-out instructions on how to use a conventional FTP client to access your site.

A URL can look like something that a cat typed by walking across your keyboard, as the following example shows:

```
ftp://ftp.science.org/pub/internetsite/info.txt
```

Despite that, using a URL is probably the most direct and simple way to tell someone how to connect to your site. The long, drawn-out alternative explanation goes something like this: "Connect to the FTP server at `ftp.science.org`, and log on as **anonymous**. Use your e-mail address as the password. Change the directory to /PUB/INTERNETSITE/. Then download the INFO.TXT file."

Setting Up Your Own FTP Server

Although using an FTP service provider is convenient, we think nothing can beat setting up your own FTP server. With your own FTP server, you can set up user accounts so that business associates and friends can log on to your FTP site securely. You can receive files from other users directly rather than through a third party, and you can provide files to others simply by copying those files to your FTP directory.

Setting up your own FTP server has one drawback: Your FTP server is available only while you're connected to the Internet. If you don't have a dedicated 24-hour connection, you probably should use an Internet FTP service provider. Using a provider is a great way to establish a permanent FTP site on the Internet, is also much less expensive than establishing your own dedicated connection, and requires less maintenance.

If your computer can communicate with the Internet by using TCP/IP, you can set up and run your own FTP server. You need only access to the Internet and FTP server software that works in the operating system you're using. Most FTP server software is straightforward — just install it and away you go.

The following sections provide detailed instructions on setting up FTP server software for either a Macintosh or a Windows-based personal computer.

Using a Macintosh NetPresenz FTP server

The best shareware FTP server software available for your Macintosh computer is NetPresenz, by Peter N. Lewis. The price is $10, and the program is worth every penny. You can find the software on the CD-ROM that accompanies this book.

Uniform Resource Locator (URL) review

Uniform Resource Locators (URL) are standardized addresses that people use to refer to Internet resources.

The first group of letters, ending in a colon, identifies the type of server providing the resource. You identify a file on an FTP server, for example, by the first three letters in the URL: `ftp:`.

The second portion of the URL, which normally begins with a double forward slash (`//`), identifies the domain name of the computer on the Internet that offers the Internet resource (`ftp.science.org`).

Following the domain name is the path name of the directory that contains the resource. (By the way, a resource is usually a file of some type.) In the case of a file on an FTP server, that portion of the URL may appear as follows:

`/pub/internetsite/`

The URL for an FTP resource can also include a specific filename. The following URL points to a file called INFO.TXT in an anonymous FTP directory on the FTP server named `ftp.science.org` at `ftp://ftp.science.org`:

`ftp://ftp.science.org/pub/`
`    internetsite/info.txt`

Some computers on the Internet don't have domain names, but every computer on the Internet has a unique address called an IP address. You can use the IP address instead of a domain name. The following example, using the IP address, also is a valid URL:

`ftp://207.92.75.100/pub/`
`    internetsite/info.txt`

NetPresenz enables your Macintosh computer to send and receive files through FTP and can also serve Web pages through its built-in Web server. Unlike many other programs that perform only one task, NetPresenz is a multifaceted server system. In addition to FTP and Web service, NetPresenz can provide files also through the Gopher protocol, a precursor to the World Wide Web. You can find out how to download the most current version of NetPresenz at the following address:

`http://computers.science.org/internet/site/setup/`

To use NetPresenz, your Macintosh must have System 7 (or later) and MacTCP Version 1.1 (or later), and you must have enabled file sharing. To enable Internet users to access your FTP server, you need some kind of Internet IP access, such as PPP (Point-to-Point Protocol) or (if you're special) a direct network connection.

Checking security

Before you install NetPresenz, you need to check the security of your computer system. Follow these steps to prepare for the installation of the NetPresenz server on your computer and to check the computer's security:

1. **Make sure file sharing is enabled.**

   Use the Sharing Setup control panel to determine the status of file sharing. Remember that you access your Macintosh control panels through the Apple menu. After you finish, close the Sharing Setup control panel.

2. **Configure sharing for your drives and folders by using the Finder to locate and click a drive or folder icon; then choose File⇨Sharing.**

   A sharing configuration dialog box appears.

3. **If you don't want anonymous FTP users to access a particular drive or folder, make sure you deselect (remove the check mark from) each of the three check boxes to the right of Everyone.**

You can change all your folders at the same time by selecting the Make All Currently Enclosed Folders Like This One check box.

Installing NetPresenz

After you check the security on your computer, you can install the NetPresenz server. After you install NetPresenz on your Mac, you see the following program icons in the NetPresenz folder:

- ✔ NetPresenz
- ✔ NetPresenz Setup
- ✔ Register

Don't click any of these icons yet; just admire their beauty. The first program, NetPresenz, is the actual FTP server program. The second program, NetPresenz Setup, enables you to configure NetPresenz. The Register program gives you a simple and flexible way to register and pay for the NetPresenz program.

You need to do a few things before you configure NetPresenz. The following four steps show you how to prepare your Macintosh to run NetPresenz:

1. **Run the Internet Config program.**

   You find the Internet Config program in the NetPresenz folder. After you run the Internet Config program, the program enables you to determine the general settings for use in many Internet applications, including

NetPresenz. You don't need to click each of the buttons in the Internet Preferences window — just the interesting ones. The important thing is that you run the application at least once so that you install the Internet Config extension (part of the program). NetPresenz uses the Internet Config extension later. Close the Internet Preferences window after you complete your setup.

2. **At some point, run the Register program (by choosing it from the NetPresenz menu) to register and pay for NetPresenz.**

   Make sure you look at the neat payment methods that are available!

3. **If you want to enable anonymous FTP logons, use the Users & Groups control panel to set up the** <Guest> **user and enable File Sharing for** <Guest>**.**

   The *Guest user* is anyone who visits your FTP site anonymously.

4. **Double-click the NetPresenz Setup icon to get started with NetPresenz.**

   The About window appears, telling you a little about the program. Close this window by clicking the Close box in the top-left corner. You're now ready to start configuring NetPresenz.

Configuring NetPresenz

After you install the NetPresenz server, you must configure the NetPresenz server correctly by using the NetPresenz Setup window. The Setup program starts after you double-click the NetPresenz Setup icon (as the preceding section describes). If you haven't done so, double-click this icon in the NetPresenz folder now.

To configure general NetPresenz settings, follow these steps:

1. **Click the FTP Setup box in the NetPresenz Setup window.**

   The FTP Setup window appears.

   The most important settings in this window are the File Access privileges, which offer the following levels of access:

   • **None:** No access

   • **Read Only:** Receive files only

   • **Upload:** Send and receive only

   • **Full:** Send and receive files and delete, rename, or modify files and folders

   You can set the access privileges independently for each of the following types of users:

   • **Owner:** The user whose name appears in the Sharing Setup control panel as the owner of the Macintosh

- **User:** Any other user you define in the Users & Groups control panel

- **Guest:** Anyone who uses anonymous FTP to access the NetPresenz server

2. **Choose an access-level privilege for each of the user types by making selections from the drop-down lists.**

   Another important setting in the FTP Setup window is Remote Mounting, which enables an FTP user to access shared file systems on other Macintosh computers on your network. To access file systems on other computers, the FTP user sends a command similar to the following example from an FTP client program:

   ```
   quote smnt MacFileServer
   ```

3. **To enable Remote Mounting, select the Enabled check box in the appropriate user-type column.**

   Enable remote mounting, however, *only* if you have a good reason to do so. Typically, you disable remote mounting.

   Enabling Remote Mounting for guests is dangerous if you have an AppleTalk network. If you enable Remote Mounting for guests, anyone on the Internet can access files from any Macintosh on your network. If you don't have a good reason to enable Remote Mounting, disable this feature by deselecting the Enabled check box.

   Other than disabling Remote Mounting, leaving the default settings for the other options in the FTP Setup window should work fine for your setup.

4. **Click the Save button after you've finished making changes.**

5. **Now check the default logon directory for FTP users by clicking FTP Users in the NetPresenz Setup window.**

   The FTP Users window appears, enabling you to set up the logon directory and logon commands for each FTP user. You also can set up defaults that apply for every FTP user.

   Login Directory is the drive or folder that you want FTP users to see initially after they connect to your FTP server. If you want the Macintosh Desktop to appear first after a user connects to your FTP server, set the Login Directory option to a single forward slash (/).

   The Login Commands box enables you to define commands to execute after a user logs on. This option enables users to perform such tasks as mounting remote shared folders and drives automatically or displaying usage statistics. You can include any SMNT or SITE command in the Login Commands box; see the NetPresenz documentation for details.

Creating an anonymous FTP directory

Your FTP server is easier for others to use if you create a /PUB directory because that is what FTP users are accustomed to finding. To create a /PUB directory, follow these steps:

1. **Use the Finder to create a new folder that you name PUB.**

2. **Create the PUB folder on the Desktop or place an alias of the PUB folder on the Desktop.**

3. **Click the PUB folder and choose File⇨Sharing.**

   The File Sharing dialog box appears, titled with the name of the folder.

4. **Select the check box labeled Share This Item and Its Contents.**

5. **In the File Sharing dialog box, you can change the owner of the folder by selecting a different owner from the drop-down list box.**

   Changing the owner is handy if a user other than the owner of the Macintosh is responsible for maintaining the FTP server.

6. **Deselect the Make Changes check box for Everyone and for each User/Group as you want.**

7. **Close the window by clicking the Close box in the top-left corner.**

8. **Start NetPresenz Setup and then click FTP Users.**

9. **Change the Login Directory for Default User to /PUB.**

10. **Click the Save button.**

Now put some files in the PUB folder. Remember that some computer operating systems don't permit spaces in filenames. A good idea is to avoid using spaces in the names of the files you make available in your FTP server. That way, everyone on the Internet can access these files without trouble. It's common practice to use an underline (_) in place of a space in filenames.

Creating special files

NetPresenz enables you to create special files to help FTP users find the files that interest them. (You must give these special files specific names so that NetPresenz will know that these files are special.) You can, for example, create in any folder a file named !Folder Info; the contents of this file appear automatically after an FTP user enters the folder. Then you can create in the PUB folder a !Folder Info file containing the following message (or something similar):

```
This is the PUB folder. In this folder, you find files and
folders that you may want to download. If you need help,
send mail to help@domain.com. (Don't blame us if your
computer blows up after you use files from this folder.)
Enjoy!
```

You also can create a startup file — another type of special file that appears after an FTP user logs on to the FTP server. You must store startup files in a Startup Messages folder, which you must put in one of the following two places:

✔ The NetPresenz folder

✔ The NetPresenz Preferences folder, which you place in the System Preferences folder

You can create a default startup file as well as startup files for each type of user. NetPresenz can display a file named Anonymous Startup, for example, after an anonymous FTP user logs on to the FTP server. If NetPresenz doesn't find a startup file for a particular user type, the program displays the default startup file (if one exists).

Make all your special files, including the !Folder Info and startup files, text-only. And press Enter at the end of each line in the file instead of using word wrap. Some FTP client programs don't perform word wrap correctly, so you must insert line endings into your files yourself for the benefit of those programs. Try to keep these special files small to improve performance. If you have a good idea of which files are most likely to catch your FTP users' interests, provide simple, direct instructions on retrieving those files. These instructions make your FTP server much easier to use.

Configuring security settings

The Security window of NetPresenz Setup controls several security settings (see Figure 9-3). Click the Security button in the NetPresenz Setup window.

You may want to disable (clear) any of the following three Security settings, because the average user doesn't need these settings:

✔ **Allow Change Password (SITE P):** This setting enables users to change their passwords.

✔ **Allow Change Privs (SITE C):** This option enables users to change their file privileges (file-level security restrictions).

✔ **Allow Process Control (SITE A):** This option enables the owner to control processes.

The rest of the settings are optional. Enabling a Connection Sounds option can prove to be helpful if you plan to be nearby as people connect to your FTP server. Connection sounds may be annoying in a busy office, however.

NetPresenz is also a fully functional World Wide Web server program. If you decide to use the Web server as well, click the WWW Setup icon in the NetPresenz Setup window. The WWW Setup window appears. Select the WWW Enabled check box to turn on your NetPresenz Web server.

```
┌──────────────────────── Security ──────────────────────────┐
│ ┌─General Security──────────┐ ┌─Connection Sounds──────────┐ │
│ │ ⊠ Log Actions to File     │ │ ◉ None                     │ │
│ │ ⊠ Hide Log in Background  │ │ ○ Speak Messages           │ │
│ │ ☐ Allow Clear Text Passwords │ ○ Play Sounds             │ │
│ └───────────────────────────┘ └────────────────────────────┘ │
│ ┌─User Restrictions───────────────────────────────────────┐ │
│ │ ⊠ Allow Get                ⊠ Allow Rename                │ │
│ │ ⊠ Allow Put                ⊠ Allow Delete                │ │
│ │ ⊠ Allow Change Password (SITE P)  ⊠ Allow Change Privs (SITE C) │
│ │ ⊠ Allow Index Search (SITE INDEX)                        │ │
│ └──────────────────────────────────────────────────────────┘ │
│ ┌─Owner Restrictions──────────────────────────────────────┐ │
│ │ ⊠ Allow Process Control (SITE A)   ⊠ Allow FTPd Shutdown (SITE Q) │
│ └──────────────────────────────────────────────────────────┘ │
│   ( Cancel )          ( Revert )              ( Save )         │
└──────────────────────────────────────────────────────────────┘
```

Figure 9-3:
Configure additional security settings in the Security window.

Checking the setup

The last step in the setup process is clicking the Summary button in the NetPresenz Setup window to open the Summary window. If you need to do anything else, the Summary window tells you what else you still need to do.

Using NetPresenz

Start the NetPresenz program by double-clicking the NetPresenz icon. This icon starts the FTP server and displays the log window. After you use your FTP server for a while, your log window should look something like the one shown for the Windows Vermillion FTP program later in this chapter.

To quit NetPresenz, start NetPresenz Setup by double-clicking its icon. Then hold down the Option key as you quit NetPresenz Setup. This action closes both NetPresenz Setup and the active NetPresenz program.

Using a Windows FTP server

Many good FTP server programs are available for Microsoft Windows. In fact, if you've installed Windows NT Server 4.0 or later, you have access to Internet Information Server (IIS), which includes an FTP server.

The process of setting up most FTP servers is similar. We chose to demonstrate the setup of two FTP servers: one called Vermillion FTP (VFTPD), written by Matte Kalinowski, and another called WFTPD, by Alun Jones. WFTPD is on the *Setting Up An Internet Site For Dummies* CD-ROM. Both programs will do the job just fine, but if you're not familiar with FTP, you may want to try out WFTPD because of its friendly and easy-to-use interface.

These programs include added security features that you don't find in other FTP servers. VFTPD, for example, has an IP-checking feature that can verify an account by IP address as well as by username. This feature is a powerful one, but be aware that many people access the Internet by using *dynamic IP addresses* (which means that they get a different IP address each time they connect to the Internet).

To use Vermillion FTP or WFTPD, you must be running a Windows operating system such as Windows 95 or Windows NT, with TCP/IP communications correctly configured in your Windows 95 or Windows NT network applet. You must also have Internet access so that other people can access and use your FTP server. For additional help in setting up TCP/IP in Windows 95 or NT, open the Control Panel, start the Network applet, and choose Help. You need this setup, along with dial-up networking or some other TCP/IP access to your service provider, such as PPP or a direct network connection.

Getting started with Vermillion FTP

The first step in installing Vermillion FTP is obtaining the software, which you usually find distributed in ZIP format. You can download the Vermillion FTP server program from the TUCOWS site at `http://www.tucows.com/`. After you contact the TUCOWS main page, select a mirror site closest to you. (A *mirror site* is an Internet site with identical information. Mirror sites are located geographically to limit the amount of international network traffic.) TUCOWS offers a Search button, which you can click, or you can follow the links to the Server Daemon page, which lists Vermillion and several other good shareware FTP servers.

Using WinZip (which is on the *Setting Up An Internet Site For Dummies* CD-ROM), extract the Vermillion FTP software into a directory in which you want the program to reside permanently. Unlike other Windows software, Vermillion FTP requires no installation process. After you extract Vermillion FTP from its ZIP file, it's ready to run.

In Windows 95 or Windows NT, choose Start⇨Run to launch Vermillion FTP. After you start Vermillion FTP, you see a status screen, shown in Figure 9-4.

If you want Vermillion FTP to launch each time you boot your computer, add a shortcut to the program in your Start folder. Remember that all program shortcuts in your Windows Start folder launch each time you start Windows 95 or NT.

Setting up Vermillion FTP

Vermillion FTP is extremely easy to set up. Click the tab labeled Setup in the main Vermillion screen. The Setup tab opens, as shown in Figure 9-5.

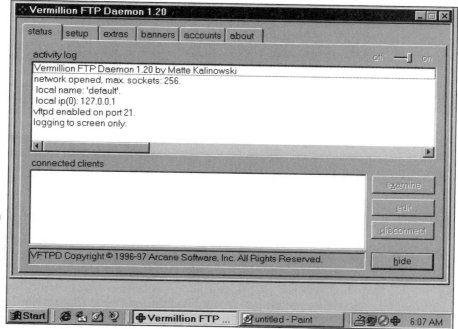

Figure 9-4:
Vermillion FTP displays its status after loading.

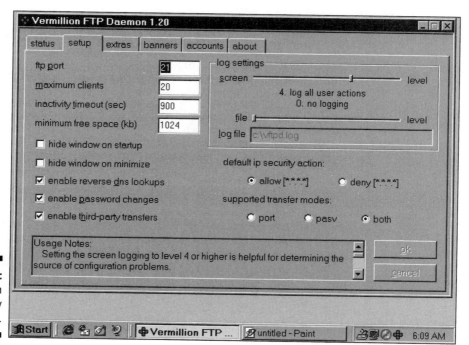

Figure 9-5:
Vermillion FTP is easy to set up.

The Setup tab contains the following options:

- ✓ **Ftp Port Number.** This option is set to 21 by default. Changing this value is not a good idea. If you change this number, no conventional FTP client programs can contact this server. All FTP clients try to contact an FTP server on port 21.

- ✓ **Maximum Clients.** This setting determines the maximum number of simultaneous connections to your server by client programs. The default is 20, which is a nice round number. Unless your machine is fast and has quite a bit of memory, stick with 20 as the maximum number of simultaneous connections.

- ✓ **Inactivity Timeout (sec).** Just how long do you want your FTP server to hang around waiting for a valid response from a connected client? The default setting — 900 — is 15 minutes, which seems to be a little long. You may consider changing this value to something shorter, such as 600.

- ✓ **Minimum Free Space (kb).** The default setting is 1024. This is a default value that should be left alone.

- ✓ **Hide Window on Startup.** Select this option if you want Vermillion FTP to run in the background, hiding itself as soon as it starts. This way, you can get on with your work without being bothered by the FTP server.

- ✓ **Hide Window on Minimize.** Select this option if you want to hide Vermillion FTP manually by minimizing the Vermillion FTP window. This option is handy if you regularly administer the FTP server.

- ✓ **Enable Reverse DNS Lookups.** Select this option if you want Vermillion FTP to look up domain names from IP addresses.

- ✓ **Enable Password Changes.** Select this option to allow users to re-motely change their passwords.

- ✓ **Enable Third Party Transfers.** This option, which allows a user to have another remote FTP server send a file to yours, is selected by default. However, it poses a security risk, so you should deselect it.

- ✓ **Log Settings options.** Logs are an important way of knowing who has accessed your FTP server, what they did when they logged on, and any problems they may have encountered. Note the sliders labeled Screen and File. The screen settings are for screen output only; the file settings cause the results to be written to a file. By moving the sliders, you can select one of seven log detail settings. The 0 setting turns logging completely off. (This setting is not recommended.) The 6 setting logs every bit of detail. (Choose this setting if you're having problems you need to troubleshoot.) Choose the amount of log detail that makes you feel comfortable. You want to watch the size of your log file so that the file doesn't fill your hard drive.

- ✓ **Default IP Security Action.** This lets you set whether you will allow or deny access from everyone.

✔ **Supported Transfer Modes.** This is set to "Both" by default, since FTP clients generally use the *port* mode for contacting your server and Web browsers use *pasv* mode.

Continuing the setup, click the Banners tab of the main screen. You can use two banners to customize your FTP server: a welcome banner and a goodbye banner. Before you get all pensive trying to think of just the right thing to say, we probably should mention that only text-based FTP clients can ever view these banners. In modern, graphical clients such as WS_FTP, these banners scroll across your screen, almost unseen, in a small status window.

If you decide to construct a banner, you can also use a number of *insertable variables* (or *tokens*). These variables are placeholders for information the computer automatically fills in for you. You can insert the time (with the %T token), the number of bytes that are free in the current working directory (with %F), the path of the current working directory (with %C), the remote host (with %R), the local host (with %L), the username (with %U), the maximum number of simultaneous connections (with %M), and the current number of client connections (with %N).

This next set of instructions, setting up User accounts, is the most important part of setting up your FTP server. Click the Accounts tab. The dialog box shown in Figure 9-6 appears. Enter a username in the Users text box, and click the Add button. A new dialog box opens, as shown in Figure 9-7, to enable you to enter the details for the User account.

Before you get into creating user accounts, you may consider creating a template. A *template* is a saved profile that you can use over and over in creating new accounts. You can create templates that act as defaults for new User accounts. This approach enables you to have several classes of users while keeping administration of user accounts fairly simple. To add a new template before you continue, click the Cancel button to return to the Accounts tab, add a name for the template in the Template text box, and click the Add button on the right side. This action launches the Template dialog box. You create settings in this dialog box that act as defaults whenever you create new accounts of the type you specified as you entered a name for the template. You may, for example, enter a name of Administration. You use this template each time you want to create an account for someone in administration. All the security settings are set by default.

If you're wondering what the upload-to-download ratio in the template dialog box is all about, this feature is a throwback to the electronic bulletin board (BBS) days. To promote file uploads to the bulletin board, someone who wanted to download files also needed to participate in uploads. In other words, for every so many bytes uploaded, you could download some number of bytes. This practice was also known as getting credits. Credits were highly sought after and became similar to a monetary exchange.

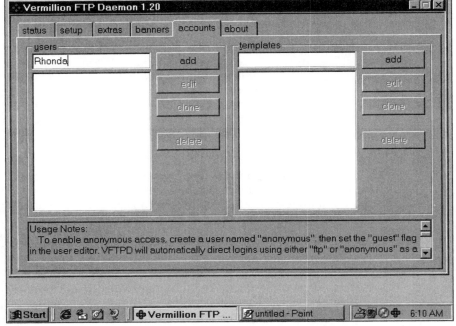

Figure 9-6:
Adding User account information in the Accounts tab is the most important part of setting up an FTP server.

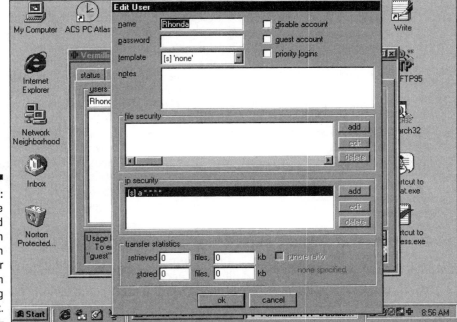

Figure 9-7:
Enter the detailed information for each user account in this dialog box.

Creating a new user account requires two additional parameters (other than the account name): file permissions and IP security permissions.

The IP Security permissions setting can remain at its default, enabling connections from any IP address. You may want to change this parameter only if your company has fixed IP addresses, and you want to restrict access to the FTP server to known hosts within your company or to trusted clients.

File security is a little more involved. Clicking the Add button next to the File Security text box launches a File Permissions dialog box. Specify only those directories and files that you want this new user to visit. Granting permissions that aren't restrictive enough opens security holes in your system. PCs are fairly impervious to hacker attack, except for this parameter.

Carefully select directories that don't contain sensitive information in setting up access to your PC through an FTP server. Creating new directories and making copies of files to which you want to give users access makes more sense than permitting access to your computer's working directories. Giving someone else access to your computer's root directory (normally, C:\) is never a good idea. Grant write and delete access to only the most trusted users. Writing programs that can launch themselves, destroying important information or causing computer hardware failure, is all too possible. You're best off limiting access to people you trust so as not to inflict these types of programs on your computer.

Carefully follow the detailed instructions that come with your Vermillion software for creating new users and templates. You have no Help button. You need to launch WordPad or Microsoft Word to read the manual that you find in the directory in which you store VFTPD.

The Windows FTP server WFTPD

FTP server software runs very well on a Windows-based computer. Although this type of setup doesn't provide the kind of performance that you obtain from a high-end UNIX workstation, the simplicity of setup and maintenance you enjoy offsets the reduced performance you experience in using Windows as your Internet-server operating system. That's why we're excited about showing you how to set up your own FTP server — in this case, WFTPD — in Microsoft Windows NT/95.

WFTPD stands for *Winsock FTP Daemon*. (*Daemon* is a program that runs in the background.) To use WFTPD, you must be running a Windows operating system, such as Windows 95 or Windows NT, with a TCP/IP communications program that's compatible with WinSock Version 1.1 or later. If you want Internet users to access your FTP server, you need some kind of Internet access, such as PPP or a direct network connection.

Installing WFTPD

The first step in installing WFTPD is to copy the software from the *Setting Up An Internet Site For Dummies* CD-ROM, unzip it onto your hard drive, and then execute the program. After you execute the WFTPD program, the main WFTPD window appears.

Setting up WFTPD security

The first and most important thing to do when you use WFTPD is to beef up your security. As soon as you start WFTPD, you add a new level of complexity to your Internet presence. Now you need to secure your computer against unwanted intruders. WFTPD doesn't fail you in this regard, because the program provides excellent security features.

To begin establishing general security settings, follow these steps:

1. **Choose Security➪General from the menu bar.**

   The General Security dialog box appears, enabling you to establish basic security preferences.

2. **Establish the level of security you want by selecting the appropriate check boxes in the General Security dialog box.**

   The most important of these preferences is the Enable Security check box. If you select this check box, every FTP user must enter a user name and a password to use your FTP server. Selecting the Enable Security check box also means that the system enforces access restrictions according to additional security settings that you make.

   If you don't select the Enable Security check box, anyone on the Internet can copy or delete any file on your system. This possibility may seem interesting if you're studying psychology or criminal behavior and want to know what some Internet users may do if they encounter a defenseless FTP server. If you conduct such a study, intentionally or otherwise, please send us the conclusions.

   The other four check boxes in the General Security dialog box are less extreme in their effect, although they're still important to your security considerations. These options function as described in the following list:

   • **Allow Anonymous.** Select this check box if you want to enable anonymous FTP access to your FTP server.

   • **Allow Uploads.** Select this check box if you want to enable FTP users to upload (send files).

- **Allow Anonymous Uploads.** Select this check box if you want to enable anonymous FTP users to upload.

- **Disable Non-reflexive PORTs.** Select this check box if you want to make sure that the return address of a PORT command is the same as that of the client issuing it.

An FTP server accepts two types of users: *anonymous users* and *users who have specific logon IDs.* Users with logon IDs have password-protected access to files in their home directories or the directories to which you give them access. The server is like a museum. You enable the public to view, touch, and feel the displays in the public viewing area. Employees, on the other hand, have a key to the back room, where you keep displays that aren't for public viewing.

3. **To limit the number of FTP users who can connect to your FTP server simultaneously, enter a number in the Maximum Number of Users field.**

   A zero in this field means that no limit applies. (If you enter a zero here and you don't want anyone to connect to your FTP server, don't run it!)

4. **Enter a number in the Timeout for Inactive Connections (Seconds) field.**

   Establishing a timeout period for inactive connections is a good idea. An *inactive connection* is an FTP user who hasn't issued any FTP commands to your FTP server in a while. Rather than having these inactive connections just sit there, consuming memory and processing time on your computer, you can tell WFTPD to boot them off after a certain number of seconds of inactivity. If you enter zero in this field, no FTP users are ever disconnected, no matter how long they're inactive.

5. **Click OK to close the dialog box after you finish setting General Security options.**

Next, you need to adjust your settings in the User/Rights Security Dialog box. This dialog box enables you to set up FTP user accounts and to control the directories that each user can access. To establish settings in this dialog box, follow these steps:

1. **Choose Security⇨Users/Rights.**

   WFTPD provides two default user names: anonymous and default.

2. **To change the directories that anonymous FTP users can access, select anonymous from the User Name drop-down list; enter a directory name in the Home directory field; and select the Restrict to Home check box.**

A user's home directory is the one that the user sees after initially logging on to your FTP server. If you restrict users to their home directories (by selecting the Restrict to Home check box), you prevent those users from accessing files in any directory that's not a subdirectory of the home directory. FTP users you restrict in this way can still access directories within their home directories. Think of the procedure as similar to grounding a child; you restrict the child to home, but he or she can still access the refrigerator there.

We usually restrict anonymous FTP users to the C:\WFTPD directory. This type of setup protects important files on your computer but enables anonymous FTP users to access files and directories within the C:\WFTPD directory.

If you enable anonymous FTP users to connect to your FTP server without restricting these users to a certain directory, anyone on the Internet can access every directory and every file on your computer.

3. **After you finish making changes for anonymous users, click the Done button or, if you want to add specific users, just follow the next procedure.**

You also can add specific users. If you have a company, you may want to give your employees their own user accounts. These accounts give the employees password-protected FTP access to their own files. To add a new user, follow these steps:

1. **In the User Name field, type a user name and then click OK.**

2. **In the New Password field, type a password.**

   The password remains hidden as you type.

3. **In the Verify Password field, retype the password and then click OK.**

   This entry confirms the password you enter in Step 2.

4. **In the Home directory field, type a directory name.**

   This directory is the one that users see first after they log on.

5. **If you want users to have full access to your computer's files and directories, leave the Restrict to Home check box deselected; otherwise, select that check box.**

6. **If you need to add more users, click the New Users button and follow these steps again.**

7. **When you've finished adding users, click the Done button.**

Now that you can add users, you may also want to delete them at some point. To delete an existing user, open the User/Rights Security dialog box and select the user in the User Name list; then click the Delete button. After you finish adding, deleting, and updating users in this dialog box, click the Done button.

As a final level of security, you can deny access to certain hosts or certain networks on the Internet. Suppose, for example, that a nasty hacker breaks into your system from IP address 127.0.0.1 and steals some important files. This act upsets you, so you send e-mail to the Computer Emergency Response Team (CERT), informing the team about the break-in. You then deny access to anyone on any host or network that begins with the number 127 by following these steps:

1. **Choose Security⇨Host/Net from the menu bar.**

   The Host Security Settings dialog box appears.

2. **Type 127.*.*.* in the Host address field.**

3. **Click the Deny radio button to the right of the Host address field.**

4. **Click the Add/Update button.**

You also can reverse your security approach. Rather than wait until a hacker breaks into your system, you can deny access to *every* host and network by clicking the Deny radio button in the Default Action section of the dialog box. Then you can selectively grant entrance to certain hosts and networks that you trust by entering their IP addresses, one at a time, in the Host Address field and then clicking the Allow radio button next to the field. Make sure that you click the Add/Update button after you type each address. Click the Done button after you finish making changes. If you want to remove the restriction, select the host address in the drop-down box and click the Delete button.

Configuring other WFTPD settings

Several WFTPD settings are both interesting and useful. First, take a look at the Messages menu. The Greeting and Farewell messages have defaults that you can't change until you pay for the software. This situation is your incentive to honesty. (Not that *you* need an incentive, of course, but many people may not pay for the software without some encouragement.) After you obtain the official version of WFTPD, you can change the Greeting and Farewell messages by choosing those commands from the Messages menu.

The MESSAGE.FTP option in the Messages menu enables you to turn on or off the display of special messages for each directory. If you choose the MESSAGE.FTP option in the Messages menu, for example, the special text file MESSAGE.FTP appears whenever an FTP user changes to a directory that contains this special file. You may want to create, in your C:\WFTPD directory, a MESSAGE.FTP file that contains the following text:

```
This is the FTP directory. Here you find several files that
   may interest you, as well as a few directories to.
   explore. If you have questions or need help using this
   FTP server, send e-mail to ftphelp@domain.com.
```

The C:\WFTPD directory then displays that message to any FTP user who accesses it.

Make sure that you press Enter at the end of each line as you create your text file for this message. Many FTP client programs don't word-wrap correctly, so you must mark the line endings in your message for these programs yourself.

If you want WFTPD to keep a log of activity on your FTP server, such as logons and file transfers, do the following:

1. **Choose Logging⇨Log Options from the menu bar.**

   The Logging Options dialog box appears.

2. **Select the Enable Logging check box.**

3. **Select the check box for each of the items that you want the program to log.**

4. **When you're finished, click the OK button.**

To log activity to a file rather than just to the screen:

1. **Choose File⇨Open Log from the menu bar.**

   The Open dialog box appears.

2. **Choose an existing log file or type the name of a new one.**

3. **Click the Open button.**

To close an open log file, choose File⇨Close Log from the menu bar. To shut down your FTP server, choose File⇨Exit from the menu bar.

Figuring Out What to Do with Your FTP Server

You can do many things with your FTP server. Whether you set up your own server or subscribe to an FTP service, the possibilities are almost endless. The following sections present some ideas that may not have occurred to you yet.

Providing World Wide Web documents

Yes, you can provide hypertext World Wide Web documents through your FTP server. Although this method isn't as common (or ideal) an approach as providing World Wide Web documents on a World Wide Web server, it works in most cases. Create your HTML document and put the file in your anonymous FTP directory. Those who have a Web browser can retrieve and view your HTML document as though they had contacted a Web server.

Providing intracompany file transfer

In addition to providing files to customers, an FTP server can provide the useful function of intracompany file transfer. One of the most useful features of FTP is its capability to limit site access to users who have passwords. This capability enables a company to set up an FTP site that only authorized employees can access.

You can also use the restricted password access technique to provide confidential files to paying customers.

An FTP site can be a valuable resource, enabling your employees to transfer files among themselves. The FTP site also can serve as a forum where you can post valuable files — such as employee manuals and general employment policies — that all employees can access and use.

Setting up a public file-exchange area

By giving anonymous FTP users permission to send and receive files through your FTP server, you can create a useful public exchange forum. Swapping files among family members, friends, and strangers around the world has its roots in early bulletin board systems (BBSs) — online forums that require user IDs — that existed before the Internet. FTP users can exchange messages and files through your FTP server just as they do by calling a BBS.

If you decide to set up a public file-exchange area for whatever reason, consider talking to a lawyer about your potential liability. A lawyer can help you create a good disclaimer that makes clear to all users of your exchange area that they use the area at their own risk and that you do not control the content or tolerate illegal activity.

Currently, no better tool than FTP exists for transferring files on the Internet, either for personal or business purposes. Depending on your requirements and skill level, you can provide FTP service by using a service provider or by running your own server on a Mac or Windows machine. The FTP system is a valuable tool and usually is essential in setting up an Internet site.

Chapter 10

Setting Up an Automated Electronic Mailing List

In This Chapter

▶ Creating a mailing list for your Internet site

▶ Using an Internet service provider to run a mailing list

▶ Turning your mailing list into an interactive information resource

Since the days of drums and smoke signals, humanity has looked for ways to broadcast information to groups of people. Automated mailing-list software is the modern answer to that age-old challenge. Send e-mail to an automated mailing list, and it distributes the mail automatically to everyone who subscribes to that list.

An *electronic mailing list* is exactly what it sounds like: a list of e-mail addresses. Similar to traditional mailing lists filled with postal addresses, an electronic mailing list is a compilation of electronic addresses. You can use electronic mailing lists to send the same message to many people at the same time, just as you use a traditional mailing list to send a printed letter to many people. The only difference between an electronic mailing list and a traditional postal mailing list is the way in which these lists deliver messages to the recipients.

Anyone can create an electronic mailing list simply by gathering a list of e-mail addresses. Many e-mail programs enable you to easily create and send messages to electronic mailing lists. Your e-mail program may, for example, enable you to define special groups such as family members, corporate departments, or project work groups to which you send e-mail on a regular basis. Then when you send a message to the group name, your e-mail program sends e-mail to each person in the group.

This type of electronic mailing list is so straightforward that we're not going to go into detail in this chapter on how to set one up. If you want to create this type of electronic mailing list, start collecting e-mail addresses of people to whom you want to send e-mail. After you have a list of e-mail addresses to which you want to send a message, just determine how to use your particular e-mail program to send a message to the entire list. Every e-mail program works differently, but most e-mail programs today enable you to create such lists.

You can't prevent people from adding your e-mail address to their mailing lists. The fact that e-mail is inexpensive to send (free, in most cases) makes electronic junk mail (unwanted e-mail, often called *spam*) a fact of life that isn't going to change any time soon. Be considerate of other people, and don't send e-mail that people may resent. Remember what your mother said when you were young: Don't talk to strangers — unless, of course, you have a good reason to do so and both you and the stranger enjoy the conversation. If you run your own mailing list, be sure to set the options so that only people who are valid subscribers can send messages to the list. This will prevent your subscribers from having to deal with spam.

This section covers a type of electronic mailing list that's more useful than the old manual type of list: *automated electronic mailing lists,* which are managed by a special server program called a *list server.* A list server still manages a list of e-mail addresses, but with a few twists, as follows:

- ✔ Anyone can add his or her e-mail address to an automated mailing list by sending a special *subscribe* request via e-mail.

- ✔ Anyone can remove his or her address from an automated mailing list by sending an *unsubscribe* request through e-mail.

- ✔ The list server enables anyone to send a message to everyone on the mailing list without compromising the privacy of the mailing-list subscribers.

People choose to be part of an automated mailing list. If they no longer want to receive e-mail through the mailing list, they remove their e-mail addresses from the list. This sense of freedom makes people much more comfortable with the idea of subscribing to the list in the first place. In some cases, people experience difficulty in removing their names from a list, but after they begin sending complaints to everyone on the list, the problem usually resolves itself quickly.

If you want to create your own electronic mailing list, seriously consider using a list server to start an automated electronic mailing list. A list server is a valuable information resource for the members of its mailing list. And because people choose to be on the list, they don't consider the e-mail that they receive to be junk. Some mailing lists that list servers manage include tens of thousands of subscribers. Such mailing lists are an excellent way to deliver timely Internet content.

Creating Automated Mailing Lists for the Listless

You can set up an automated electronic mailing list in two ways: You can establish a mailing-list service by using a service provider on the Internet, or you can set up your own automated electronic-mailing-list server on your personal computer. Either way, the setup process is straightforward if you know the anatomy of an automated mailing list.

One of the mailing list's vital organs is its e-mail address, which is known as the *mailing-list address.* This address is where people send e-mail if they want that mail to go to the entire mailing list. A mailing-list address can look something like the following example:

```
computers.enthusiast@science.org
```

The mailing-list address connects to the *list-request address* — the address to which people send subscribe and unsubscribe requests for the mailing list. Remember that all messages sent to a mailing list end up in all subscribers' electronic mailboxes. No one wants a mailbox full of "Please add me to the mailing list" requests, so you need to send commands of this sort to the list-request address instead. The list-request address usually is the name of the mailing list, followed by `-request`, although many mailing lists also have a list-request address that includes something such as `majordomo` or `listproc`, as shown in the following example:

```
listproc@science.org
```

The list-request address connects to a *mailing-list server* — the program that makes the mailing list possible. The server maintains the list of e-mail addresses for the mailing list and responds to commands sent to the list-request address. If you subscribe to mailing lists on the Internet, you may have encountered two common mailing-list-server programs: *majordomo* and *listproc.*

The mailing-list server connects to the mailing-list manager's (or administrator's) e-mail address. The *mailing-list manager* is the person who oversees the operation of the mailing-list server. Members of a mailing list need to know who the mailing-list manager is so that they can send messages to a human being if problems occur. The mailing-list server software also needs to know the address of the mailing-list manager so that the program can send error reports and other useful information to the administrator.

If the mailing list is a *moderated* one, the mailing-list moderator's e-mail address also connects to the mailing-list server. A *mailing-list moderator* is a person who reads each message that anyone sends to the mailing list and then approves or rejects the message. If the moderator approves the message, that message goes to everyone on the mailing list; otherwise, members of the mailing list never see the message.

Mailing-list moderators can be valuable — if they do their jobs. By reviewing all the mail that comes to a list before the messages go out to everyone, a moderator can screen messages that not everyone on the entire list needs to read. The moderator may choose to eliminate duplicate messages on a subject, messages that have nothing to do with the subject of the mailing list, and solicitation posts (product sales, announcements, and so on) that the moderator deems to be wasteful of the reader's time. The work of a good list moderator can save the members of the list a great deal of time, because members don't need to weed out unnecessary or irrelevant e-mail.

Using an Internet automated-mailing-list service

Alternatives to running your own list server are available. Several companies on the Internet can host your mailing lists for you. Using a list-hosting service is much like posting your Web pages on someone else's server; you get the benefit of a fast connection, support staff, and expertise.

Many Internet service providers offer automated-mailing-list services. Best Internet Communications (at www.best.com) hosts one of the most popular mailing-list services, called *bestserv*. To set up a new mailing list through best.com, you simply fill out a form on a Web page (see Figure 10-1). Users still interact with your mailing list by using e-mail; best.com just simplifies the process by enabling you to establish a new list through a Web page.

Other service providers' mailing-list services may not be as easy to use as best.com's, but you shouldn't have too much trouble as long as the provider you choose gives you reasonable instructions. Unfortunately, all the services provide different mailing-list server programs and give you different instructions for creating a new list; otherwise, we'd tell you exactly how to set up a mailing list by using a service provider. Just remember the following key elements of setting up a list:

- ✔ Your mailing list needs a name and a mailing-list address.
- ✔ Your mailing list needs a list-request address.
- ✔ You must provide the mailing-list manager's e-mail address at some point.
- ✔ You need to decide whether to set up a moderated or an unmoderated mailing list.

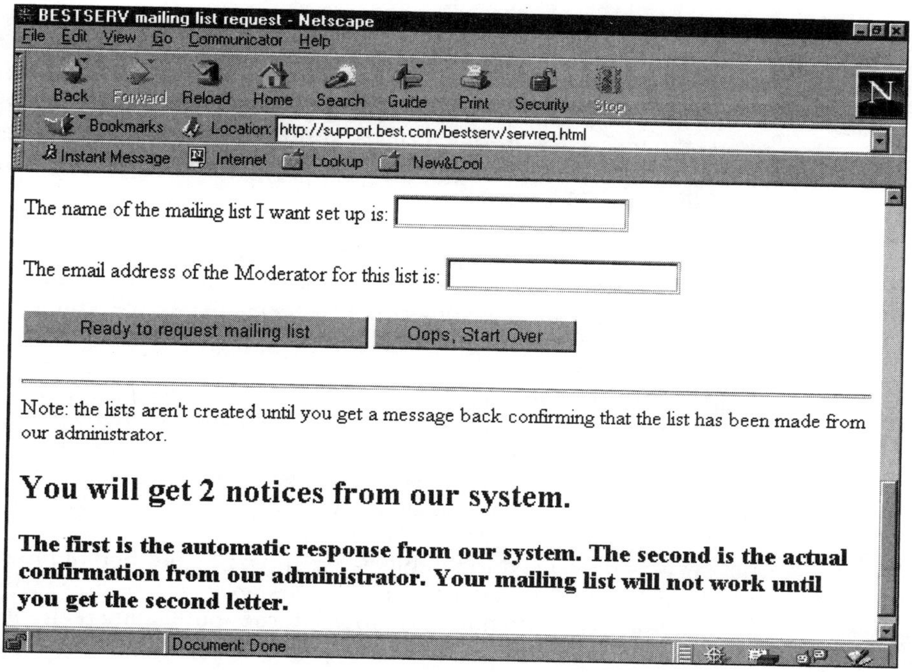

Figure 10-1:
Setting up a
new mailing
list is easy
if you use
a Web
interface.

You probably want your mailing-list address to use your registered domain name. This setup makes the process much simpler for people trying to associate your list with your organization. Using your registered domain name is something you need to work out with your service provider. (See Chapter 3 for information about domain names.) Typically, you need to send the provider a monthly fee in exchange for using the provider as your domain-name server. Your domain-name service also applies to other services that your provider may offer, such as a Web-publishing service.

L-Soft offers a list-hosting service called EASESM. Using EASESM (or another list-hosting service) is a convenient way to run electronic mailing lists on the Internet without running your own server. Using a list-hosting service is a good idea because list servers can become resource hogs while running mailing lists with many subscribers. These servers become resource hogs because every time someone sends a message to a list, an e-mail message must go out to each subscriber on the list. Continually sending e-mail messages to an active list can burden an underpowered server. The other advantage of using a service is the fact that an expert sets up and manages the mailing list for you. You can find L-Soft at this address:

```
http://www.lsoft.com/
```

Unlike other Internet server programs, list servers don't need a dedicated connection to the Internet. The list server retrieves e-mail bound for any of the lists it manages each time a connection to the Internet is established. You can send outgoing messages while you're connected to the Internet or queue the messages for delivery at another time. For busy lists, however, placing the list-server software on a machine with a dedicated connection provides superior results.

Note: You still need to keep an Internet e-mail account, even if you use someone else's list-hosting service. Your continued participation in the lists that you run is vital. Remember that to keep a list active, you need to seed the list with information on a regular basis.

Of all the Internet information utilities that you may run, a list server is one of the easiest and most effective. List servers already follow the publish-and-subscribe paradigm that Web technologies are moving toward. Running electronic mailing lists enables you or your organization to broadcast information efficiently and effectively.

List servers have used the publish-and-subscribe method of Internet broadcasting for several years. This method has proved to be so successful that the technology is creeping into other Internet-publishing technologies, such as the World Wide Web.

Subscribing to your automated mailing list

Mailing lists can be *public* (advertised to the public) or *private* (reserved for family members or internal company communications, for example). Chapter 12 provides tips on how to advertise your mailing list to the public.

Whether your mailing list is public or private, Internet users normally need to join your mailing list before they can send or receive mailing-list messages. To join your mailing list, a user must send to your list-request address an e-mail message that contains a command such as that shown in the following example:

```
subscribe ListName
```

ListName is the name of the mailing list to which the user wants to subscribe. Giving instructions to people on how to subscribe to your mailing list is simple. The following text provides instructions on subscribing to a mailing list at science.org called computers.enthusiast:

```
To join the SCIENCE.ORG mailing list for computer
enthusiasts, send e-mail to listproc@science.org and
include, in the body of your message, the following:
subscribe computers.enthusiast FirstName LastName
```

Another option is to tell people how to obtain help on using your mailing list. Your mailing-list software responds to a request for help automatically by sending instructions to the user. Here is an example of instructions that you can give to people so that they can get help from your mailing-list server:

```
For instructions on using SCIENCE.ORG's automated
electronic mailing list server, send e-mail to
listproc@science.org, and include, in the body of your
message, the following word: HELP
```

After a person subscribes to your mailing list, he or she can send a message to the other subscribers on the list by sending e-mail to the mailing-list address. After a person subscribes to the science.org mailing list computers.enthusiast, for example, that person can send e-mail to computers.enthusiast@science.org to communicate with the other mailing-list subscribers.

Running Your Own Mailing List

To get started creating your own electronic mailing lists on your personal computer, you need the server software that can manage your lists. This list-server software enables people to perform such tasks as these:

- ✔ Subscribe and unsubscribe from lists.
- ✔ Get a Help file via e-mail.
- ✔ Obtain a list of mailing lists that the list server manages.
- ✔ Obtain a list of other list subscribers. (You can turn off this option for security reasons.)
- ✔ Tell the list to send e-mail messages in a batch rather than one message at a time. (This method of sending e-mail is called *archiving*.)

An *automated-mailing-list-server program* is a cross between an automatic-reply e-mail system and a simple electronic mailing list. Instead of responding to file requests, however, the automatic-reply component of a mailing-list server accepts subscription and cancellation requests from Internet users.

Setting up an automated-mailing-list software package involves the following two general steps:

1. **Configure an automatic-reply account.**
2. **Create a mailing list.**

The following sections show you how to perform these steps in detail using Windows and Macintosh mailing-list software.

Setting Up a Mailing List for Windows

The same software that enables you to run a full Internet e-mail server on your Windows-based PC — SLmail — also enables you to set up automated mailing lists. The following sections describe how to use SLmail to set up a mailing list. SLmail is on the *Setting Up An Internet Site For Dummies* CD-ROM.

Using SLmail to set up the list

In this section, you use SLmail to set up a list called setupshop — a mailing list for discussions about setting up shop on the Internet. Follow these steps:

1. From SLmail, choose <u>S</u>ystem⇨Configure.

The configuration dialog box appears.

You can access the configuration dialog box from the SLmail program and also from the Start menu (by choosing Start⇨<u>P</u>rograms⇨ SL Products⇨SLmail Configuration).

2. Click the Users tab, which is shown in Figure 10-2.

3. Click the Create New User button (which is labeled in Figure 10-2).

The menu shown in Figure 10-3 appears.

4. Select <u>L</u>ist from the menu.

An icon labeled *new_list* is created, as shown in Figure 10-4.

5. Simply type over the phrase *new_list*, replacing it with the user ID for the new account. For this example, type setupshop.

Note: The user ID should not contain spaces.

6. Press the Enter key.

The Edit Mailing List dialog box appears, as shown in Figure 10-5.

Delete Selected User(s)

Create New User — ┌ Edit Properties

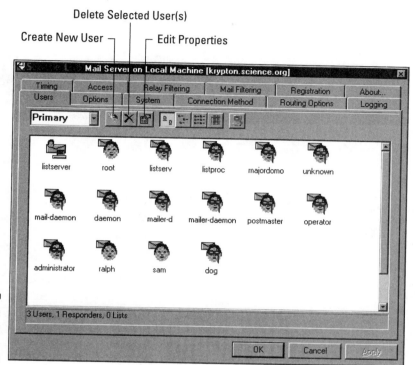

Figure 10-2:
The Users
tab.

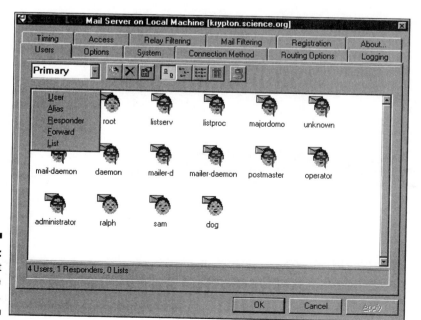

Figure 10-3:
Choose List
from the
menu.

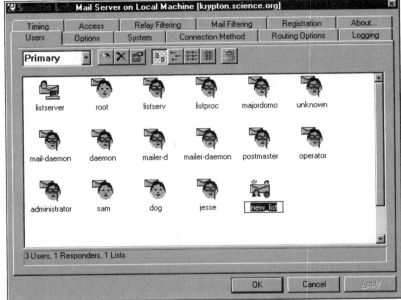

Figure 10-4: Add List accounts to create mailing lists.

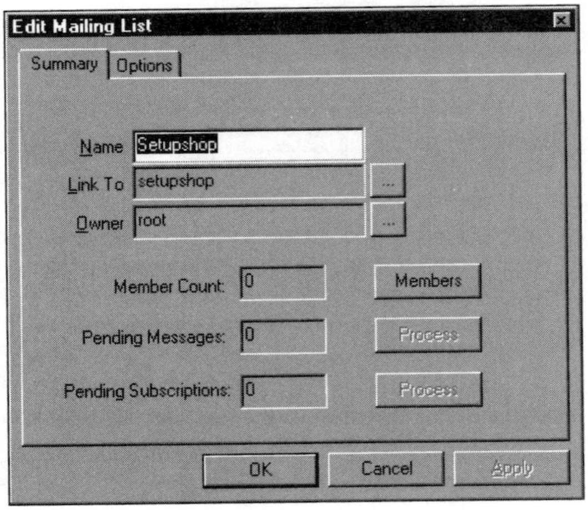

Figure 10-5: The Edit Mailing List dialog box.

7. **If you want to assign another name to identify the list, type the name in the Name text box.**

8. **Click the OK button to add the mailing list.**

Configuring the mailing list

Now follow these steps to configure your new mailing list:

1. **On the Users tab, select the mailing list's icon and then click the Edit Properties button (labeled in Figure 10-2).**

   The Edit Mailing List dialog box appears.

2. **Click the Options tab, which is shown in Figure 10-6.**

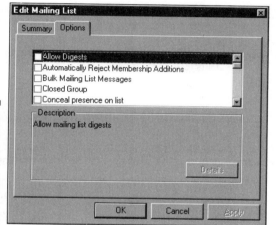

Figure 10-6:
Configure
your mailing
list so that
it operates
the way
you want.

3. **Select or deselect the configuration item check boxes to set up your mailing list.**

   The default settings are good ones for a typical mailing list. Be sure to select the Send Welcome and Send Footer check boxes, and a file to send for each. Your software automatically adds a welcome message and footer information to each message it sends.

4. **Click OK.**

   You return to the Users tab.

Your mailing list is ready.

Editing the mailing list

To manage the mailing list, select the mailing list's icon in the Users tab, and then click the Edit Properties button. In the Summary tab of the resulting Edit Mailing List dialog box, click the Members button. The List Members dialog box shown in Figure 10-7 appears, displaying the member list. (Remember that list members usually add their own names to your list.) You can add, modify, and delete members. Notice that no members of the list appear in Figure 10-7.

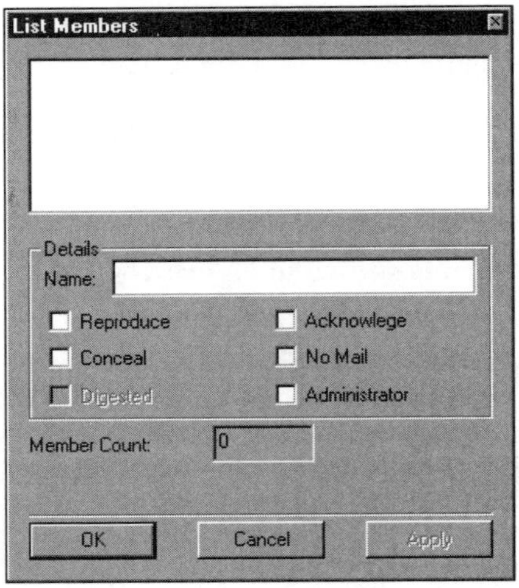

Figure 10-7:
The List
Members
dialog box.

To add a new mailing list member manually, follow these steps:

1. **Press the Insert key (or right-click and select Insert from the pop-up menu).**

   The Select List Member dialog box appears, as shown in Figure 10-8.

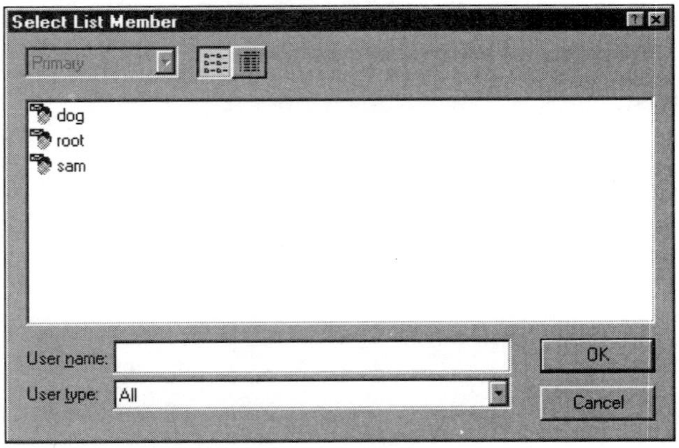

Figure 10-8:
The Select
List
Member
dialog box.

2. **Type the address of the person.**

   If you don't know the person's address, click the Browse button (...) that appears when you press the Insert key. Select one of the users from the Select List Member dialog box, shown in Figure 10-8.

3. **After you select a user from this dialog box, click the OK button.**

   You are returned to the List Members dialog box.

4. **To change any of the settings in the Details group, select the member name from the list and then click in the appropriate check box.**

   You may want to alter two of the options. The list is set by default to reproduce any message sent to it, which means a copy of a particular message will go to all list members, including the person who sent it. If you want to override this default, click the Acknowlege check box. Now, only a brief acknowledgement is sent to that user when he or she sends a message to the list. Also, if you want a person to remain invisible to other list members, click the Conceal check box.

5. **After you finish adding people to the membership, click the OK button.**

Deleting a member is easy; just select the member's e-mail address in the List Members list box, and then press the Delete key. To modify a member's entry, select the member in the List Members list box, make your changes, and then click the OK button.

Using LISTSERV to set up a list server

Another automated electronic-mailing-list software package for the Windows environment is LISTSERV, an L-Soft product. Created in 1986 for IBM mainframes, LISTSERV is now available for several operating systems, including Windows NT, Windows 95, and UNIX. You can download LISTSERV at the following URL:

```
http://www.lsoft.com/
```

You do the basic configuration of LISTSERV during installation. After the files finish installing, you get a series of dialog boxes, beginning with the one shown in Figure 10-9.

Click the Continue button to display the dialog box shown in Figure 10-10, and then follow these steps to complete the basic installation:

1. **Type the host name of the computer on which you have installed LISTSERV and then click the Continue button.**

   The Internet Hostname Aliases dialog box appears.

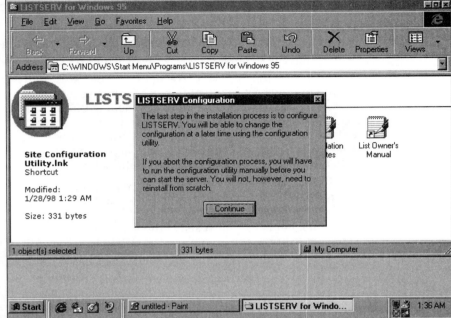

Figure 10-9:
Basic
configuration
is the last
step in
installing
LISTSERV.

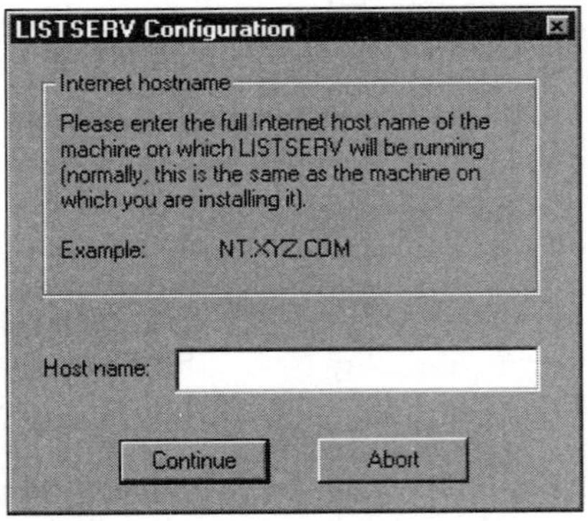

Figure 10-10:
LISTSERV
Configuration.

2. **Type the alias for the host computer; if the host computer doesn't have an alias, just click the Continue button.**

   The Organization Name dialog box appears.

3. **Type the name of your organization and then click the Continue button.**

   The List Creation Password dialog box appears.

4. **In the Password text box, type the password you want to use for list creation. Press the Tab key to move the cursor to the Verification text box, type the password again, and then click the Continue button.**

   The LISTSERV Maintainer dialog box appears.

5. **Type the e-mail address of the LISTSERV maintainer and then click the Continue button.**

   The Mail Delivery Machine dialog box appears.

6. **Type the host name of the computer that you want to designate to handle the mail for your list and then click the Continue button.**

   The dialog box shown in Figure 10-11 appears.

Figure 10-11:
The Web
Archives
Interface
dialog box.

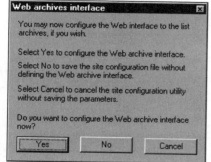

7. **If you are not going to establish a Web interface to your list archives, just click the No button to finish the basic configuration. Otherwise, click the Yes button to continue.**

   Clicking Yes displays the dialog box shown in Figure 10-12. If you click No, you're done now.

8. **Fill in the text boxes.**

   In the first text box, type the path to your cgi-bin directory. (Use the Browse button if you don't know the path.)

   In the second text box, type the URL to the Web archive script.

   In the third text box, type the path to the archives directory. (Use the Browse button if necessary to search for the path.)

9. **If you want to define which lists to archive, click the Lists button in the Web Archive Interface Setup dialog box. Otherwise, just click the OK button to complete the basic configuration. (If you click OK here, you're done now.)**

   Clicking the Lists button displays the Web Archive Lists dialog box shown in Figure 10-13.

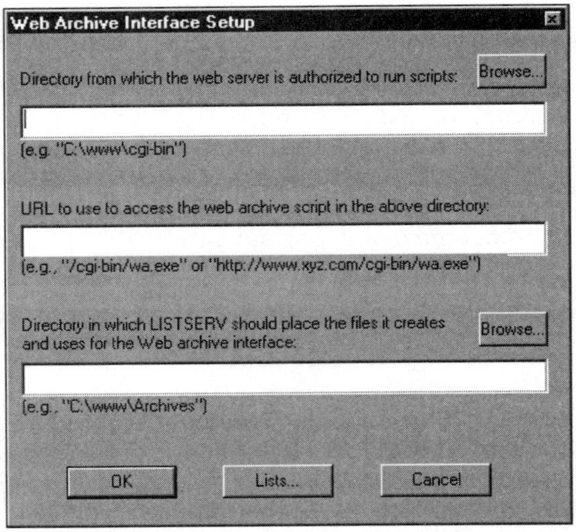

Figure 10-12:
The Web
Archive
Interface
Setup
dialog box.

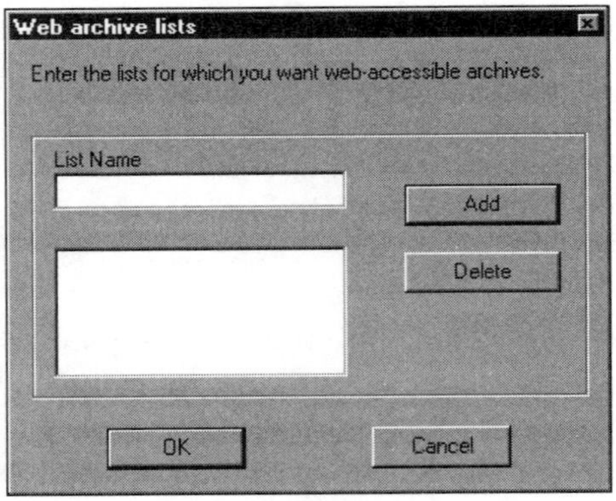

Figure 10-13:
The Web
Archive
Lists
dialog box.

10. **In the List Name text box, type the name of the list you want to archive and then click the Add button to add it to the list.**

   To remove a list from the archive lists, select it and click the Delete button.

11. **When you are finished, click the OK button.**

   You return to the Web Archive Interface Setup dialog box.

12. **Click the OK button.**

   The Web archives script file is copied to the URL you specified in Step 8, and a confirmation dialog box appears.

13. **Click the OK button to complete installation.**

   You are now looking at the LISTSERV main window, shown in Figure 10-14.

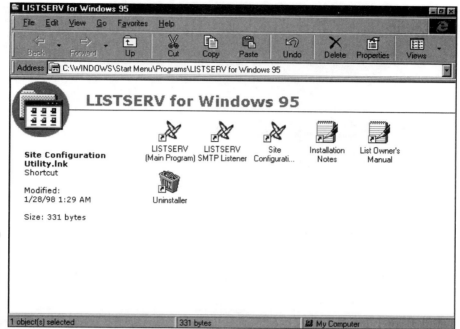

Figure 10-14:
The
LISTSERV
main
window.

LISTSERV advanced configuration

Although the basic configuration process during installation is simple, you may want to change some settings. And you probably want to set some of the more advanced configuration options that aren't included in the basic configuration process, too.

To change a setting, start the LISTSERV Site Configuration Utility program from the Windows Start menu or by clicking its icon in the LISTSERV main window. The LISTSERV Configuration Utility dialog box appears, as shown in Figure 10-15.

You can change the basic configuration parameters by clicking the Basic Configuration button to display the Configure LISTSERV dialog box, which is shown in Figure 10-16.

You can set advanced parameters by clicking the Advanced Configuration button in the LISTSERV Configuration Utility dialog box. This displays the Advanced Site Configuration dialog box, which is shown in Figure 10-17. From here, you can view and set all the advanced LISTSERV parameters, which are described in Table 10-1.

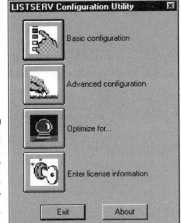

Figure 10-15:
The
LISTSERV
Configuration
Utility
dialog box.

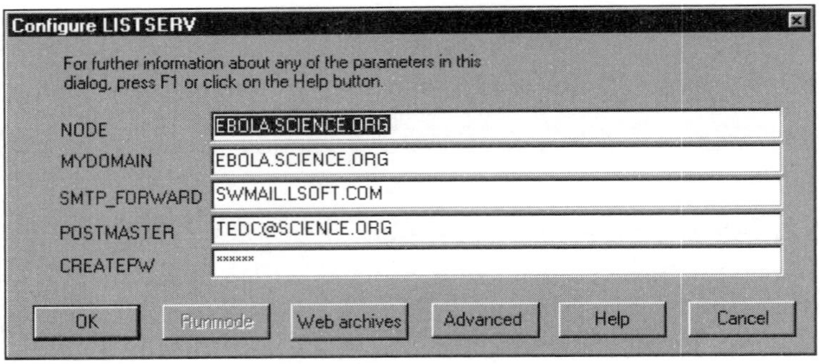

Figure 10-16:
The
Configure
LISTSERV
dialog box.

Figure 10-17:
The
Advanced
Site
Configuration
dialog box.

Table 10-1	Advanced LISTSERV Parameters
Parameter	*What It Does*
BITNET_ROUTE	This parameter is important only if you have a gateway to BITNET. Most Internet sites can ignore this parameter.
CREATEPW	This parameter is the password set by the administrator for creating new lists. (*Warning:* Giving this parameter to the public may not be a good idea. Your list server could quickly become swamped.)
DBRINDEX	Sets reverse indexing for database functions.
DEFAULT_SPLIT	If your site is behind a firewall or if your mail server has a maximum mail-file size, set this parameter to something less than that maximum size so that you can split mail files into smaller files.
FILTER_ALSO	This parameter defines a list of users whom you want to block from using your list server.
FIOC_TARGET	This parameter defines the size of the cache in kilobytes. You normally set this parameter by clicking the Optimize For button in the LISTSERV Configuration Utility window.
FIOC_TRIM	This parameter sets the point at which the program aggressively trims the cache to free virtual memory. You set this parameter by clicking the Optimize For button in the LISTSERV Configuration Utility window.
FIOC_WARNING	Defines the cache size in kilobytes.
LICENSE_WARNING	Turns license expiration warnings on or off.
LIST_ADDRESS	Ignore this parameter, which is for BITNET machines migrating to Windows.
LIST_EXITS	Specifies special custom programs that run whenever a list exits. See the product manual for more information on using this advanced feature.
LOCAL	Identifies the domain for local hosts.
MAILMAXL	Specifies the maximum size of incoming e-mail messages.
MAXBSMTP	Sets the maximum number of recipients for a single e-mail message. You normally set this parameter by clicking the Optimize For button in the LISTSERV Configuration Utility window.
MAXDISTN	Ignore this parameter, and leave the default value (1000) alone.

(continued)

Table 10-1 *(continued)*

Parameter	*What It Does*
MYDOMAIN	A list of all possible Internet domain names for the machine running LISTSERV. If you have only a single domain name, this parameter is the same as the NODE parameter.
MYORG	The name of your organization. The parameter appears in the header of e-mail messages sent from the list server.
NODE	The Internet host name of the machine running LISTSERV.
POSTMASTER	A colon-delimited list of e-mail addresses of the maintainers of the list server. If bad things happen, these people automatically receive notification by e-mail.
PRIMETIME	Specifies when the machine running LISTSERV is busiest. LISTSERV can delay sending e-mail until a time other than prime time.
QUALIFY_DOMAIN	Internet domain that should be appended to all partial (nonqualified) addresses.
SMTP_FORWARD	Lists the host name of the machine running the mail server.
SMTP_FORWARDn	Spreads e-mail delivery among several mail servers. Used for a busy site.
SMTP_RESET_EVERY	Enables Sendmail (if your mail server is running on a UNIX system and using Sendmail) to run more efficiently by resetting the connection on a regular basis. (Sendmail is the program that many UNIX machines use to correctly direct e-mail messages.)
SORT_RECIPIENTS	Enables mail servers running on UNIX machines to receive the recipient list in presorted form. You normally set this parameter by clicking the Optimize For button in the LISTSERV Configuration Utility window.
SPAM_DELAY	Sets how many minutes to give LISTSERV to analyze messages for spam content.
TRAPIN	A list of blacklisted addresses from which LISTSERV is not to accept e-mail.
TRAPOUT	A list of blacklisted addresses to which LISTSERV is never to send e-mail.

Parameter	What It Does
WEB_BROWSER_CONFIRM	Determines whether to confirm commands sent through a Web browser interface.
WWW_ARCHIVE_CGI	Relative URL-to-Web archive script. Already set during install.
WWW_ARCHIVE_DIR	Path to Web archive directory. Already set during install.

Most of the parameters in Table 10-1 are set automatically by LISTSERV, have default values that are sufficient to run LISTSERV, or are set by clicking the Optimize For button in the LISTSERV Configuration Utility window. A handy thing to know is that you can view or change these settings in the configuration utility. You may want to make a note of the default values of these parameters in case you accidentally set a value that causes the LISTSERV program to misbehave.

Creating an electronic mailing list by using LISTSERV

The first step in creating an electronic mailing list is deciding what topic your mailing list covers. No one is going to subscribe to a mailing list unless the list covers a topic of interest. Topics can range from personal family mailing lists to end-user and product support lists. Many special-interest groups also find that electronic mailing lists are an excellent way to disseminate information to people who are interested in their cause.

Your excitement about running your own list, now that you have LISTSERV installed, may lead you to start electronic mailing lists that already exist on the Internet. Don't reinvent the wheel. No law or technical reason prevents you from starting electronic mailing lists on a topic that's identical to someone else's, but you may want to simply subscribe to that group and start your own list on a different topic. (Trying to steal subscribers from someone else's mailing list is never a good idea.) The spirit of cooperation has helped Internet information systems, such as mailing lists, become as successful as they are.

An easy way to determine whether someone else is running a group similar to the one that you want to start is to send an e-mail message to a list server running at L-Soft. Put the following line in the body of the e-mail message:

```
LIST GLOBAL <search_string>
```

Address the e-mail to the following address:

```
LISTSERV@LISTSERV.NET
```

You then receive a long list of existing electronic mailing lists by e-mail.

The following list describes some additional ways to find out what lists already exist:

- ✔ Visit the Mailing Lists section of Yahoo! on the World Wide Web at the following URL:

  ```
  http://www.yahoo.com/
  ```

- ✔ Obtain a copy of the Interest Groups List of Lists, which is maintained by a company called SRI. Point your FTP-enabled Web browser to the following address:

  ```
  ftp://sri.com/netinfo/interest-groups
  ```

- ✔ You can also use an FTP client program and access the FTP site at sri.com. Change directories to `netinfo` and download the file `interest-groups`. (See Chapter 9 for more information on using an FTP client.)

Using commands to control LISTSERV

You create mailing lists and perform all other administrative functions by sending e-mail messages to the LISTSERV software. The e-mail messages that you send to the list server contain command words and parameters that tell LISTSERV what to do. You can send the following seven types of command keywords to LISTSERV:

- ✔ **Access control.** This type of command keyword specifies who can post to the list, who can obtain the list of subscribers to a list, and whether the list is open to general subscription.

- ✔ **Distribution.** These command keywords determine how LISTSERV distributes postings to subscribers. Some of the settings determine whether posters receive acknowledgments. Other settings specify the maximum number of postings that can go through the list daily and indicate whether the list is available in digest form (messages that the server sends out in a group instead of delivering one at a time).

- ✔ **Error handling.** This group of commands sets automatic deletion, loop checking (when e-mail sent from the server ends up returning, only to be sent again and again and again), and the e-mail address of the list administrator.

- ✔ **List maintenance and moderation.** These commands set the list owner, list editor, and list archive notebook (which tells you about archived copies of the list). The commands also set other subscription parameters, such as the person to contact if users subscribe or unsubscribe.

- ✔ **Security.** These keywords control who can view the list and whether a list is password-protected.

> ✔ **Subscription.** These keywords determine whether a list is open to general subscription and what user options are set as the default if someone subscribes.
>
> ✔ **Other.** These keywords include miscellaneous and rarely used commands.

Note: The LISTSERV software comes with complete documentation on the command keywords you use to control LISTSERV. Refer to the LISTOWNR.MEMO file in the MAIN directory for detailed information on creating lists.

Giving birth to the new list

The PUT command is the one you specifically use to create a new electronic mailing list. Only the person you designate as the postmaster or anyone you authorize to create new lists can use this command. Creating a new mailing list makes you the list's *list owner*. You use this list as shown in the following example:

```
PUT <listname>
```

A good idea for protecting your list is to password-protect the list-header information by using the PW command, as follows:

```
PW=xxxxxxx
```

Making changes to your list

If you want to change your list's configuration parameters, first fetch a copy of the list's header information by using the GET command, as in the following example:

```
GET <listname> PW=yourpassword
```

The GET command returns a header file that looks something like the following example:

```
PUT SUPPORT.SAWBLADES PW=XXXXXXXX
* This is a list for the support of saw blades
*
* Owner= TEDC@SCIENCE.ORG (Ted Coombs)
* Notebook= Yes,A,Monthly,Public
* Errors-To= Owner
* Subscription= Open,Confirm
* Ack= Yes    Confidential= No    Notify= No
* Files= No  Mail-Via= Distribute  Validate= No
* Reply-to= List,Respect Review= Public Send= Public
```

(continued)

(continued)

```
* Stats= Normal,Private X-Tags= Yes
* Default-Options= NoFiles,NoRepro
*
* This list installed on 97/01/01, running under L-Soft's\
* LISTSERV-TCP/IP version 1.8b for Windows NT.
*
* Comments:
```

Edit this header file and send it back to the list server. This file is what instructs the list server to set a list's configuration.

You modify a list's configuration by using the GET and PUT commands in concert. First, you GET the list's header file. Next, you make any modifications. Finally, you include the PUT command in the first line of the header file to replace the current header with the new, modified version.

Using a list server

Sending the INFO command to a LISTSERV list server in the body of an e-mail message returns a list of commands available to subscribers and potential subscribers. This information can vary from server to server, depending on how the postmaster configures the list server.

You can activate and deactivate the digest feature, for example. (The *digest* feature is the capability to receive postings as a group in a single e-mail message on a regular basis.) How you configure this feature affects whether a subscriber can have messages sent in digest form instead of receiving many e-mail messages at random intervals.

Almost all list servers support the SUBSCRIBE command. The SUBSCRIBE command always includes the name of the mailing list as its first parameter. Some list servers require that you enter your name and sometimes your e-mail address as second and third parameters. Other list servers grab this information from the e-mail header.

Obtaining subscriber information from the e-mail header has its pros and cons. On the pro side, no one can enter your subscription to various mailing lists without your knowledge or approval; all e-mail automatically goes to the e-mail address in the From field of the e-mail header. The downside of this setup is the confusion that sometimes results from a company's e-mail server configuration. If you subscribe from one machine and the e-mail address includes the name of the machine, this machine is the only one that you can use to post messages to the mailing list. Postings from a different machine, even in the same domain, aren't acceptable.

After you subscribe to a list, you automatically receive messages from the list. You can respond to messages in one of the following ways:

- **Respond only to the person who posts the message.** You accomplish this action by sending e-mail to the sender's personal e-mail address, which usually is part of the original message.

- **Respond or send new e-mail to the list address** (which usually is *listname@domain*.com). These messages go out to everyone on the list.

To unsubscribe from an electronic mailing list, send the UNSUBSCRIBE command (usually including the name of the list as a parameter) to the same e-mail address that you used to subscribe — *not to the e-mail address of the list*. The address of the list server depends on what type of list-server software the list owner uses, as shown in the following examples:

```
majordomo@domain.com
```

```
listserv@domain.com
```

You send all commands, including the UNSUBSCRIBE command, to the list server. The list server e-mail address is probably going to look like one of the examples we just listed. Sending a wrong command or a badly formatted command usually results in an error message sent back to you. The error message usually includes instructions for receiving help from the list server. Sometimes, you can start receiving help by sending either the word HELP or the word INFO within the body of the message. (By the way, sending both words, just to make sure that you get help, is a safe bet.)

If you use words that the server can't understand in the body of your e-mail message, most list servers ignore those words or just complain. If your e-mail client includes a signature file along with each of your e-mail messages, for example, the list server may complain that it doesn't understand each word in your signature file. If you can send e-mail without sending a signature, the list-server software is much happier (if a list server can even *be* happy).

Using Your Automated Mailing List

Automated mailing lists are excellent interactive tools, and running a list of your own presents several interesting possibilities. Two possibilities that we're excited about (and that we describe in the following sections) are using your mailing list to serve World Wide Web pages and to distribute files.

Sending World Wide Web documents to the mailing list

One of the best aspects of a mailing list is the fact that you can send World Wide Web documents to all the subscribers. You can send any World Wide Web HTML document to any mailing list without requiring additional configuration or any special type of mailing-list service. The HTML documents simply end up in the electronic mailboxes of the list's subscribers.

Why would you want to send Web documents via a mailing list? The answer is access. Remember that the World Wide Web is not available to all people on the Internet. The graphics that Web pages use place a heavy load on connections to the Internet. Dial-up connections to the Internet over older, slower modems make surfing the Web painfully slow and annoying. In many cases, surfing the Web is not even a viable option because of the time that downloading a graphically rich page takes.

If your objective is to distribute information, an automated mailing list is an efficient and widely accessible means of delivery. The connection demands of e-mail file distribution can be insignificant compared with those of delivering the same information via the Web. The Web may be more glamorous, but e-mail can be more effective in delivering information to a larger user base of Net surfers.

To view a World Wide Web document, a subscriber simply saves the e-mail message to a file and opens that file with a World Wide Web browser. Any hyperlinks within the HTML document are accessible, provided that the subscriber has an Internet connection. If some of your subscribers don't have access to the World Wide Web, they can still view your basic World Wide Web documents as long as they have browsers; they just can't access any links to other Internet sites that may be on your page.

A mailing list becomes even more like a magazine if you send World Wide Web documents to your subscribers. Using a mailing list this way gives you a great deal of flexibility in content, format, and advertising, and also opens new possibilities for interactive publishing.

Distributing files using a mailing list

Another great use for a mailing list is the distribution of binary files (such as word-processing documents). To send a binary file through e-mail, you first must convert the file to text-only format; e-mail can handle only text. The most common way to perform this conversion from binary to text is to use a program called _UUEncode_. After you UUEncode a binary file (turn it into text), you can send the file to your mailing list, and the file ends up in the electronic mailboxes of the list's subscribers. Users must UUDecode the file to return it to its original binary form.

More information on UUEncode and on sending files via e-mail is available on the Setting Up An Internet Site page on the World Wide Web, at the following address:

```
http://computers.science.org/internet/site/setup/
```

Making Money with Your Automated Mailing List

An automated mailing list is similar to a traditional magazine: A mailing list has subscribers, each message sent to the mailing list is like a magazine article, and a successful mailing list can attract advertisers. If your mailing list is especially useful, you may be able to charge for subscriptions to the list.

You can charge for subscriptions in several ways. One popular means of charging for information is the voluntary approach. Put the information out there and indicate that, if the information is useful, the user may elect to pay a specified fee. You can collect the money via traditional snail mail (you know — the mail that the person in the uniform delivers while walking down the street accompanied by yipping dogs) or through some type of online commerce system.

The voluntary approach is a low-pressure means of generating revenue from your mailing list. A more aggressive method involves requiring a subscription fee before you distribute information. In this method, you structure your mail-delivery system to provide information on how to subscribe to your list as part of the autoresponse system (the message that they receive after they contact you). After a person subscribes, you add that person's name to the list; then the person can begin receiving your information. How you decide to collect fees for your information depends on the information you have to deliver and on the methods you use to attract interested users to your site.

Other money-making opportunities exist with an automated mailing list, depending on how you configure your list. If you use a moderated list, you can charge to distribute messages to the mailing list. If you distribute World Wide Web documents through the mailing list, you can charge users a fee for including hyperlinks to their Internet resources in your documents. If you're going to charge, of course, you need a loyal subscriber base, and your mailing list must offer enough value to support fees or advertising.

Mailing lists have a great deal to offer, both to potential subscribers and to your Internet site. An automated electronic mailing list is, in some ways, better than the World Wide Web. You can reach anyone who has an e-mail account, for example, and you know exactly who subscribes to your list — capabilities that the World Wide Web doesn't offer yet.

A mailing list is more interactive than most World Wide Web sites. And a list has a greater chance of becoming a regular tool for its users because mailing lists rely on the one resource that all users have in common: e-mail. Remember that, to extend the capabilities of your mailing list and make the list even more useful to you and your business, you can distribute World Wide Web documents to the subscribers, thus combining the benefits of a mailing list with the power of the World Wide Web. Take advantage of the fact that e-mail is easy for people to read and respond to and that list servers are simple to set up and easy to maintain. A mailing list is an important addition to any Internet site.

Part IV
Site Builder Skills
for Today's Internet

The 5th Wave   By Rich Tennant

Well, there's your Web page, Crypto. Designed like you asked. But personally, I think it has too many spinning spirals and blinking lights. It makes...hard reading. Make...tired... look...at...lose...all... con...cen...tra...tion...

Perfect!

CRYPTO THE HYPNOTIST

In this part . . .

Companies big and small have flocked to the Internet. Commercial sites, whether run by the world's largest corporations, individual entrepreneurs, or anything in between, are everywhere in cyberspace. In this part, you discover the problems they all face and the solutions that have evolved.

Whether or not your site is a storefront, it doesn't make sense to have a site that no one can find. So we also show you how to let the zillions of people on the Internet know where you are. You find out how to register with the popular search engines, partner with other site developers, understand who your audience is, and adapt traditional marketing methods to your new needs.

Chapter 11

Electronic Commerce

· ·

· ·

*E*very commercial Internet site needs the capability to conduct secure and reliable online transactions. After all, what good is a storefront without a cash register? Just as commerce involves more than sales, electronic commerce encompasses more than the online sale of goods and services. Commerce, electronic or otherwise, entails some or all of the following elements:

- ✔ Marketing
- ✔ Sales
- ✔ Invoicing
- ✔ Purchase orders
- ✔ Payment
- ✔ Delivery of products and services

Even charitable or association sites whose only involvement with money is accepting donations or annual dues can benefit from doing so online.

Understanding Electronic Commerce

Preparing your site for electronic sales is the focus of most discussions of electronic commerce. Some of the same considerations for safe and reliable sales transactions also prepare your site to handle electronic invoicing, an electronic purchase-order system, electronic funds transfer, and even the reliable and safe delivery of some products and services.

Following are some aspects of electronic commerce:

- ✔ **Shipping.** If you've ever used (or seen the commercials for) the major shipping companies, you already know that shipping information is online now. Check out the sites for Federal Express (`http://www.fedex.com/`) and United Parcel Service (`http://www.ups.com/`) for examples. Setting up your Internet site to query these information systems automatically and then integrating the shipping information with your billing system is an important step in electronic business.

- ✔ **Inventory.** As stores stock new consumable and durable goods, they update their inventory systems. In the world of global networking, nothing prevents these inventory systems from linking directly to the suppliers or to an automated reorder system.

A key component of most successful forms of electronic commerce is a secure Internet site. After you set up a secure environment, you can establish each area of electronic commerce with little fear that anyone can compromise corporate secrets or misappropriate electronic funds.

After they establish secure environments, not-for-profit organizations can receive electronic donations, product manufacturers can sell directly to consumers, and service companies can collect fees. Creating a secure sales environment isn't difficult, but it can be expensive. To simplify the process, this chapter gives you a solid overview of the technology you need and explains each step of setting up a secure environment.

The chapter covers no single solution; instead, it gives you the foundation you need so that you can decide which solution is right for you. The specific product manufacturer or Internet shopping-mall service provider that you choose can give you a great deal of support and guidance. You can expect quality technical support as part of the service or product for which you pay fees to your service provider.

If the thought of spending money to gain security support makes you queasy, remember that, if you're generating online sales or contributions to your cause, you're making online money. Making money on the Internet takes money, so dive right in and do it!

Authentication

Most Internet security measures include the use of public-key cryptography (that is, the use of public and private keys to encrypt and decrypt information). Encryption guarantees privacy. *Authentication,* on the other hand, verifies the identity of the party with whom you communicate. Creating a secure communications link doesn't do much good if you really aren't sure who's at the other end of the link. Without authentication, you have no way of being certain what person or organization is sending an encrypted message, and an impostor could use someone else's computer.

Imagine, for example, the problems that could arise if the U.S. military were to accept and carry out encrypted orders without first verifying that the orders come from the president. Authentication has been part of important military command messages for many years. So you can see that, without authentication, encryption solves only half the security problem of online communications.

Using a digital signature

You accomplish authentication by using a *digital signature* (an electronically encrypted authentication). In the same way that you sign a letter or memo, you can apply a digital signature to an encrypted message.

The term *signature* may be a little confusing. A digital signature is not a graphic picture of your actual written signature; think of it as being more like an electronic watermark.

Public-key encryption works well for the creation of digital signatures for the following reasons:

✔ A recipient can decrypt information that you encrypt with a public key only by using the corresponding private key.

✔ A recipient can decrypt information that you encrypt with a private key only by using the corresponding public key.

You can digitally sign an encrypted message by using your private key to encrypt a message. Then someone must use your public key to decrypt the message. If the recipient can decrypt the message by using your public key, the message must be from you. The recipient of your message, therefore, establishes the authenticity of your message — establishes that you really sent it — by using your public key.

Again, the need for official public-key directories becomes apparent. Here's why. Suppose that you have someone's public key. How do you know where that key came from? Having the Internet industry create an official — and trusted — public-key directory gives users one more level of trust and authentication in using digital signatures. If you can check a public directory to authenticate a public key, you can feel confident that the message you decrypt with a public key is, in fact, from the person whom you believe sent the message. Unfortunately, this trust issue can go only so far. At some point, you must believe (within reason) that you can trust the public key you've received.

Authenticating a public key

One way to further authenticate your message is to authenticate the key that you have in your possession. You do so by using a *key certificate* — a digital document that attests to the ownership of a public key by a particular person or organization. *Certificate authorities* (CA) issue key certificates, and a higher authority in turn authenticates these certificate authorities. At the top of the authentication hierarchy (the most trusted people in the world concerning keys) is a private company, entrusted as the keeper of the keys, so to speak. Only after verifying the key certificate for a particular public key can you be reasonably certain that the key belongs to the person or organization that appears to be using that key.

The *Public Key Certificate Standards* (PKCS), the Internet standard that deals with public keys, states that every digital signature must point to a certificate that validates the public key of the signer. This setup enables software (such as Netscape's Navigator and secure e-mail software) to authenticate digital signatures automatically by contacting the appropriate CA and then viewing the corresponding official public-key certificate.

 With all this talk about business on the Internet, a great idea may be to start a new certificate authority. The assignment and management of key certificates and corresponding public-key directories soon may be critical for all secure Internet communications. Contact RSA Data Security, Inc. (at `http://www.rsa.com/`) for more information about starting your own CA.

Public-key certificates create confidence in the authenticity of certified public keys. Two or more certificates may link in such a way that the certificates certify the authenticity of the other certificates. This link is known as a *certificate chain*. This chain continues from certifying authority to certifying authority until you reach the company or organization considered most trusted.

To obtain a public-key certificate, you first must generate a public-key/ private-key pair. (See your server documentation for the procedure or, if you are using an ISP or a virtual server supplier, simply ask them to generate the key pair for you.) Then you must send the public-key part of the key pair to an official CA, along with proof of your identity — a notarized copy of your driver's license, for example. After validating your identity, the CA sends you a key certificate, verifying that you registered the public key and that the CA officially recognizes the key as belonging to you. (The section "Getting a digital ID and public-key certificate" later in this chapter provides a little more detail on this process.)

The CA maintains your public key in a public-key directory and gives a copy of your key certificate to anyone who requests one. If your private key ever becomes compromised, the CA can add your key certificate to a *Certificate Revocation List* (CRL), which invalidates the previously certified public key.

World Wide Web Security

With its simple graphic interface, the World Wide Web is now the home of the Internet marketplace. Most of the encryption technologies discussed in this chapter focus on making the World Wide Web a secure place to transact business.

A typical World Wide Web sales transaction may proceed something along the following lines:

1. Joe Smith views an online catalog and finds things that he wants to buy.

2. He accesses a secure order form, in which he enters the items that he wants to purchase and his credit-card information.

3. He transmits the order and payment-method information to the secure server, on which a program is set up to verify the payment method.

4. The company notifies Joe Smith that his order is accepted and tells him when to expect the shipment of goods or how to access online goods or services.

This typical transaction involves the following main components:

✔ The nonsecure online catalog and the secure World Wide Web form

✔ The secure World Wide Web server

✔ An electronic payment method

The following sections explore these elements as they relate to secure business transactions on the Web.

The online catalog and the Web order form

Products such as Microsoft's Merchant Server (`http://www.microsoft.com/products/prodref/100_ov.htm`), Netscape's SuiteSpot (`http://merchant.netscape.com/netstore/servers/suitespot.html`), or Covesoft's Database Shopping Cart (`http://www.covesoft.net/script.htm`) can help you create complete catalogs and secure sales environments. Most of the commercial online-sales products, however, are still fairly expensive. These products normally provide the following elements:

✔ **A database or access to a database.** This is where you store product information.

✔ **A dynamic Web catalog-page-creation utility.** Each time someone accesses your online catalog, the utility dynamically creates catalog Web pages. This way, the pages automatically add price changes, catalog changes, and specials based on information that you store in the database.

> ✔ **A credit-card processing system.** These systems handle complete credit-card processing, normally using an additional service that a bank or other credit-card processing service provides.
>
> ✔ **Digital cash processing.** We cover this feature in greater detail in the section "Electronic money" later in this chapter.

After you establish a secure environment, the information in your Web order form is transmitted securely from the purchaser to your secure Web site. If you're worried about how safe these transactions are, the fact that some banks are now using secure Web pages to enable people to access their bank-account information should reassure you.

For a good example of a securely transmitted form, check out Wells Fargo Bank's On-Line Banking page at http://www.wellsfargo.com/. Figure 11-1 shows the bank's site certificate. This certificate is your way of authenticating your connection to the bank. As you can see in the figure, a certifying authority issued the site certificate.

The secure World Wide Web server

Not all Web servers are created equal. Shareware Web servers run on just about all computer platforms but usually don't include any type of encryption capability. Other Web servers, such as Netscape's Commerce Server, provide secure communications by using the Secure Sockets Layer (which we explain in the section "Using the Secure Sockets Layer (SSL)" later in this chapter).

After purchasing and installing a secure Web server, you need to perform some setup functions to activate its security capabilities. Most important, you need a public-key/private-key pair for the server to use. This key pair is used to create the server's *digital ID*. Typically, secure Web server software includes utilities that generate a public-key/private-key pair and a certificate request that a CA accepts. (For a background discussion of key pairs, certificates, and CAs, refer to the section "Authentication" earlier in this chapter.) If your secure Web server doesn't provide such a utility, contact the company that sold you the software and ask how to generate these keys. Or, if you are using a virtual server (see Chapter 4), simply ask your server supplier to generate the keys for you.

If you're using a digital ID for authentication, your digital ID incorporates your host name. This way, the URL of a site includes the same host name as the digital ID. Web browsers such as Netscape Navigator automatically verify that the host name matches the one embedded in the digital ID and display a warning if they detect a discrepancy.

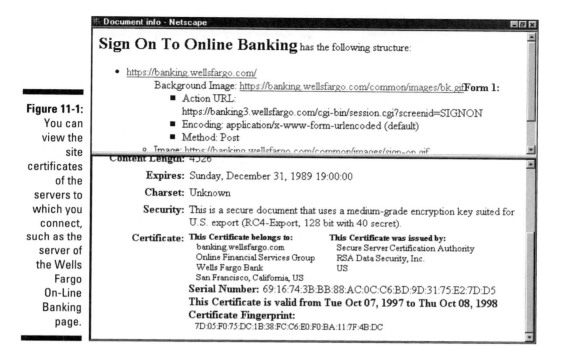

Figure 11-1:
You can
view the
site
certificates
of the
servers to
which you
connect,
such as the
server of
the Wells
Fargo
On-Line
Banking
page.

For detailed information on how to set up your site to use a digital ID, visit the following Web site:

```
http://www.verisign.com/pr/pr_ns_secure.html
```

VeriSign's current price for issuing a digital ID is $349 for servers located in the U.S. and $449 for servers located outside the U.S. If you plan to run a Netscape Commerce Server or a Netscape News Server, you need to obtain a digital ID from VeriSign, which for now is the most trusted certifying authority. VeriSign is a private company that manages many of the authentication-management techniques that we describe throughout this chapter.

Getting a digital ID and public-key certificate

If you operate or plan to operate a secure Web server, you should apply to VeriSign for your digital ID. For information specific to your Web server, contact the VeriSign Web page at the following URL:

```
http://www.verisign.com
```

Processing your request for a digital ID takes about a week, so apply for a digital ID before you try to open your Internet shop. Follow these steps to obtain a digital ID:

1. **Install your secure Web server software and name your site.**

2. **Create a distinguished name for your Web server.**

   Follow the instructions that come with your Web server to create a *distinguished name,* which is the trusted name of your server. This name is the one you give your server. (Sometimes the domain name of the server is also the distinguished name.)

3. **Document your Web server.**

   This documentation includes a letter that identifies the *Webmaster* (the Web administrator) for your site and a "Proof of Right to Use" the distinguished name. You find detailed information and the complete text of a sample letter on the VeriSign home page. After you fill out this letter, send the letter with your Proof of Right to Use application.

4. **Based on the distinguished name that you chose, generate an RSA key pair (public-key/private-key pair).**

   Your Web server documentation tells you how to perform this procedure.

5. **E-mail your application to VeriSign, requesting your digital ID.**

   The appropriate e-mail address for your application appears on the VeriSign home page (at `http://www.verisign.com/`). The VeriSign Web page lists specific e-mail addresses for each type of secure Web server.

6. **After you submit your request, mail a signed authorization letter with your payment arrangement, such as credit-card number or purchase order.**

   Send the letter to the following address:

   > VeriSign, Inc.
   > 2593 Coast Avenue
   > Mountain View, CA 94043
   > USA

7. **After you receive your digital ID, follow the instructions in your Web server documentation for installing the ID.**

For additional information on obtaining digital IDs and public-key/private-key pairs, contact RSA Data Security, Inc., at the following URL:

`http://www.rsa.com/`

Using the Secure Sockets Layer (SSL)

The *Secure Sockets Layer,* or *SSL,* was developed by Netscape and then adopted by other server makers. It is the most popular protocol that provides security and encryption for all communications between a client and a server. To provide this security, authentication of the server is a requirement, and authentication of the client is an option. With the client authenticated, the server knows who is communicating with it.

Software developers use the Secure Sockets Layer in writing programs that need to communicate securely at all times. Unlike the security that's built into secure Web servers, public-key encryption programs use SSL for all data communications.

One of the main advantages of the Secure Sockets Layer is the fact that SSL is indeed a layer — in other words, application programs (such as FTP and the World Wide Web) run on top of SSL. SSL negotiates all the security between the client and the server program before an application program exchanges even one byte of data, so all the data goes out securely.

The Secure Sockets Layer enables a special type of security known as channel security. *Channel security* provides the following basic features:

- **The communication channel your program uses is always secure.** After the Secure Sockets Layer negotiates the connection by exchanging keys, all transmissions are secure.

- **You always know to whom you're talking because the channel (the communication session between two computers) is always authenticated between the client and the server.** This type of authentication is the same that we discuss in the section "Authentication" earlier in this chapter, except the programs perform this authentication automatically.

- **The transport protocol (TCP/IP) provides reliability.** You can depend on the fact that messages you send reach their intended destinations. (Macintosh computers include a message integrity check.)

The Secure Sockets Layer provides a comforting level of security. Using programs that have built-in security is far easier than handling security yourself — and certainly better than having no security at all.

Electronic payment methods

One of the main reasons for setting up a secure environment for online sales is to collect the money. Boy, *that* term's ready for the scrap heap. Who uses *money* anymore? Electronic financial transactions are quickly replacing hard currency, both online and on the street. You can use your ATM card for just about everything now. Credit-card companies are moving to create *smart cards* with embedded chips to process cash debits.

The Internet presents an entirely new set of challenges involving collecting money from customers. One of the biggest concerns about online sales is the security of credit-card transactions. But as many people argue, this fear is overblown. After all, you risk your credit-card number every time you hand the card to a store clerk or waiter, leave the number with your travel agent, or print your number on some type of mail-in order form. During a single serious trip to a shopping mall, you may hand half a dozen credit cards to 20 total strangers, each of whom gets to keep a copy of your information and signature when you walk away. And, unless you shred your receipts and eat the scraps, there's probably more of your financial information in your trash can than on the entire Internet. Given current computer security, online transactions probably are safer than most of the other credit-card transactions you make every day.

What makes Internet transactions scary for many people is the apparent anonymity of the transactions. The buyer probably doesn't know the person who's receiving the credit-card information. But you can make the same argument about mail-order transactions or even purchases in stores. Just last week, a clerk asked us for identification and we asked him to prove that he worked for his company. We had ID. He failed to produce a corporate contract. Authentication (as we discuss in the section "Authentication" earlier in this chapter) takes some of the fear out of anonymous electronic transactions.

After the fear is gone, however, the question of how you carry out transactions over the Internet remains.

Credit-card transaction systems

The simplest and most obvious way to transact business over the Internet is to have customers pay for goods and services by providing their credit-card numbers. Many companies are working diligently to make this method the most secure type of transaction that can possibly take place on the Internet. VISA and Microsoft teamed to develop a technology called Secure Transaction Technology (STT) to facilitate secure electronic payment systems.

VISA and Microsoft also extended SSL to create Private Communication Technology (PCT). PCT provides better authentication than Secure Sockets Layer by extending SSL, but it remains 100 percent compatible with the SSL standard.

After you know that you can transmit credit-card information securely, you need to figure out how to handle the rest of the transaction. VeriFone, Inc., a supplier of transaction automation system solutions, offers a suite of products that delivers software products for processing payment transactions over the Internet. The company's products include an electronic wallet for consumers (a little like a debit or ATM card for the Internet), a virtual point-of-sale terminal (or cash register) for merchants, and an Internet gateway (a way to make a payment) for Internet shoppers. These products go beyond simply accepting credit-card transactions; they offer a complete solution for vendors who want to accept online transactions. These solutions can take a transaction from the buyer's order through credit-card approval at the bank.

VeriFone's system is not limited to credit cards. The company's software can handle many of the new electronic payment forms that we discuss in the following sections. Check out the company's Web page at the following URL:

```
http://www.verifone.com/
```

Many companies that issue credit-card merchant accounts also have a variety of software for handling online payments.

Electronic money

Another option for a secure Internet sales environment is the use of electronic-money technology. Because you can't pay for things on the Internet by shoving dollar bills into the floppy-drive slot on the front of your computer, someone needs to create a way to pay for things on the Internet electronically. One method may be plastic money (credit cards). With credit-card transactions, however, you have a certain amount of uncertainty. (Is the card good? Is it going to be good when the transaction goes through? Is someone using the card fraudulently?) The solution for these uncertainties is a relatively new concept known as electronic money, which has some advantages over traditional credit-card sales. Electronic money is normally defined as some type of secure document (digitally signed) that has some value based on the purchase price of the document. This special signed document is transferred over the Internet after you purchase something. The vendor can then convert the document to cash from the company that created the document.

Several companies offer secure electronic-money systems for the Internet. One such company is DigiCash, which uses digital signatures to authenticate digital cash. In this system, the user's computer generates a random number, which becomes a note that the user can send by using electronic mail or a World Wide Web form. The vendor receives the note and submits the note to DigiCash, which credits the vendor's account with electronic cash. This electronic cash is a little like a Las Vegas poker chip; vendors can choose to cash in the notes whenever they want the real, hard cash.

For those of you who worry about the privacy of your personal finances, a technique called *blinding* keeps the bank from knowing who generates the note. By using blinding, you make these electronic transactions work just like cash transactions; no one can track them.

Merchant accounts

Before you can accept credit cards, you need to get a credit-card merchant account. Without one, you have no way to handle credit cards, nor any place to deposit the funds from a credit-card transaction. Neither a regular bank account nor a typical business account will do. Although most banks currently are not eager to issue merchant accounts for small or home-based businesses operating on the Internet (and many will not issue one for any online business, including an online branch of an existing customer), some companies specialize in this market. CardService International was one of the first to specifically seek out Internet entrepreneurs. Their Web site is at

http://www.cardservice.com/

Other companies in this field include Commerce Today, at

http://www.commercetoday.com/
    web/merchant-account.htm

Internet Merchant Access, at

http://www.paymentsonthenet.com/

and Master Merchant, at the following address:

http://www.mastermerchant.com/

When dealing with any credit-processing company, make sure that you understand exactly what your obligations are, and what it will cost to do business with them. Typically, you'll have to pay an application fee that may run as high as $100; some companies, however, waive this fee. They will also take a percentage of each transaction (called a *discount fee*) and hit you with a small monthly accounting charge. Different companies have different rates, and it pays to shop carefully. It may be worthwhile to pay a larger startup cost to get a lower discount fee.

In addition, you need to lease or purchase software to process the credit-card orders and submit them for payment. These companies may also offer you a variety of gadgets for handling face-to-face transactions (called, no kidding, *card swipers*). If you're just on the Net, you don't need 'em, so don't buy 'em.

Some credit-processing companies want you to maintain a business account at a bank of their choice. Run, don't walk, if this is required, and choose one that will deposit the funds in your own business account at your local bank.

After you've applied, you need to undergo an inspection. This is a holdover from ancient times when people had stores with products and employees and all that stuff. You'd figure they'd want to look at your Web site, which is where your store actually is, but — believe it or not — they want to come out to your home or office and see your computer sitting on your desk. The inspector, who is a part-timer at the pinnacle of his career, will arrive either two hours early or two hours late and complain about the drive out to your place. Odds are pretty good that the inspector will need to be shown which object in the room is called a computer. He or she will take two pictures of the computer, fill out a form saying that your business has been inspected, and leave you alone forever after.

For more information, see the DigiCash Web site at the following address:

```
http://www.digicash.com/
```

CyberCash is an electronic-transaction-processing company with a few twists. Unlike other companies, CyberCash doesn't require consumers to have a relationship with CyberCash to use its system. Consumers simply need to download the CyberCash Wallet software, which is available at no charge on the CyberCash Web site. This software creates the link between the consumer, the seller, and their respective financial institutions.

To receive CyberCash from people on the Internet, you set up accounts directly with CyberCash. These accounts are noninterest-bearing holding accounts. You can transfer digital cash into or out of the accounts. CyberCash also enables you to set up financial transactions on an as-needed basis, such as to transfer money from one person to another across the Internet.

For more information, check out the CyberCash Web site at the following URL:

```
http://www.cybercash.com/
```

Other electronic-money systems are likely to emerge. Watch these developments with interest, because the future of privacy in electronic commerce is at stake. All types of companies currently conduct online sales by using combinations of all the technologies that we discuss in this chapter. Visit some of the online malls and shopping networks to see how companies are handling Internet sales today. Search for the term *online malls* in any of the search engines to find online malls and shopping networks.

Note: Some companies charge a fee to accept and process transactions. We don't recommend using such companies if you can avoid doing so. If you consider conducting business with one of these companies, make sure that you read all the fine print in the contract; you may find some real eye-openers.

What direction the industry may take with regard to digital cash isn't completely clear at this point. The ideal is standardization on a single digital monetary unit and ways to transfer, protect, and spend the digital cash. This type of standardization is unlikely to occur in the short term. For now, you have to put up with many competing standards. Having your money backed by a private company that could go out of business in a volatile emerging marketplace is a little scary, so buyer, beware!

Chapter 12
Promoting Your Internet Site

● ●

In This Chapter

▶ Figuring out your promotional needs

▶ Knowing your audience

▶ Marketing with the Web search engines

▶ Using new marketing strategies in cyberspace

● ●

*W*ell, you have your site set up, it's full of wonderful features and useful stuff, and now you can sit back and watch the online world beat a path to your door. In a matter of minutes, hours at most, you'll be world famous. Your only real concern is that the volume of visitors might melt the high-speed lines.

As they say in the Navy, "Wakey, wakey!" The truth is, you've just begun. Sad to say, nobody knows you're there. And they're not gonna find you unless you stand up and shout and wave your arms, metaphorically speaking.

Before you start trumpeting your site, though, give some consideration to what you want to achieve. You need to cover three key points:

✔ What purpose does your site serve?

✔ Who are you trying to reach?

✔ What do you want from them?

After you cover these three points, you'll understand what it is you're promoting, who your audience is, and how to know if your promotion efforts have been successful.

What's It All About?

If you're running an online publication that depends on advertising or subscription-based access, you'll need to consider how to get as many people as possible to visit your site. After all, the bigger the numbers you accumulate, the more advertising revenue or subscription prospects you have. You need to aim for the same goal if you're using the Internet to sell products directly to the general public. Sometimes, the "product" is a political or social view, but the approach is still the same. If you don't "sell" your ideas effectively, your site won't generate much interest.

Some organizations — even commercial ones — are not interested in the vast numbers of the general public, though. They are interested in a small number of dedicated buyers, called a *niche market.* They are, however, terribly concerned with the *type* of visitors they get. Dealers in pre-Han dynasty Chinese maps, for example, want to attract a certain type of person to their site, and would be happier with a few hundred affluent geographers than with two million gaming enthusiasts who mistakenly thought the site offered a new level for DOOM. In fact, such sites will want to take great care in marketing to ensure that their site isn't so overloaded that real potential customers cannot get through.

So now you know something about two different types of Internet sites: One depends on the greatest number of people landing on the site, and the other depends on the right people finding the site. You need to promote these two types of Internet sites somewhat differently. We begin in this chapter with some of the basics common to both types of sites, such as getting a listing in the various Internet search engines.

Users have coined many new words over the Internet; one of the better ones is *netiquette,* derived from *Net* and *etiquette.* Because the Internet has no rules — only guidelines — you need to become familiar with the netiquette of your area of the Internet, just as you'd need to discover all the different customs and protocols should you move to a new country. Be sensitive to cultural differences on the Internet. Take the time to study the customs and protocols of a particular group of Internet users before using shared Internet resources to promote your Internet site. That way, your site has a chance to become famous rather than infamous.

Graduating from being known to being famous

You can make your Web site known among Web surfers — or you can make your site *famous*. Before you launch any cyber-marketing attempt, therefore, take time to ask yourself which one you want. Then answer your own question. To help determine the answer, consider these factors: If your Internet site offers resources that you intend for only a small group of people to use, being known may be quite enough for your purposes. On the other hand, if your goal is to reach as many people as possible on the Internet, you definitely want your site to become famous.

Being famous, of course, always has its price. In the case of a famous Internet site, you must work to keep your site fresh and exciting. Just like movie stars, Internet sites must keep taking on new roles to stay in the public eye.

If you want to transcend being known and enter the realm of being famous, try to get your site listed as a cool site. Several pages on the Web offer a "cool site of the day." Getting chosen as a cool site can take you from having only hundreds access your Web site to having tens of thousands of visitors. (See the "Cool Site of the Day" section later in this chapter for more information.)

Whose Site Is This, Anyway?

Whose site is it? Well, it's yours, obviously. But, in another sense, it belongs also to a whole lot of other people. Marketers call this *brand loyalty,* and you see it all the time when people say things like "That's my beer" or "Honey, you got the wrong kind of hand grenades." It's what made us trade our old Jeep in for a new Jeep instead of going to all the trouble of hunting up a classic Yugo. And it's what keeps people coming back again and again to your site.

People will never develop loyalty to your site (or any other product) until it achieves a certain level of performance that people find satisfactory. You have to earn loyalty by giving people what they want and keeping up to date.

Whether you want your site simply to be known or your goal is to own the hottest site on the Internet, you must know your audience. Not knowing the people for whom you create your site is like trying to paint in the dark. Fortunately, defining Internet audiences is now the subject of research by some of the top marketing agencies in the world. Even Nielsen, famous for its TV ratings, has joined the Internet survey game. Internet users are literally as diverse as the cultures of the world, and the analysis of that diversity results in data known as *demographics*. The studies that advertising companies and organizations such as Nielsen conduct help define who is using the Internet and for what purpose.

On the Internet, the one thing that you can count on is the fact that everything's always changing. By *everything,* we mean any and all of the following characteristics:

- ✔ **The profile of the average user.** The Net used to be the exclusive territory of the young white male technonerd, a strange bipedal creature chiefly noted for its ghastly eating habits and plaintive cry of "More RAM!" Today, normal people are often found encroaching on its former grounds.

- ✔ **The number of people connected.** The Global Village is undergoing the biggest population explosion since the Baby Boom. Pretty soon, everybody's middle name will be @.

- ✔ **Improved technology.** Any hardware or software is obsolete by the time you remove the shrink wrap. By the time you get it installed, it's a museum-quality antique. Don't expect the pace of technological improvement to slow down any time soon. As better methods of connecting to and surfing the Internet become available, your site will need to become more and more sophisticated to effectively compete for audience share.

Just what is the potential audience? How many people are on the Net, and what are they like? Fortunately, this is a burning question to a whole bunch of people who actually like using calculators and figuring out means and chi squares and things like that. The only real problem now is, if you ask 200 different statisticians what the number is, you'll get 400 different answers.

To get a handle on what the experts have to say about who's on the Net these days, take a crack at the sites in Table 12-1.

Table 12-1	Internet Demographic Info
Service	*URL (Internet Address)*
CyberAtlas	`http://www.cyberatlas.com/`
GVU's WWW User Surveys	`http://www.cc.gatech.edu/gvu/` `user_surveys/User_Survey_Home.html`
Nielsen Media Research	`http://www.nielsenmedia.com/`
The NPD Group	`http://www.npd.com/`
NUA Internet Surveys	`http://www.nua.ie/surveys/`
Win Treese's Internet Index	`http://www.openmarket.com/intindex/`

It's one thing to know in general what the overall Net population is like (statisticians call that the *Net universe*). But what about the people who actually come to your site? It's a really good idea to find out as much as you can about them. At the very least, you should have a good log analyzer program such as Statbot by Dave Tubbs, which will enable you to track how many people are visiting your site, which ones are repeat visitors, and what type of domains you are appealing to most. For instance, if most of your visitors are from domains ending in .edu, which denotes an educational institution, you are most popular with students or professors. On the other hand, if they end in .mil, you're appealing mainly to the military. You can find Statbot at `http://www.xmission.com/~dtubbs/club/cs.html`.

Don't bother with page counters if you're really serious about knowing your audience. They're cute and come in such a variety of looks that they can fit into just about any design, but they don't give you any real, meaningful information. All they'll tell you is how many times a particular page was accessed; you have no way of knowing if those 20,000 *hits* you got yesterday were from one obsessed person or from thousands of different people. And the page counters you get from services outside your site really increase the download time for the page you put them on, because the page has to wait for a separate server to respond before it can complete loading.

You may also want to post a questionnaire form that can be voluntarily filled out. If you have something people really want, like the beta for a hot new piece of software, you can make the questionnaire a condition of getting the software, although many people find this annoying and you will very likely get some truly bizarre answers to innocent questions.

In most localities, it is illegal to require people to answer the very questions a marketer is most interested in, such as age, sex, and race. Make sure that your form has these as *optional* responses and says in no uncertain terms that they are not required. If in doubt, check with your attorney.

The Little Search Engine That Could

The cliché "If you build it, they will come" may be true for baseball fields but not for Web pages and other Internet resources. If nobody knows about your presence on the Internet, that's exactly who you can expect to visit your site — nobody. Just as you can advertise your business by putting your phone number in the local Yellow Pages, you can advertise your Internet site in online directories and through search engines.

A *search engine* is a program provided as a Web page that enables you to search for key words and phrases found in Web pages indexed by this program. Many types of programs, known as *crawlers* and *spiders,* wander around the Web creating these indexes so that people can navigate through the hundreds of thousands of Web pages on the Internet without getting lost.

One of the most successful types of Internet business has been the World Wide Web search engine. Without search engines, finding what you need on the Internet is a near impossibility. Figuring out how to make the best use of the search engines in promoting your Internet site is of great importance. Search engines are usually the first place everyone starts in visiting the World Wide Web. In fact, most search engines use a customized screen that loads each time users who have made the search engine their home page start their Web browser.

We suggest configuring your Web browser to load a popular Web search engine, such as Yahoo!, as the default home page. You can set your browser's default home page or start page by using your browser's configuration menu. The search engine, a logical starting place, therefore becomes an "Internet Main Menu" for the average Internet user.

Taking advantage of search engines in promoting your site is the single most important thing you can do in marketing your site. In the following sections, we take a look at some of the different types of search engines, as classified by the following list:

✔ Edited lists of sites

✔ Web crawlers, spiders, and worms (sounds creepy, doesn't it?)

✔ Site-published resource lists

Yippee! Hurray! Yahoo!

One of the most popular types of search engines is the edited list of sites. Yahoo! is a good example of such an edited list. People submit their Web pages and newsgroups for inclusion in the Yahoo! directory. One reason for Yahoo!'s success is that a real, live human being manually visits the submitted resource and determines whether to include it in the directory. Each page is submitted to Yahoo! in a specific category or categories. The person at Yahoo! checking out the resource makes certain that the submitted page is appropriate for the category for which it was submitted. This screening process results in an edited but still very complete list of Internet resources. Having Yahoo! include your Internet site in its directory is very important.

Sometimes you must be persistent in your efforts to get Yahoo! to include your site in its directory. The number of requests for a listing in the Yahoo! directory has resulted in a long waiting list. Our experience is that a certain number of requests simply fall through the cracks. Be patient and don't bombard the folks at Yahoo! with requests. But if your site doesn't appear after a week or two, checking to make sure that your site is still in the running for a listing is a good idea.

Submitting your Internet site to Yahoo! is a little trickier than getting a listing with some of the other Web search engines. Because a human reviews each site for Yahoo! and because the service is free, the Yahoo! folks expect you to do some of the work of figuring out exactly where in their directory to list your resource.

You can enter your Internet site into more than one Yahoo! category. Your first step is to access the main Yahoo! page at the following URL (see Figure 12-1):

```
http://www.yahoo.com/
```

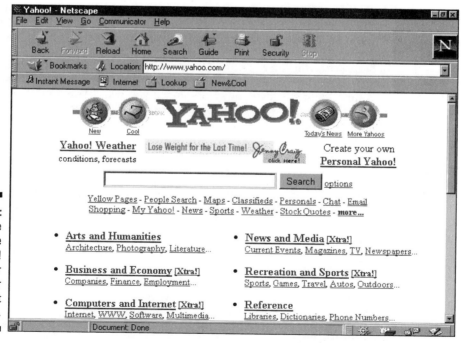

Figure 12-1: Locate the appropriate Yahoo! category for your Internet site.

Notice in Figure 12-1 that you have several categories from which to choose. For complete instructions, you can scroll down to the bottom of the main Yahoo! page and click the link entitled "How to Suggest a Site." Or you can go directly to adding your site. Find the category that best fits your Internet site. After you locate the correct category, click the Add URL icon at the top of the Yahoo! page. This action launches a new Yahoo! page containing instructions for adding your URL to the Yahoo! directory.

If you choose a category that's too general, you receive a notification to choose a more specific category. If you receive such a notification, select the subcategory that's closest to the topic of your Internet site.

After you have finished reading the page of instructions, click the Proceed to Step One button. This will lead you to a form composed of four steps. In Step One, you need to fill in the title, location (URL), and description of your site. Be careful to enter the URL of your resource correctly and completely. Remember that an Internet resource can be a Web page, a newsgroup, a mailing list, or many other possible Internet information types. Don't be confused because the `http://` part of your URL is already filled in for you. If your Internet resource is not a Web page — you have a mailing list, for example — you can delete the `http://` part and enter the correct URL. (You may, for example, need to enter a `mailto:` or a `news:` URL type in place of `http://`.) When you have finished with Step One, click the Proceed to Step Two button.

In Step Two, you can type any other categories you think your site should be listed under (you must enter the category title exactly, or it will be rejected by Yahoo!) and suggest a new category if you want. You don't have to make any entries in this step. When you are ready to proceed, click the Proceed to Step Three button.

In Step Two of the Add URL form is a place where you can add categories for your site. To include your page in more than a single category, you really need to have already browsed through the different Yahoo! categories and made a note of the page titles of each appropriate category. You should click the Add URL icon only after you're on the category page you feel is most appropriate to your Internet site. That category automatically appears on the form. Then, in the box provided on the form, enter the additional category names. Make sure you enter them exactly as they appear on the Yahoo! category pages.

In Step Three, you give contact information. Type your name and e-mail address into the appropriate text boxes. Yahoo! people use this address to notify you after entering your resource into the Yahoo! directory. They may even contact you with questions about accessing your Internet resource, although this situation is rare. You can optionally give the geographical location of your site. Entering the location of your Internet site on Yahoo!'s Add URL form is important only if your site contains region-specific information or resources. If, for example, you own a bagel shop that takes local delivery orders from your Web page, you want to note your locale. Bagel connoisseurs in Algiers can then avoid disappointment because you can't deliver hot, fresh bagels to their door. When you are finished with this step, click the Proceed to Step Four button.

In Step Four, you can enter the dates during which your site will be available. This is an optional process, and is of importance only if you are operating a site that will have only a temporary existence, such as a holiday site that you plan to take down after the holiday. You can also enter any additional information that you think will be useful to the Yahoo! staff in handling your submission. When you have finished Step Four, click the Submit button to complete the submission.

Figure 12-2 shows the Yahoo! Add URL form. Fill out a separate form for each Internet resource you want Yahoo! to list.

Directory assistance, please

Another type of Internet directory does not rely solely on people submitting their resources for indexing. Lycos, AltaVista, Infoseek, and Inktomi are examples of search engines that use special programs to search the Internet, looking for Internet resources to index in their directories. These search programs have all sorts of bug-related names, such as *worms* and *spiders*.

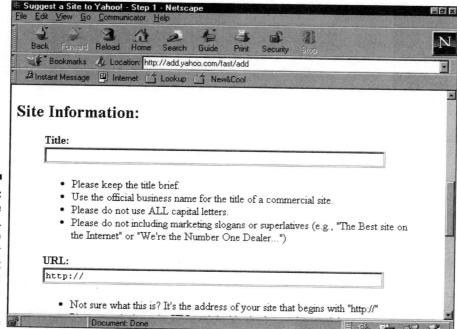

Figure 12-2:
Fill out the Add URL form to have your Internet resources added to Yahoo!.

(Perhaps these programs would be better named Internet ferrets.) The programs constantly search the Internet for new resources to list.

Such programs primarily search the World Wide Web for new Web pages, moving link by link from page to page and site to site. Some also search the Usenet newsgroups, indexing newsgroup information. This kind of program has its good aspects and its bad aspects. On the good side, these programs — we henceforth call them *spiders* for simplicity's sake — collect keyword information from hundreds of thousands of Web pages throughout the Internet. Whether someone specifically submits a URL or keeps a low profile on the Web, these Web spiders seek out and locate new Web pages and include those pages in their keyword index. If you're searching on an obscure topic, you have a much better chance of finding what you're looking for by using the search engine of an Internet directory that employs a spider.

The downsides to using a spider-based search engine are that you often receive not only too much information but a lot of out-of-date information as well. Searching on a keyword or phrase may return results numbering in the thousands. Most search engines return their results ranked by *relevance*. In other words, the first results in the list are more likely what you're looking for than are those farther down the list. But such is not always the case, and searching through thousands of results is both time-consuming and tedious.

Domo arigato, Mr. Roboto
Thank you, Mr. Robot

Doing your part to make Internet directories more useful is easy. An important file to have in your Web-publishing directory is a ROBOTS.TXT file. Spiders, Web robots, worms, and other wandering Web-indexing engines use this file primarily to exclude directories and files you don't want them to index. You may, for example, create several Web pages as tests. Because these pages aren't a permanent part of your site, you probably won't want them showing up in searches through Lycos and AltaVista.

A ROBOTS.TXT file is a simple text file that you create by using any text editor. You save your completed ROBOTS.TXT file in your Web-publishing root directory (which is the same directory in which your main home page normally resides).

The following sample displays a comment line, beginning with a pound sign, that states that it allows any user-agent (crawler, spider, and so on), plus a few lines specifying directories that we want robots to stay out of. These lines begin with the word Disallow. The following is a sample of a ROBOT.TXT file:

```
# SCIENCE.ORG Robot File
User-agent: *
Disallow: /test
Disallow: /graphics
```

You can find the full specification for creating a ROBOTS.TXT file at http://info. webcrawler.com/mak/projects/ robots/norobots.html#format.

One reason why so many results return from spider-based searches is that the searches include Web pages, which were never really meant to be indexed. Suppose, for example, that you want to learn more about Visual Basic, the Microsoft programming language. You perform a search on the words *Visual Basic* — and wind up with thousands of results. You find that these results include listings for everyone who's ever used the words *Visual Basic* in their online resumes as well as anyone who's ever put up a job posting looking for Visual Basic programmers. Often, wading through these inappropriate Web pages to find the specific information you want just isn't worth the trouble.

Expired and broken links also are problems you encounter in using both spider-based directories and hand-entered indexes. Many Internet information resources are time-sensitive or temporary. Many others simply either move, usually by changing service providers, or stop publishing their resources. People searching through these types of indexes for information should consider wearing a hat to keep from pulling out their hair in frustration. Even so, without these types of search engines, finding information on the Internet would be nearly impossible.

Be sure to check out Chapter 5 to see how to use the META tag and keywords so that search engines can index your site more effectively. Also, make sure you update your pages regularly so that the search engines see that the pages are not stale.

Table 12-2 gives the URLs of various Web sites that either evaluate the different search engines or deal with using search engines for business promotion.

Table 12-2	Search Tool Information
Service	*URL (Internet Address)*
The Art of Business Web Site Promotion	http://www.deadlock.com/promote/
did-it.com	http://www.did-it.com./
Evaluation of Selected Internet Search Tools	http://www.library.nwu.edu/resources/ internet/search/evaluate.html
Internet Search Tool Details	http://sunsite.berkeley.edu/Help/ searchdetails.html
Interwave Marketing Group	http://ibmc.com/interwave/
The Spider's Apprentice	http://www.monash.com/spidap.html

Feeding the worms and spiders

Instead of waiting for a spider, worm, or Web robot to find your Internet resource, you can increase your chances of getting indexed by submitting your URL to different search engines. Table 12-3 lists in alphabetical order several of these search engines, along with their URLs.

Table 12-3	Internet Search Engines
Internet Search Engine	*URL (Internet Address)*
AltaVista	http://www.altavista.digital.com/
Excite	http://www.excite.com/
Galaxy Search	http://galaxy.tradewave.com/search.html
goto.com	http://www.goto.com/
HotBot	http://www.hotbot.com/
Infoseek	http://www.infoseek.com/
Inktomi	http://www.inktomi.com/
Inter-Links	http://alabanza.com/kabacoff/Inter-Links/search/search.html
LinkFinder	http://www.linkfinder.com/
Lycos	http://www.lycos.com/
Magellan Internet Guide	http://www.mckinley.com/
Open Text Index	http://index.opentext.net/
WebCrawler	http://www.webcrawler.com/
World Wide Web Virtual Library	http://vlib.stanford.edu/Overview.html

Each search engine or directory in Table 12-3 includes its own mechanism for enabling you to add your URL to its index or directory. Using your Web browser, go to the Web pages listed in the table and look for the link or button on the page that enables you to add a URL. This process is much simpler than that of submitting your URL to Yahoo!. In most cases, you simply type the URL of your resource and perhaps a brief description, and then click a Submit button. The search engine takes care of adding your site to its index. It usually sends some sort of spider to index your entire site (all your Web pages).

Submitting your URL the easy way

Hundreds of search engines and directories are on the Internet. Probably no one really knows how many are there. Some guesses put the number of these services at somewhere slightly less than 500. If you just became a little faint at the thought of having to enter your Internet site URL into all those different search engines, however, take heart. Services exist that enable you to automatically enter your URL into many different search engines at once.

Because the different search engines have widely varying content and requirements, you may find that you are limiting your site's exposure if you use a mass submission service. Make sure that the service takes these differences into account before you go with them.

One such service, WebStep Top 100, estimates that adding a link to 100 different search engines takes a professional about ten hours. The WebStep site lists 100 different directories and search engines, rating each with from one to four stars. You can save time by choosing to add your site to only three- and four-star directories. You can use the WebStep site as a quick access guide to each of the 100 search engines and directories the site lists.

But don't expect any real shortcuts. You still must manually enter the information about your resource into each directory's Add URL form. If you're in a hurry, however, and time is more important to you than money, WebStep offers to add your URL to 100 search engines and directories for $295. WebStep can be contacted at the following URL:

```
http://www.mmgco.com/top100.html
```

!Register-It! is another company offering a free service that enables you to enter your information once and, by doing so, automatically enter the information into 16 of the top directories and search engines (see Figure 12-3). Of course, !Register-It! also offers a commercial service that enters your site into 100 directories for $39.99. You can surf to the !Register-It! site by pointing your Web browser to the following address:

```
http://www.register-it.com/
```

Submit It!, the very first service of its kind, offers more than 20 submissions and several other commercial rates for submitting your resource information to more than 400 search engines and directories. The service also offers special rates to Webmasters who need to submit URLs for several different companies. Submit It! Online, a commercial service, advertised rates of around $200 for 10 companies and around $300 dollars for 20 companies. You can reach the Submit It! site at the following URL:

```
http://www.submitit.com/
```

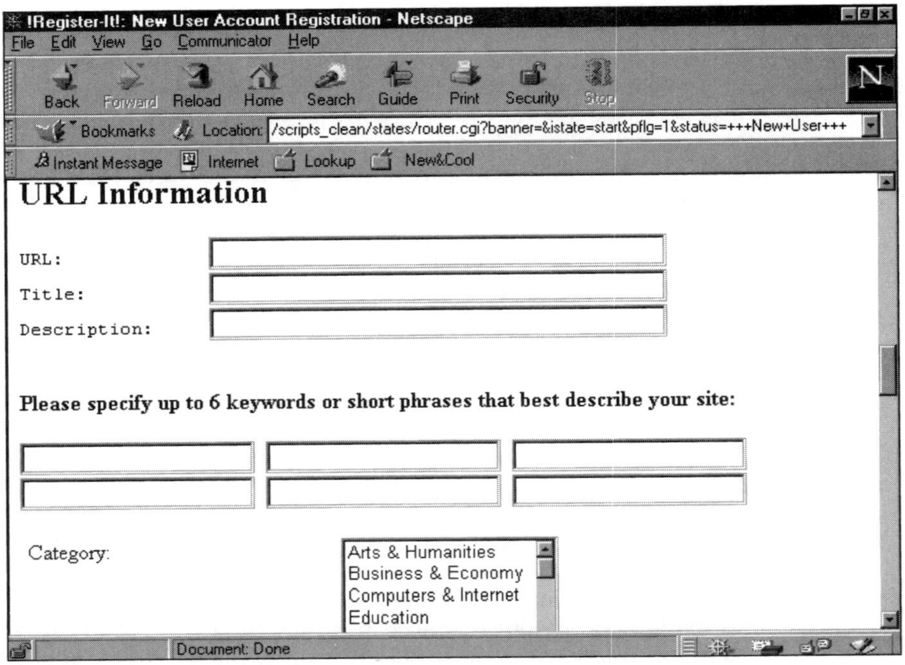

Figure 12-3:
!Register-It!
offers both
a free and a
commercial
URL
registration
service.

The last service we cover here is Postmaster. This service is similar to the others in this section, with a few exceptions. The folks at Postmaster offer to add your site to around 400 different directories and search engines. They also offer to send your URL to more than 10,000 individuals. This service is aimed mainly at organizations with a bit of cash. The company offers to submit 80 posts, for example, for $2,999. You can reach the Postmaster site at the following address:

```
http://www.netcreations.com/postmaster
```

Using a service saves you time, whether you choose to take advantage of the free offers or pay a fee to have your site added to many directories. Be aware, too, that some search engines to which you submit your URL may offer additional exposure for your Internet site for an additional fee. Some value-added services include posting an announcement on a special page that highlights new submissions; others may post your listing in their directory in a larger and colored font. As many of these registries grow to rival the traditional printed phone books, having your listing stand out from the many other listings becomes a challenge. You must decide for yourself whether the additional exposure these marketing features add is worth the extra money.

Using an online ad agency

Sit back and relax while Internet promotion specialists take your Internet site from obscurity to fame. Traditional ad agencies have only recently become aware of the potential of the Internet. Most agencies don't fully understand how to go about marketing someone's online presence. Several companies, however, have performed really well in online marketing. One of these companies, DoubleClick, provides a full service ad agency devoted to online promotion.

You can contact DoubleClick at the following URL:

```
http://www.doubleclick.net
```

Aliweb, alakazam!

You need no magic to add your Internet resources into Aliweb's directory. The Aliweb directory compiles its listings using a different method than Yahoo! or any of the Web spiders. Aliweb builds its index by reading special *index* files on your computer. You (or the person who maintains your Internet site) build these index files, named SITE.IDX. Then, after you register your site with Aliweb, the service visits your site several times a week to read your SITE.IDX file for the most current site information.

The following list describes advantages to using a system such as Aliweb:

- ✔ **Resources in Aliweb are always up to date.** (You find few expired or broken links.)

- ✔ **You have complete control over what resources appear in Aliweb.** (No pages appear that you do not specifically enter into the SITE.IDX file.)

- ✔ **Update-to-implementation time is relatively fast.** (Changes you make appear as soon as the Aliweb engine queries your site, which means that the wait before the updates appear may be two or three days maximum — quite speedy compared to that of any other service.)

One requirement to using the Aliweb system is that your Internet site must be available over a dedicated connection. The Aliweb queries come at regular intervals. If the engine can't reach your site several times in a row, Aliweb removes your site's information from its database. This practice helps ensure that the information in the Aliweb database is always current.

The first step in getting your site ready to register with Aliweb is to create a SITE.IDX file. To create this file, you must use a text editor or a word processor that can save to text-only (TXT) format. The SITE.IDX file contains *records* — blocks of information that describe your entire Internet site. Each record contains specific *name-value pairs* that describe each resource or *template type.* A name-value pair is a fancy way of saying that for each *name* (what is known in a database as a *field,* or a *column*) you have a *value.*

The following table is an example extracted from a SITE.IDX file. The names appear in the left column and the values appear on the right.

```
Template-Type:    USER
Title:            Joe P. Macandsun
Handle:           joe@virtualcorporation.com
Email:            joe@virtualcorporation.com
Work-Phone:       800-555-1234
URI:              http://www.virtualcorporation.com/joe/
```

This table is an example of a record that describes a USER. A SITE.IDX file contains records that describe different template types.

Your SITE.IDX file always begins with two records, one that describes your Internet site and the other that describes your organization. The following is another example of a typical SITE.IDX file:

```
Template-Type:             SITEINFO
URI:                       /
Host-Name:                 SCIENCE.ORG
Admin-Handle:              webmaster@science.org
Owner-Organization-Name:   SCIENCE.ORG (tm)
Description:               The WWW Server at SCIENCE.ORG
Keywords:                  Research, Science, Technology

Template-Type:             ORGANIZATION
Organization-Name:         SCIENCE.ORG
Organization-Handle:       SCIENCE
Organization-Phone:        619-943-9382
Organization-Fax:          619-944-6888
Organization-Email:        info@science.org
Organization-Postal:       258 Neptune Avenue
City:                      Encinitas
State:                     California
URI:                       http://www.science.org/
Description:               SCIENCE.ORG (tm) is a non-profit
                           science and technology research
                           and development lab.
Keywords:                  Research, Science, Technology
```

Use the preceding two record types to describe your site and organization in as much detail as you want. An important point to keep in mind is that you can't deviate from the template. To describe users, services, and documents, you must use the correct associated template type. The first example in this section demonstrates the template type for users. The two most common template types are SERVICE, which you use to describe an Internet service such as FTP, Finger, or some other service, and DOCUMENT, which you use to describe a document that's available through a service. Examples of documents are Web pages and files available through Gopher or FTP.

If you find this confusing, check with your favorite programmer types. They love this kind of stuff.

The following are examples of both the SERVICE and DOCUMENT template types:

```
Template-Type:      SERVICE
Title:              FTP
URI:                ftp://ftp.science.org/
Description:        FTP site for sharing research info
Keywords:           Anonymous, FTP
Admin-Handle:       jasonc@science.org

Template-Type:      DOCUMENT
Title:              ActiveX Source
Admin-Handle:       tedc@science.org
URI:                http://ebola.science.org/ActiveX/
Description:        A source for ActiveX controls
Keywords:           ActiveX, COM, DCOM, Microsoft, WWW, Web
```

When you are ready to register with Aliweb, go to their Web page at http://www.nexor.com/aliweb/register/doc/register.html and fill out the online form there. Once you have done this, Aliweb will automatically keep your site on file.

Promoting Yourself

Not everyone who wants to promote an Internet site is a business or an organization. Some people may want to promote their personal site or possibly tell people how to reach them by e-mail. Most of the search engines and directories listed previously in this chapter enable you to submit a personal Web page URL.

A hint about getting people to visit your personal Web page is to have an interesting theme. You can relate this theme to one of your interests or hobbies. Having a focused content about a specific topic makes placing your page in a directory much easier and also attracts people who share your interests to your home page. Making the page interactive keeps them coming back. A good example of this is a fun page we created a few years ago: the Coombs Family Reunion in Cyberspace page (`http://www.science.org/coombs/`). Visitors to this page could leave their own messages and family histories. Pretty soon, we had wonderful messages from distant relatives all around the world.

Most of these people came across our page doing something most people do at least once — use one of the search engines to search for their name. (Where do you think the idea of the Coombs Family Reunion page came from?) Finding other people with the same name can be fun, especially if you get to meet them, as one of the authors of this book did.

The first directory that enabled people to enter their home page, e-mail addresses, and favorite URLs was People On the Net. Soon after People On the Net was started, a really wonderful service called Four11 started up. Four11 not only provides the most complete listing of people on the Internet, but also offers access to all U.S. telephone directories. If you're looking for someone in the United States, we know of no quicker way to find who you seek than if that person is listed in the phone book or has an e-mail address registered with Four11. Even Yahoo!, which used to maintain its own listing of people, now uses the Four11 service.

The Four11 directory includes the following directories (among others):

✔ **E-mail addresses.** This directory is an important one in which to appear.

✔ **Telephone.** This list comes straight from the telephone white pages.

✔ **Netphone.** Want people to call you on your Internet phone system? Add your name to this list.

✔ **Celebrities.** This directory includes lists of celebrity mailing addresses and e-mail addresses. If you're a celebrity actor, model, author, or VIP, make sure you add yourself to the celebrity directory.

Four11 also offers additional services to paid members. You can maintain a Web page on the Four11 server, create searches that continue searching even while you're offline, and use several other services such as the iName service. Get an iName personalized e-mail address for life that redirects e-mail to any e-mail account of your choice. While you're getting yourself set up with an iName, go ahead and register yourself in the Four11 directory so that people can find you online. Entering your name in the directory is free. Simply go to the Four11 home page at the following URL and click the Add Me link under the My Listing category:

```
http://www.four11.com/
```

Table 12-4 lists some of the places you can add your name and personal profile so that people can find you on the Internet. One of these sites, the InfoSpace page, is shown in Figure 12-4.

Table 12-4	Personal Internet Directories
Service	*URL (Internet Address)*
Bigfoot	`http://www.bigfoot.com/`
Four11	`http://www.four11.com/`
InfoSpace	`http://www.accumail.com/iui/index.htm`
WhoWhere	`http://www.whowhere.com/`
World Wide Profile Registry	`http://www.wizard.com/wwpr.html`

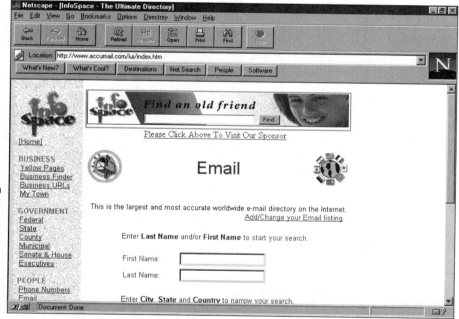

Figure 12-4: InfoSpace is one place to add your name when promoting yourself.

Cool Site of the Day

If traffic to your site is what you're looking for, your goal is to shoot for a listing in one of the *Cool Sites of the Day* pages. The idea started several years ago with Glen Davis launching the first Cool Site of the Day page. His Internet site was so overrun with people trying to load his page that his

Internet service provider could barely handle the traffic. Every day, these pages feature a different Web page as a cool site. Thousands of people make a point of finding out where clicking the link to the Cool Site of the Day takes them.

Becoming the Cool Site of the Day probably means that your site is going to receive visits from tens of thousands of people in a single day. Make sure that your connection, your computer, and your software can handle that many connection attempts. If your site becomes overloaded, replace your Web page with a brief explanation that your site is overloaded with requests and for visitors to try back later. Don't just turn your computer off or shut down your Web server. That upsets people, and they may never return to your site. Another alternative is to find someone with a very fast connection and a powerful computer and ask that person to temporarily host your Web site. Create a simple home page with a link that takes people to the temporary site.

Infinet, now several years old, runs the Cool Site of the Day page (see Figure 12-5). As always, Infinet takes recommendations for the day's cool site. (Recommending your own Web page as the Cool Site of the Day is okay.) To correspond with Infinet or to find out for yourself just what's cool today, go to the following address:

```
http://cool.infi.net
```

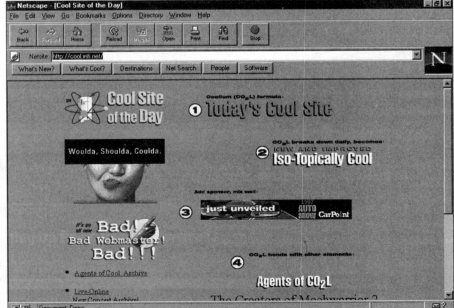

Figure 12-5: The bonanza of all cool site pages, Infinet's Cool Site of the Day page.

A good idea doesn't stay lonely for very long. Just about everyone now has a list of cool links. Netscape Navigator, for example, provides a button for "What's Cool?" as part of the Navigator interface. In case you use a different browser, clicking the What's Cool? button in Navigator takes you to the following URL:

```
http://guide.netscape.com/guide/whats_cool.html
```

Yahoo!, the mother of all Internet directories, used to point to Glen Davis's Cool Site of the Day. That support probably helped make the site as popular as it is today. Not to be outdone, the Yahoo! main Web page now has its own Cool icon at the top of the page. Clicking the icon takes you to the following address:

```
http://www.yahoo.com/Entertainment/Cool_Links
```

If you're going to diligently pursue becoming a cool site in one or more of the lists of cool sites, you want to make sure that your Web site

- ✔ Is graphically appealing
- ✔ Contains interesting content
- ✔ Loads quickly — go easy on those Java applets!

Don't be discouraged if no one immediately selects your site. The number of Web sites is rapidly approaching the one million mark. The companies that run the lists of cool sites receive a large number of requests every day for consideration as the cool site. Your persistence and creativity is bound to pay off eventually. (See Chapters 5 and 6 for tips on creating a great Web page.)

Extra! Extra! Read All about It!

Make your site big news. Newsgroups were among the first popular gathering places on the Internet — so popular, in fact, that the words *newsgroups* and *Internet* were once almost synonymous. A newsgroup, by the way, is one of the many discussion areas available on the Internet. Newsgroups were originally formed (and are still formed today) to enable users to share information or carry on electronic dialogue about anything and everything. If you tell people in newsgroups that you have an online presence, you automatically increase your visibility.

Certain newsgroups work better than others as places to post an announcement of your new Web page. Begin with general newsgroups that were specifically created for posting announcements. One recommendation is the comp.infosystems hierarchy of newsgroups, especially the following:

```
comp.infosystems.www.announce
```

You can use *newsreaders,* such as the ones that come with either Microsoft Internet Explorer or Netscape Navigator, to read and post messages to newsgroups. In writing your posting, tell newsgroup readers a little about what to expect after they log onto your Web page. Remember to include your URL. Getting caught up in the description of your site while completely forgetting to tell people how to get there is all too easy.

The following list offers guidelines to keep in mind if you post your site to newsgroups:

- Post messages to newsgroups with the same topic or focus as the Internet site you're promoting.

- Read the newsgroup before you post to it. Reading posts completely unrelated to the information pertinent to the newsgroup is aggravating.

- Don't post the same message to hundreds of similar newsgroups.

- Don't advertise specific items as you would in a magazine or a newspaper; save specific product or service information for the people who are interested enough to seek out your online presence.

- Newsgroups archive their messages, so they erase your posting after a period of time. The more active a newsgroup is, the quicker the messages disappear. Posting to a newsgroup one time doesn't guarantee that your message is around forever.

- Make certain that your posting and the content of your Internet site appeals to the audience of a particular newsgroup before you post your message with that newsgroup. If you post to alt.wolves, for example, don't post a "Humans Against Wolves Home Page" message unless you're looking for a fight.

It's a Jungle out There — How Amazon.com Does It

Whether you're marketing fresh lobster from Maine, tours of the Holy Land, coffee from Hawaii, or rare books from your attic, you can sell your wares on the Internet. You don't need to be a big mall, like the Internet Shopping Network, to be a big success. The Internet is often called the "great equalizer." You have as much opportunity to sell your products in this electronic village as the bigger guys do. You just need a few tricks up your sleeve.

Awards

Ever notice how many people will watch any movie that wins an award? Well, awards exist in every field, not just movies, and the Web is no different. Whether it's the Top 5% of the Net or George's Grungy Gonzo Award, there's something about winning one that just plain ol' feels good. But it also means that lots and lots of people will be heading your way as a result. They'll find your site listed among the other prestigious winners and know right off the bat that there's something special about it.

A word of caution here: You can get some awards that have no criteria for winning. In other words, anyone can put these awards up without passing any judging. You can have a truly shallow and meaningless experience by putting one on your site. But you won't be taken seriously if you apply for any of the real awards.

You might also consider issuing an award. It's a bit of work, but most Webmasters would be happy to get one, and that means a reciprocal crosslink back to your site. Translation: free promotion. If you do this, though, don't do it indiscriminately or your award will be cheapened and your reputation will suffer. You'll have to actually go to the sites that apply and decide whether they merit your award or not. It's a lot of work but can be truly fulfilling.

Here are a couple of award sites to get you started:

- The Most Meaningful Awards on the Web at `http://www.konnections.com/outpost/bestawards.html`

- So You Want to Win an Award? at `http://ucsu.colorado.edu/~hundley/win.html`

A wonderful success story began in 1994 when Jeff Bezos founded Amazon.com. This Internet-only bookstore has one of the world's largest selection of books and is the leading bookstore on the World Wide Web. If you're wondering what the Amazon has to do with books, the company is named after the Amazon River, which is more than eight times the size of the next largest river in the world. Amazon.com claims that its catalog of books is more than eight times the size of the largest physical bookstore.

One of the tricks up Amazon's sleeve is to partner with Internet site developers. Just about anyone can become a "branch store" for Amazon.com by listing books in a Web page and linking to the Amazon.com site. This partner program benefits Amazon.com by having thousands of Web pages selling their books, and the commissions paid back to the partners is a great incentive to continue selling books through Amazon.com.

Find out about the Amazon.com partner program by going to the Amazon.com home page at the following address:

`http://www.amazon.com/`

You can use this same strategy in promoting your own products or services. Create partnerships and pay commissions to people who promote your products. To do so correctly, you need the assistance of a network programmer. The programmer must create a program that tracks how purchasers of your online product land on your Internet site so that you can appropriately credit whoever promotes your product.

Forming partnerships certainly fits with the overall cooperative model of the Internet. Many other business models certainly can find their way successfully onto the Internet. Perhaps your ideas can create the next huge success.

Promoting Your Electronic Mailing Lists

Information is one of the hottest products going on the Internet. After all, aren't we currently in the Information Age? If information is your product, one of your most important considerations is how to distribute what you know.

One great way to distribute information is by creating an *automated mailing list* — which is nothing more than a vehicle that enables people to sign up to receive your information automatically or to participate in e-mail conversations. (See Chapter 10 for complete instructions on how to create an electronic mailing list.) More and more people subscribe to automated mailing lists every day. Some electronic mailing lists, such as the one run by Robert Seidman, have more than 15,000 subscribers.

Follow these significant ways to increase participation in your mailing list:

✔ Post messages in newsgroups about your mailing list. (If you're working with newsgroups, follow any guidelines they have for posting. Newsgroups usually post such guidelines in a newsgroup *FAQ,* which stands for frequently asked questions.)

✔ Mention the mailing list on your home page and tell people how to subscribe.

✔ Enter your mailing list in some of the search engines that post mailing list information.

As we mention in the preceding list of suggestions on how to promote your electronic mailing list, placing a link from your home page is one of the best ways to promote your list. You can offer a complete description of the list and provide a `mailto:` URL that enables people to send a *subscribe* e-mail message to your list server.

Entering your mailing list in a search engine doesn't guarantee that people can find your list, but doing so does increase the chances enormously. Yahoo!'s list of mailing lists is the most complete resource of electronic mailing lists on the Internet. You can begin browsing their resources at the following address:

```
http://www.yahoo.com/computers_and_internet/internet/
mailing_lists/index.html
```

Many "lists of lists" are available through the World Wide Web. Yahoo! is only one of the sources. You can find another significant index of mailing lists at the following URL:

```
http://www.internetdatabase.com/maillist.htm
```

Many people get caught up in advertising their Web pages and forget about promoting all their other Internet resources. Getting people to subscribe to your electronic mailing lists creates an online community centered around your Internet site. Forming this type of community can prove much more valuable than simply trying to get hordes of people to see your Web page.

Remember that e-mail isn't limited to text. Your electronic mailing list can distribute full multimedia files, HTML files, or even sound files. Sending a lot of multimedia can possibly lower your list server's efficiency but certainly makes your mailing list more interesting.

Advertising Your Anonymous FTP Site

Anonymous FTP sites are wonderful places to store and share programs, information files, or other types of electronic information. If you decide to run an anonymous FTP site, you quickly find that advertising the site is simple. Archie, started in the late 1980s at McGill University, is a search utility that checks a database containing the filenames of files stored in anonymous FTP and Gopher sites around the world.

Adding your anonymous FTP site to the Archie database is simple. Just find the Archie server nearest you and send an e-mail message to the administrator. If you need help finding the Archie site nearest you, check out the Archie page at Yahoo!.

Figure 12-6 shows a Web-based Archie request form. Using this form, you can search an Archie database for keywords that match the names of files stored in anonymous FTP sites. If you're offering files from your anonymous FTP site, you can see the importance of registering your site in the Archie database.

Figure 12-6:
You use the
Archie
Request
Form at
NCSA to
find files
stored in
anonymous
FTP sites.

You can access the NCSA Archie Request Form at the following address:

```
http://archie.rutgers.edu/archie.html
```

In addition to Archie, the University of Illinois has put together the Monster FTP Sites List. You may want to contact the university to add your site to the list. You can access the Monster FTP Sites List at NCSA's Web site at the following URL:

```
http://hoohoo.ncsa.uiuc.edu/ftp/
```

Remember to advertise your anonymous FTP site on your Web page. You can create lists of files and documents available in your FTP site with links directly to the file by using an `ftp:` URL. That way, people can download files from your anonymous FTP site by clicking a link in your Web page.

Sending Electronic Postcards

Postcards don't sound very high-tech, do they? But electronic postcards provide a fun and interesting way to announce your Internet resources to friends, clients, and prospects.

Today, most people pay more attention to the information they receive through e-mail than they do to the mountains of paper that the postal service delivers. A nice break from the usual e-mail is an electronic postcard or greeting card. Point your Web browser to the following URL to find out how you can send electronic postcards:

```
http://postcards.www.media.mit.edu/Postcards/
```

To send a postcard, go to the electronic postcard rack at the URL we've listed and pick a card — any card. You find many different categories, including holiday cards, famous art, photographs, bug drawings, science, and pictures from outer space. Some even include music.

After you choose a card (actually a graphic), enter the e-mail address to which you want to deliver your card. (You don't actually deliver a card. Instead, you send an e-mail message to the recipient notifying that person that a postcard is waiting.) Finish creating your card by entering a private message and your name. Your card goes out as soon as you click the Submit button.

The recipient, armed with a password, can then use his or her Web browser to go to the postcard Web site and view the card you sent. Even though viewing a postcard takes longer than reading an e-mail message, receiving an electronic postcard adds something special to the communication. Whoever you sent the card to isn't likely forget that you sent it.

You can find all sorts of variations on the postcard theme. You can send everything from virtual bouquets to virtual vacations. Table 12-5 shows a sampling of the things you can do.

Table 12-5	Postcards and Suchlike Fun
Service	*URL (Internet Address)*
Cybear Gram	`http://www.bearisland.com/cyb.html`
Postcard Desk	`http://www.webjunkie.com/christmas/cardrack.html`
Virtual Florist	`http://www.virtualflorist.com/`
Virtual Vacation	`http://www.virtual-vacation.com/`
Zodiacal Zephyr Card Shop	`http://www.zodiacal.com/cgi-hts/htmlscript?cardshop.hts`

Physical World Promotion Techniques

Getting lost in the marketing possibilities offered by your connection to the Internet is easy. But you want also to remember some of the more conventional marketing methods, such as radio, TV, and print magazines. These days, you see URLs at the end of movie trailers, TV shows, TV commercials, and in magazine ads. People now expect to find along with these forms of communication an Internet address that takes them to a site where they can get more information. You must find out how to use the resources around you, whether through word of mouth or corporate letterhead, to promote your Internet site.

Never pass up an opportunity to plug your site. At the very least, add your Web address and e-mail address to your business cards. Consider putting them in the return address portion of your snail mail (that's what techno-geeks call the U.S. Postal Service).

Word of mouth

Tell people you're online. You are the best marketer of your information. Gone are the days when you needed to give a lengthy description while waving your arms trying to describe the Internet or the World Wide Web to people. The Internet is now a ubiquitous part of life in North America and parts of Europe and Asia. Tell people that you have an e-mail address, a Web site, and other electronic resources that you provide online.

A side benefit to discussing your online presence with others is the fact that they discover that you keep up with the times and use the resources around you to succeed. Of course, having someone grab a pen (if the person can find one), ready some paper (other than the restaurant napkin), and then write out *h-t-t-p-:-/-/* can prove time-consuming and frustrating; by the time everything is written down, the person may have lost interest. So try combining word-of-mouth advertising with printed materials.

Printed materials

Online advertising hasn't replaced printed advertising yet; printed materials remain one of the most effective ways of telling people that you have an Internet site. Putting the URL of your site on your business card, along with your e-mail address, makes finding and contacting you online fast and simple — no one must struggle to find a pen, paper, and a place to write down your information. In fact, including your e-mail address and URL in all your printed material, such as stationery, advertisements, business cards, newsletters, brochures, and slide presentations, is always appropriate now.

The following list provides some additional suggestions for advertising your Internet address:

✔ Run small advertisements in appropriate media.

✔ Add your URL and e-mail address to coffee mugs, pens, floating key chains, and other advertising specialty items.

✔ Add your home page URL to greeting cards. You may be surprised how much closer contact you maintain with distant associates or even family and friends from long, long ago if you keep in touch electronically. Aunt Marsha and Uncle Herb might have an e-mail address and a home page, too.

The telephone

The telephone remains one of the most important business tools in the world; the Internet hasn't replaced Ma Bell yet. But the problem with the phone is the fact that most people use it only to talk to people during business hours or to leave the ubiquitous voice mail. You need to take advantage of current telephone technology to direct people to your more interactive technologies. Your company's interactive voice response system (you know — the electronic voice that answers the phone) can offer electronic alternatives for customers looking for more information about your products or services. Direct them to your Internet site. You could use a recorded message such as the following example:

> "If you want further information, you can browse our World Wide Web site at [*address*] or download the most current specifications from our FTP site at [*address*]. You can also contact the sales department directly through our NetMeeting connection. Connect to [*address*]."

Millions of people still use the telephone to transact business, provide information, and talk with friends. No reason on Earth exists why you shouldn't take advantage of this old technology to direct people to your exciting online presence.

Part V
The Part of Tens

The 5th Wave — By Rich Tennant

"OH, I'LL GET US IN — I USED TO RUN TECH SUPPORT AT AN INTERNET ACCESS COMPANY."

In this part . . .

This part of the book is the most fun. Each Part of Tens chapter highlights ten things that we thought you'd like to know about but that didn't fit anywhere else in the book. Among these are ten Internet services you can't live without. You also discover ten technology add-ons for your site, ten easy ways you can enhance your site, ten lords-a-leaping, and anything else we could think of that had anything to do with the number ten.

Chapter 13

Ten Trends in the Interactive Global Village

• •

In This Chapter

▶ Coping with the change that is upon you

▶ Finding out how the Internet is the key to shared diversity

▶ Creating the future with Internet programming

• •

*T*he Internet of today is still a confusing environment for many people, and it's not going to get any less complex. Just about everyone now recognizes the *potential* of the Internet, but few realize that the Internet is already transforming the future of communications and the structure of society.

Predicting the future direction of the Net is like trying to predict the weather, but we think a few solid trends will hold true.

Science on the Internet

The Internet has its roots in the scientific and research communities. Expanded communications and collaboration tools have increased the speed at which information disseminates in these communities. Scientists and science students are realizing truly remarkable advantages from the Internet.

One resource that has been in the news lately is The Visible Human Project, a large set of digital images that displays every detail of human anatomy, 1 millimeter at a time. You can access the project, which includes both male and female anatomy, at the following URL:

```
http://www.nlm.nih.gov/research/visible/visible_human.html
```

To science, The Visible Human Project represents the opportunity to incorporate a precise electronic anatomy model into all kinds of biological research. Now programmers can write new software, giving researchers around the world an interactive biology laboratory in which they can conduct endless experiments. Only the capabilities of the computers and software involved limit the potential of such an interactive biology lab.

Another exciting Internet science project involves astronomy. The Hubble Space Telescope has helped renew interest in astronomy, but its effect is much more significant now because of NASA's use of the Internet. Through NASA's Web site, you can download astrophotographs taken by the Hubble, sometimes within hours of their transmission back to Earth. The NASA Web site is located at the following URL:

```
http://www.nasa.gov/
```

Interactive Shopping

The Internet Shopping Network (at `http://www.internet.net/`) is reporting a significant increase in sales, primarily because of shoppers from outside the United States. This trend makes a great deal of sense, if you think about it. Although many Americans live just around the corner from a physical shopping mall, people in other countries (especially developing ones) don't have this luxury; their shopping options are severely limited. The Internet Shopping Network and other operations like it offer an excellent solution to their problem.

Along with enabling retailers to reach the overseas market, the Internet is proving to be an excellent sales vehicle for retailers that offer unique or specialty items. If a product is hard to find in the real world, the Internet is the place to sell that item. In fact, specialty retailers generated impressive sales even before the Web offered security features. People who wanted to purchase specialty or hard-to-find items were willing to take the chance that a hacker could intercept their credit-card numbers; more often, they found alternative ways to make their payments.

Even among affluent people who have good physical shopping facilities easily available, the Internet is bound to become a major alternative to the hassle and hustle of old-style shopping. Already, mail-order catalog companies — which also keep a strong presence on the Net — are gaining a distinct edge over shopping malls, offering better pay, working conditions, and benefits than the stores can. As Net commerce expands, you'll be able to sit around the house in your underwear and take your pick of the exact thing you want at the best price you can get. The days of fighting traffic, battling for a parking space, elbowing your way through a snarling crowd, and settling for whatever's on the shelves will fade into the footnotes of history. A few decades from now, historical preservation societies will lobby to save the crumbling ruins of the last shopping mall, and professional actors will be hired to staff it and recreate what it was like in the old days. Tourists will come from all over the world to see the mall reenactment, complete with screaming children, husbands complaining that they're missing the football game, surly clerks, and muggers in the parking lot.

A new technology called digital ID (which we describe in Chapter 11) promises to make Internet shopping as simple as clicking the ad for the product you want to buy. Personal digital IDs for individuals prove to the Web sites you connect to that you are who you say you are. Companies such as Verisign (http://www.verisign.com/) that handle digital IDs for Web servers also handle the personal ones. In fact, the operation of generating key pairs is virtually identical, except you can generate them on the Web at Verisign's site instead of messing about with all that server nonsense or bothering your ISP. Your browser will generate the appropriate keys and connect with Verisign to complete the process. You can do a free trial run with a temporary, but fully functional, digital ID for 60 days to see if you like it. Web browsers such as Netscape Navigator and Microsoft Internet Explorer will supply customers' digital IDs (if they have those IDs) to merchants automatically after those customers decide to make a purchase. This type of setup means you no longer need to fill out a long form and type your credit-card number each time you make a purchase.

Online Advertising

If you create an Internet site that includes online sales, you're going to be confronted with two specific areas of concern: advertising and selling. Advertising and purchasing are going to become interactive, with sales generated instantly if you place the right ad in front of the consumer at just the right time.

Network agents

In the future, your customers are likely to use personal network agents that can filter ads that don't interest them. The network agents that are being developed can describe customers' interests and buying habits to auto-mated advertising generators so that these programs can dynamically create ads to appeal to a specific customer. You want to stay abreast of agent technology so that you can make maximal use of this technology to further target your customer base. To read an excellent article on the JavaWorld site, check out http://www.javaworld.com/javaworld/jw-05-1997/jw-05-hood.html.

Credit checks

The new intelligent advertising-generation programs may have access to credit ratings and the current bank-account balances of the customers who are viewing your advertising. More likely, your Internet commerce site is going to access an Internet credit agency that doesn't reveal confidential information but does track (and score) the purchasing habits of your potential customer.

This type of automatic credit checker may be a little scary to the average consumer, providing personalized and targeted advertising at the expense of consumer privacy. Even if legislation doesn't end up restricting it, as the developer of an online store, you must weigh the pros and cons of using such a system. No matter what happens, Internet shopping is certain to have a unifying effect on global society.

Access to Government

Another trend that is certain to develop in the future is a set of Internet tools that change the way in which private citizens throughout the world interact with their representatives. Through the Internet, voters can inform elected officials of their opinions, as well as track the performance of officials through voting records and multimedia political archives. Keeping abreast of government activity can become simple, and real facts about government actions may be available at everyone's convenience.

Ideally, the cumulative effect of these changes will be positive. Interactive Internet government presents the possibility of a more accessible governing process that could revolutionize the way government officials and the governed relate to one another.

In addition, it seems likely that, with the emergence of digital IDs, online voting is not far away.

Virtual Communities

Another exciting development is the emergence of virtual communities. Entire towns are organizing to establish a presence on the Internet.

Electronic villages

The city of Blacksburg, Virginia, for example, worked in cooperation with Virginia Tech to create the Blacksburg Electronic Village. You can visit this impressive creation at the following address:

```
http://www.bev.net/
```

The electronic village has helped bring the people of Blacksburg together, even though they clearly were very "together" to begin with.

Internet coffee shops

Another interesting trend in community development is the emergence of Internet coffee shops. These establishments, which are appearing in all parts of the world, offer Internet access along with a hot cup of java and a friendly atmosphere. Internet coffee shops are a great way to build real-world relationships surrounding the Internet.

The desire to associate and conduct business within our own communities seems to be human nature. Becoming part of the online community can bring about the same sense of camaraderie and, with it, trust, relationships, and business. As in any community, the responsible store owners are the ones who help shape the neighborhood.

Recently, some people have discussed the possible harmful effects of the Internet on cultures — how the Internet may work to water down or homogenize cultures around the world. But this is nothing new. Port cities such as New York, Los Angeles, Miami, London, and Hong Kong have always been a mix of cultures. You can think of the Internet as the biggest port in the world, but without the oil slicks. And the capability to communicate with people in other cultures, as we now regularly do through the Internet, can work to increase understanding by sharing the unique aspects of those cultures with all people who have online access.

We also hear the ridiculous statement that the Internet, in reducing the diversity of the global community, may wipe out the incentive for creativity. We believe quite the opposite: The Internet acts as a place to share diverse ideas, spawning new creativity.

Virtual Workplaces

You may already be one of the millions of Americans who telecommute. If so, you know how significantly telecommuting changes your life. Although you may still be employed by a company, you're empowered to create your own work environment and develop your own work habits. This opportunity can be challenging, but the rewards are well worth the extra initial effort required to get your bearings and develop good telecommuting skills.

The benefit of telecommuting to companies is also significant. Studies have shown that worker productivity increases if management puts effective telecommuting practices into place. Telecommuting has become such a mainstream and important effort that even the State of California's transportation department, CalTrans, is researching ways to implement telecommuting practices in California companies, in the belief that reducing the number of cars on the road will also reduce air pollution. Recently, the idea of a paperless office has engaged the imaginations of companies everywhere. According to *Wired* magazine, however, the excitement about the paperless office is over; now companies are on to the idea of an *officeless* office.

Internet Programming

Internet software is no more difficult to build than traditional software is, and anyone who has computer programming experience can build these programs. We've watched Internet programming evolve from laboratory experiment to corporate technology to its current Web-oriented phase. Developments in Internet programming technology are sure to become some of the most important keys to the future of the Internet and to the world that the Net helps create. Many companies have products that make Internet programming simple and fun. Macromedia's Backstage product, for example, helps you create powerful Web-based database applications. Check out the following URL for more information:

```
http://www.macromedia.com/
```

Some other Internet programming technologies, such as Java and ActiveX, have made network-application development a reality for almost any programmer and removed such work from the arcane world of the UNIX gurus. For more information about ActiveX, you can visit the Microsoft home page at the following URL or find more information on the science.org Web site:

```
http://www.microsoft.com/
```

Anyone setting up an Internet site needs to become familiar with Java and find out more about some of the exciting standards that are going to change how software communicates. For more information on Java, point your Web browser to the following address:

```
http://java.sun.com/
```

Chapter 14

Ten Internet Services Your Internet Site Can't Live Without

*T*his book covers many details about getting your site online, setting up the software to provide services, marketing your site after you're online, and more. Now is our chance to tell you about some of the services on the Internet that we think you're going to love using.

Link Exchange

You've seen banner ads gracing thousands of Web pages. The cost of some of those ads can be astronomical. But what if you could place your banner ad on tens of thousands of Web pages for free? Well, you can do that, through Link Exchange, which is one of the most valuable services on the Internet because the service is a barter arrangement. You agree to place on your page banner ads that the Link Exchange provides, and for every two times someone views the Web page on which you place the ad, your banner ad appears on the Web page of another Link Exchange participant.

The great thing about the way the service works is that the more people who visit your page, the more your ad appears on other people's Web pages. The thing can really snowball. By using Link Exchange, you can easily keep track of how many people visit your pages, how many people click your banner ad to visit your page, and how many times your banner appears on other Web pages. Using Link Exchange is fun and costs you nothing.

Link Exchange gives you a special ID, which tells Link Exchange when someone loads a banner from your page. Apply for this ID at the following URL:

```
http://www.linkexchange.com/
```

Commonwealth Network

The idea of bartering banner ads, as you do in Link Exchange, is useful and interesting but does not generate any income. Commonwealth Network, on the other hand, actually pays you for running banner ads. Check out the Commonwealth Network's Web site at the following URL:

```
http://commonwealth.riddler.com/
```

Add to your Web page the HTML code you get from Commonwealth to load a new banner ad from Commonwealth Network, and each time someone visits your page Commonwealth records the visit. You get paid each time a unique host visits your page within a 24-hour period. (In other words, if the same host visits five times in a single day, you get paid for one visit; if the same host visits once each day for a week, you get paid for seven visits.)

For each 20,000 paid hits to your Web page, you earn about $150. On high-volume sites, you can earn up to $20,000 a month, and even on lower-volume sites, you sometimes can pay your monthly Internet fee with the money you earn.

The company that runs the Commonwealth Network, Interactive Imaginations, pays royalties monthly. Make sure you read all the rules before you sign up.

Because of large demand, the Commonwealth Network sometimes closes its membership application. If you're excited about the possibility of having your Web site make money and don't want to wait, consider the Internet Banner Network (at `http://www.banner-net.com/`) This network pays only a third of what Commonwealth pays but is another option.

Webrings Keep Visitors Coming Back

If cyberspace is truly an online community, it could use some community planning. That's exactly what an online organization called Webring is attempting to do: bring organization to some of the content on the World

Wide Web. If you use this new organizational structure for Web pages, your site can become part of an Internet community instead of just one more page in someone's directory.

Webring is a ring of Internet sites and Web pages that have a common theme or similar content. If you click a Next or Previous link in one Web page in the ring, you travel to a different page. If you click long enough, you return to the page from which you started.

Instead of managing the links in a ring manually, Webring manages a database of rings on the Webring site at `webring.org`. That way, if someone leaves or joins the ring, no one must change the HTML code on any Web pages. The ring and all associated changes are completely managed by Webring.

No limits exist to the size or number of rings you can form in Webring. You can create your own ring or join an existing ring. Hundreds of rings, on just about any topic that you can imagine, await you.

Visit the Webring site at the following URL:

```
http://www.webring.org
```

Like many services on the Internet, Webring is a free service, supported through sponsorships.

The Amazon.com Associates Program

Wanna buy a book? Amazon.com is a huge online bookstore, offering more than a million titles available for purchase online. Amazon.com maintains an excellent site that offers descriptions of each book, plus some reviews and even interviews with the authors. What makes the company stand out in our minds isn't so much the fact that it has a successful online bookstore as the fact that it has an interesting business model — one that you can take advantage of.

Just about everyone has a favorite book. Why not try selling that book from your Web page? Amazon.com makes this task simple. Instead of setting up everything that you need to become an online bookstore yourself, you can become an Amazon.com associate. For every book that you sell through your Web page, you're paid a referral fee. With a catalog of more than a million titles at your disposal, however, you can do more than just recommend your favorite book; you can also promote books that support your industry or special-interest organization. That way, you provide an excellent service to people who visit your Internet site.

To become an Amazon.com associate, fill out the application form at the following URL:

```
http://www.amazon.com/exec/obidos/subst/assoc-
application.html
```

You begin earning referral fees for sales that you generate through your links. Every week, you get an update that tells you what links people clicked, how many people clicked links, how many books were sold through your site, and (the best part) how much money you earned.

VeriFone Moves Money

Three distinct parties are involved in the Internet sales transaction of the future: the merchant, the customer, and the acquirer/processor. The *merchant* is anyone who has an Internet application, such as a Web page, with a catalog of goods or services to sell. The *customer,* who wants to buy something from the vendor's catalog of goods or services, either enters information in a Web form or uses a special electronic wallet. Where else would you keep electronic money other than in an electronic wallet? Then a bank or other processor of credit-card information (known as an *acquirer* or *processor*) processes the transaction. The acquirer/processor with which the vendor has a merchant account debits the credit card and pays the vendor.

We present this scenario so that you can better understand the products that VeriFone offers for completing the entire electronic purchase transaction. This transaction involves the following three products:

- ✔ **vGate.** Banks or providers of merchant credit-card processing use this software.

- ✔ **vPOS.** Internet merchants use this point-of-sale software for selling their products online.

- ✔ **vWallet.** A customer who wants to purchase something online can use this software. The vWallet software can process the transaction by using a variety of methods, including credit cards and smart cards.

For those who are setting up their own Internet site, the vPOS software is important. Products such as Microsoft's Merchant Server and Oracle's Project Apollo incorporate the vPOS software today, and some version of vPOS is likely to end up on just about every Internet site in the world at some point.

If you're getting into the online sales business, you should know that conventional businesses pay a smaller discount fee on credit-card transactions — around 1.65 percent less than online businesses. Unfortunately for the online businesses, most acquirer/processors consider them to be high-risk, and make them pay fees of between 5 percent and 6 percent.

Extra! Extra! Read All about It!

According to Individual, Inc., the company that runs NewsPage, you have two excellent ways to create a high-traffic Web site. One way is to provide highly relevant, useful information to your Web site's visitors; the other way is to keep updating your information frequently so that people want to visit your site again. NewsPage gives you a hand both in providing the content and keeping it updated automatically. Nothing's better than a Web page that updates itself every day with the latest pertinent information.

To find out how you can become part of NewsPage, point your Web browser to the following URL:

```
http://www.newspage.com/
```

Some people say that no news is good news, but that's not true in the reporting business. Adding news to your page increases the number of people who visit your page on a regular basis. Adding such news is also an excellent way to provide meaningful content with a minimal amount of effort.

Keeping Track of Your Guests

So you're not a programmer, and you think that the letters *CGI* mean "Can't get interested"? You can offer visitors to your Web page all sorts of services that require no CGI (Common Gateway Interface) programming whatsoever. One of the features that many people like to add to their Web pages is a guestbook for people to sign.

Think of a guestbook as being something like an answering machine. If people call you on the phone and no person (or machine) is home to answer, or if you don't subscribe to Caller ID service, you'll never know who called. The same is true of your Web page. Sure, your Web server can give you the IP address of everyone who visits your home page, but having that information is not the same as knowing exactly who was there.

You can add this nice implementation of a programming-free guestbook to your Web page. For instructions on using the guestbook on the GuestPAD Web site, go to the following address:

```
http://www.GuestPAD.com/
```

Testing Your Web Pages

Few things are more laborious and time-consuming than maintaining Web pages. If you have many Web pages, you can spend more time maintaining the pages than you do creating new, interesting content. We found a solution to this problem: Doctor HTML. You can use the program at the Doctor HTML site to test your Web page automatically. It not only checks for errors in your HTML code, but can also spell check and run link verification tests.

You can access Doctor HTML at the following URL:

```
http://www2.imagiware.com/RxHTML/
```

Doctor HTML performs all available tests by default. If you don't want the Doctor's entire bagful of tests, select only the tests you want it to perform. While choosing which tests you want the Doctor to perform, you can choose also the amount of detail you want Doctor HTML to display in its final report.

Doctor HTML can also test your entire Web site. This test is a fee-based service that first maps your site and then runs tests on each page of the site. Contact the folks at Imagiware, Inc., for more information about this pay service.

Beyond the Simple Counter

PAGECOUNT is a service that Web International offers. If you don't mind having a banner ad on your page, you can receive free counter and Web-statistics services from the company. Most counters merely count the number of people who visit your page. This service gives you all the great statistics you'd expect from a full-blown Web-statistics package. True, many Web-statistics packages are available. In using those statistics packages, however, you must make sure that your logs are up to date, remember to run the statistics program regularly, and then wait while the program chugs through the numbers. You don't need to do any of these things if you use PAGECOUNT.

The banner that appears on your page displays the count of accesses. By the way, you can start the count at any number you want (to avoid embarrassment if you're just starting out). Changing the start number doesn't affect your statistics; PAGECOUNT still keeps an accurate count of the true total.

To start using this service, access the PAGECOUNT home page at the following address:

```
http://www.pagecount.com/
```

NetDelivery Service

Electronic online delivery is quickly becoming one of the most exciting businesses on the Internet. By using the publish-and-subscribe model, companies have started offering many types of content delivery on the Internet.

One of the services that we find particularly interesting is NetDelivery. This Colorado-based (actually, Internet-based) Internet company offers a unique service, both to Internet site operators who need to deliver products or information over the Internet and to NetDelivery's customers (who are called *members*).

You can find the NetDelivery Web site at the following address:

```
http://www.netdelivery.com/
```

This service is perfect for you if your Internet site provides content, merchandise, or information services. Your clients don't need to come to your site to fetch their data; you can deliver the information right to their desktops daily, weekly, or monthly by using the NetDelivery service.

NetDelivery is a young company, and we expect it to eventually have a lot of competition on the Internet. The field of online delivery offers a great deal of opportunity. You may even consider providing this sort of service yourself.

Chapter 15

Ten Technology Add-ons
for Your Site

- -

- -

*M*ost Internet sites provide the same old set of server software as part of their Internet presence. You get the Web server, the e-mail server, the FTP server, the list server, and the news server — and then what? After all, you can't just paint your Internet site a different color and give the site a red tile roof to make it look distinctive. The services you offer are what make your site stand out from all the rest.

But not all services you offer are for the sake of visitors to your site. Remember that your Internet site also provides Internet access and services for others in your organization. The first technology add-on that we describe in this chapter, for example, enables people to provide their own services right from their desktops.

The Internet Utopia

Netopia Virtual Office, a Farallon product, is one of the new ways to communicate with people on the Internet or on your local intranet. All you need is a Web browser. In addition to collaboration capabilities, the product enables you to create your own World Wide Web address where you can leave files for others to pick up and pick up files others have left for you. The virtual office metaphor even extends to placing the files in your in basket and out basket.

Find more about Netopia software at the following URL:

```
http://www.netopia.com/
```

And what office doesn't have a conference room? The Internet enables you to conference with many people across the world. The Netopia software works with Microsoft NetMeeting to provide such services as a shared whiteboard (much like the one you scribble on in your office, except it's electronic and on the computer), application sharing, and Internet telephony. With these features and the inherent power of Netopia's screen sharing, messaging, and simple file sharing, you could hardly ask for a more powerful office tool.

Using the Voice Chat feature is simple, but you must have a compatible sound card and microphone. (We find that using a high-quality microphone helps the quality of the conversation.)

To have two-way, telephonelike conversations, you need a special full-duplex sound card. *Full-duplex* communications enable people at both ends of the conversation to speak and listen at the same time (as they can on a telephone).

A quieter type of chat — text chat — is available. This option enables two people to communicate by typing text. You enter the text and then transmit it to the other party every time you press the Enter key or click the Send button. After your text appears on-screen, your name appears before the text.

Digital Camera

A picture may be worth a thousand words, but today, pictures are measured in kilobytes. Almost all the major camera manufacturers are coming out with digital cameras. Depending on how much you want to spend, you can get digital pictures that rival the finest film. Whether you have a high budget or a low one, you can find a digital camera that captures images without the hassles of film and development (and, ultimately, scan the developed print into your computer).

Look for a camera that comes with a motorized zoom feature, automatic focus, a built-in flash, and a PC-card memory-expansion slot. If you expect to take a significant number of pictures, you can purchase memory-expansion modules to increase the camera's memory capacity.

Flatbed Scanner

Scanners have been around for years and now come in all shapes and sizes. Little photo scanners can scan 4×6-inch color photographs; paperport scanners take up little room on your desk and can quickly scan black-and-white documents. The flatbed scanner, however, is still the most versatile and useful of all the scanner types.

Most flatbed scanners can scan larger document sizes (11×14 inches) than can other scanners and have higher scanning resolutions. The other advantage of flatbed scanners is that, if you're going to do a great deal of scanning, you can purchase automatic sheet feeders for the devices. This addition can make scanning multiple-page documents a snap.

Stereo Mixer and Microphone

Sound is becoming a common technology on the Internet. Simple text and graphics are being replaced by an audio-media type that is just as important as visual media (as radio has shown us). People now use more than one technology to present sound over networks. Many people still use historical means of providing sound by capturing sounds in a sound file and then publishing the file (the same way that they publish any other file type) for others to download and hear.

The quality of the sound recording is directly proportional to the resulting file size: The better the quality of the recording, the larger the file's size. Users frown on large file sizes because of their long download times, however, so few people consider sound quality to be important.

Then someone introduced a second technology into the sound publishing arena: *MIDI.* MIDI's special files do not really contain sound. Instead, MIDI is a special control protocol that musical instruments use to record and play back sound. Most sound cards today have the capability to record and play back MIDI sounds. The advantage of this technology is that MIDI files tend to be very small. Not only did MIDI background music across the Internet become possible, but MIDI brought the first really useful sounds to the Internet. But MIDI does have one huge limitation: It limits you to sounds that your sound card can generate. Therefore, you may hear not the sounds you record but a reasonable facsimile. You also can't hear sounds (such as voices) that a MIDI-compatible instrument can't create.

An even newer technology than MIDI now enables you to hear sound files that previously were too large to reasonably download and play. This technology, available for both audio and video, is called *streaming*. A file of any type that you stream across the network "plays" (or processes) while the file continues to download. So instead of waiting for an entire file to download and write to a file on your machine before you can listen to its sounds, you can begin listening nearly immediately, as the data transfers from the source to your computer.

Purchasing a higher-quality microphone is a good investment if you're providing audio content from your site. In the same way that professionally produced graphics give your site a quality look and feel, professional-sounding audio also leaves a good impression of your organization. Upgrading your microphone is a small price to pay for quality. Check out the offerings at http://www.surplusdirect.com for cheap computer audio gear.

An additional piece of equipment that can add to the quality of your sound recording is a mixer. A *mixer* is a piece of sound equipment that recording studios and live performers use to better control the sound coming from musical instruments and microphones. Mixers can have many features. The basic mixer has a place to plug in one or more microphones or musical instruments and has some sort of output plug. At a minimum, you should look for a mixer with two microphone inputs and a stereo output.

You can use mixers with added features to enhance the quality of sounds you send to your sound card. A basic mixer, for instance, may also include an equalizer. This feature enables you to boost certain frequencies while reducing the signal of other, less desirable frequencies. Such an inexpensive mixer should also feature fader controls that enable you to fade from one channel into the next. This control is useful for disc-jockey-type use of the mixer.

Internet Broadcasting

Internet audio broadcasting is becoming an important new wave in entertainment. With the equipment that we recommend in the preceding section and additional music inputs, such as a CD player, you can create your own Internet audio-broadcasting channel.

No laws currently govern the use of the Internet as a broadcast medium. Our hope is that people use this powerful capability to broadcast globally for little or no money. Don't let the big companies that are already in the conventional broadcast markets become the companies that end up controlling this medium as well. Make certain, however, that you comply with any licensing requirements before you embark on an Internet-broadcasting career.

Fax Servers

Fax has become a household word. Almost every business now has a fax machine; most modems are now fax/modems; and many people have fax machines at home, in their cars, and built into their cellular phones. Networks and the Internet have taken fax technology, which was already a great idea, and made it even better.

FaxBack, Inc., a spinoff of Intel, offers network fax solutions. You can find the company's Web page at the following URL:

```
http://www.faxback.com/
```

Some people believe that Internet document delivery may one day do away with the need for fax machines. This belief may or may not be accurate. In any event, the fax machine isn't going away soon — fax-machine use still far outweighs personal-computer use. The interesting aspect of fax server technology is that it now enables people who have no computer to view the contents of the World Wide Web. Fax-on-demand systems, which are becoming popular for corporate delivery of public information, can also deliver fax Web pages on demand. You use a touch-tone phone to select the Web page you want, and the page comes directly to your fax machine.

Fax technology has had one major drawback, in that it's long been tied to the conventional phone system. Every fax you send gets billed at the normal phone charge. International business phone charges have decreased, because information has been condensed into a fax that's often transmitted in less than a minute's time. Still, sending a fax requires making an international long-distance phone call.

Systems called *Internet fax servers* route faxes across the Internet, rather than through the public phone system. Any computer you connect to the Internet can send a fax anywhere in the world through a fax server. The fax server in the remote location can deliver the fax via the network or dial a local phone number and then deliver the fax to a conventional fax machine.

Network delivery of fax documents enables a wide range of add-on capabilities, such as these:

  ✔ Fax mailboxes
  ✔ Storing and forwarding of fax documents
  ✔ Document-type conversion
  ✔ Encrypted (secure) delivery
  ✔ Registered delivery and document tracking

The savings in fax delivery costs alone are enough to make this Internet-site technology one of the most useful imaginable.

Network Modems

If your company has an investment in several computers that connect on a network, you can probably find a way to improve the cost-effectiveness of your computer system. Several of the computers on the network, for example, probably have modems, either internally or via serial attachments to external modems.

But your network can easily support a single modem that you connect not to a computer, but to the network itself. With such a setup, any computer on the network can access the modem, which itself connects to a single phone line.

We tested the Shiva NetModem E and found the device to be an effective network tool — one that we recommend to anyone who has a small network and light modem usage. You don't need to purchase a modem for every computer on the network, and you realize annual savings from running a single phone line. (You can buy two network computers for that amount of money.) You not only save money by going this route, but also overcome future limitations and costs.

Bear in mind, however, that the number of modems required in a pool depends on the average traffic generated by all computers accessing the modems. This in turn depends on the nature of the modem usage. If the usage is high, you may not save much with the networked solution, given how cheap modems are today. If you have an office PBX, it costs you little to use extension lines instead of direct external lines. The other factor to consider is the required speed. The highest speed that this modem can achieve is 28.8 Kbps. Modems today can do 33.3 Kbps and 56 Kbps pretty cheaply.

For more information, contact Shiva at the following URL:

```
http://www.shiva.com/
```

Citrix WinServer

Applications that take advantage of skinny clients are more efficient and easier to maintain than those that require fat clients.

A program called Citrix WinServer (or WinFrame Server), based on Windows NT, enables you to run almost any Windows program within a skinny client. Imagine running a large accounting program — not simply a Web front end for an accounting program, but the actual accounting program — from within a Web browser. WinServer enables you to provide client/server capabilities and run your old legacy software remotely through a Web browser.

If you need to run applications from your Web browser, Internet Explorer automatically loads the appropriate ActiveX control; Netscape Navigator requires you to load and install the Citrix plug-in to do so.

The exciting part is that you don't need to wait for your application to load across the network before you run the application. By using the Citrix ICA technology, you transfer only keyboard commands, mouse movements, and display data across the network. In other words, you see the display information as the server sends it, and you can respond to the data by using your own keyboard and mouse.

By using remote node functionality (the capability to connect to a remote server), based on the Windows NT Remote Access Server system, WinFrame Server delivers access to all network applications and network resources across a dial-up connection as though the remote node were directly connected to the network. You can set up applications to run remotely or locally on your machine. You can quickly switch between remote and local applications by using a hot key.

The WinFrame Server supports remote access from thousands of remote clients. This capability enables your company to set up a powerful telecommuting system, as well as to support traveling executives, salespeople, and support people.

For more information, contact the Citrix home page at the following URL:

```
http://www.citrix.com/
```

PointCast I-Server

PointCast was one of the first (and best) Internet information services. The PointCast service uses a publish-and-subscribe model, making PointCast an extremely useful news service. By using publish-and-subscribe, you no longer need to go surfing around looking for information. Instead, you can download news, weather information (with maps), several magazines, market information, and more right to your desktop. Even if you aren't running the PointCast client application, you can use the PointCast screen saver, which continually displays updated news. The PointCast I-Server is an excellent add-on to your Internet site.

Setting up and maintaining I-Server is easy. The server works closely with the Windows NT Internet Information Server. One of the setup procedures configures your Internet Information Web server to use two of the special administrative I-Server directories.

For more information about the PointCast I-Server, go to the following Web site:

```
http://www.pointcast.com/
```

Macromedia Flash

Macromedia Flash enables you to create powerful interactive Shockwave multimedia content for your Web site. Shockwave is the Macromedia player that enables viewers to view content in a Web page. Shockwave content includes animations, graphics, and special interactive objects that do your bidding whenever someone clicks those objects in a Web page.

You may think that something this fancy in your Web page may take a long time to load over a slow modem connection, but it doesn't. By using special vector technology that keeps your files small, and because your files stream over the Internet, your animations begin playing immediately. And the Shockwave Flash client is free to anyone who wants to view the Flash content in your Web pages.

For more information, contact the Macromedia home page at the following URL:

```
http://www.macromedia.com/
```

Chapter 16

Ten Easy Ways to Enhance Your Site

*T*he Common Gateway Interface *(CGI)* is often seen as a terrifying and mysterious thing, one that many site builders prefer not to deal with at all, but it's really quite simple. CGI is a way that information is passed from your site to a program that processes that information. Fortunately, you don't have to be a programmer to use it on your site. Other people have already written tons of programs you can just plug in and run, making your site better than it would be without them.

Usually, adding a CGI program to your site means including a form on your Web site (see Chapter 6 for how to make forms) and adding a single line at the beginning of the HTML code for the form that tells the form where the program is so the information can be sent to it. You may also need to fill in a few variables in the program code itself, but don't let that scare you. Each program comes with instructions, either as a separate text file or as notes within the program code (called *comments*). Program code is nothing but a document, and all you need to do is load the code into any text editor (such as Windows Notepad) and type what the program's notes tell you to. Usually, that's something straightforward such as the URL of your site or the directory containing the program (which is almost invariably called *cgi-bin*).

You won't need to concern yourself with the program structure itself unless you want to. If you have any questions about what to do, you can usually find the answers from your ISP. Or you can e-mail the program's author, whose address should be either in the instructions or at the top of the program code.

We've included as many of these programs as possible on the *Setting Up An Internet Site For Dummies* CD-ROM.

Search Me

Darryl Burgdorf's WebSearch program is a good example of the ease with which Web sites can be enhanced. WebSearch enables the people who visit your site to type in keywords and sit back while the program reads through all the pages on your site to see which ones contain those terms. WebSearch is a modified version of Matt Wright's famous Simple Search. It takes about five to fifteen minutes to get a fully-functional search engine running on your site, complete with scoring that indicates how likely a given HTML page will be the one you're looking for. Installing WebSearch is a simple process:

1. **Fill in the name of the directory where you're going to put the WebSearch file, the name of the directory your HTML files are in, and the URL of your site.**

   If you don't know this information, ask your ISP.

2. **Save the file.**

   Make sure that you save CGI files in plain-text ASCII format. If you're using a simple text editor such as Notepad, the CGI files will be automatically saved as plain-text ASCII. If you're using a word processor, you need to save the CGI files using a Save As option similar to one of the following: text only, ASCII, txt, or some combination such as ASCII (DOS) Text.

3. **Transfer the WebSearch file to your site.**

   Copy the file to the directory if you're running a local site, or FTP the file if you're running a remote site.

4. **Copy the HTML code from WebSearch into your Web page.**

5. **In the first line of the HTML code, after** `"ACTION="`**, add the URL where the WebSearch file resides.**

6. **Transfer the new Web page to your site.**

That's it. Six simple steps and you have a search engine that adds to your site's usefulness and appeal. If you want to see WebSearch in action, you can take a look at it on the LinkFinder site at `http://www.linkfinder.com/` — just click the Search button on the upper-left side of the screen and you'll be off and running (see Figure 16-1).

You can add several different search engines. Table 16-1 shows where you can find them.

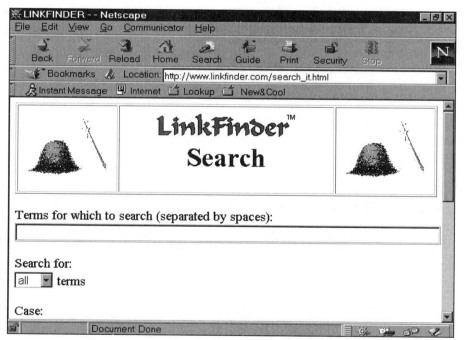

Figure 16-1:
The
WebSearch
page at
LinkFinder.

Table 16-1	Search Engines
Program	*Web Address*
ICE	`http://www.informatik.th-darmstadt.de/mitarbusers/~neuss/ice/`
Intermediate Search	`http://www.xav.com/scripts/search/index.html`
Selena's Keyword Search Script	`http://www.extropia.com/Scripts/keyword_search.html`
Simple Search	`http://www.worldwidemart.com/scripts/search.shtml`
Site Search	`http://www.agl.uh.edu/~saljxk/site_Search/`
SWAT	`http://www.chriscrawler.com/swat/Overview.html`
WebSearch	`http://awsd.com/scripts/websearch/index.shtml`
Xavatoria Indexed Search	`http://www.xav.com/scripts/xavatoria/index.html`
Zone Coaster Search	`http://www.zonecoaster.com/shop/?Enter`

Just Leave a Message

In Chapter 7, we cover how to add a news server to your site. If you read that chapter, you'll recall that we said there was an easier way to add messaging capabilities to your site. Message boards are that way. Message boards are similar to newsgroups, but without the hassle of setting up and maintaining your own news server. They allow your users to leave messages, read the messages others have left, and respond to them. The more sophisticated message boards include message threading, which means that they can follow a chain of responses to one message regardless of the order in which they were posted. Some message boards also enable users to sort messages by date, subject, or author, and even to search the messages for keywords. Table 16-2 points the way.

Table 16-2	Message Boards
Program	*Web Address*
Dream Catchers Message Board	http://dreamcatchersweb.com/scripts/messageboard.html
Message Bulletin	http://www.stepweb.com/messagebulletin.shtml

Can We Talk?

Chat rooms allow several users at a time to communicate with one another. If you've ever been on one of the major online services such as CompuServe, you've probably been in a chat room at some point. Typically, the program shows the names of the people who are present at any given time. When one of these people types on his or her keyboard, the words show up in a common screen where they can be seen and responded to by all the participants. Chat rooms are a great way to hold a long-distance meeting or to conduct distance-learning classrooms. Table 16-3 lists some chat programs.

Table 16-3	Chat Programs
Program	*Web Address*
Chat	http://www.freescripts.com/html/chat_main.shtml
Chat Group!	http://www.covesoft.net/script.htm
Zone Coaster Chat	http://www.zonecoaster.com/shop/?Enter

Too Much Time on Your Hands

We're a world obsessed with time. We have clocks in nearly every room, calendars on every desk and in every purse and briefcase, and it's a rare person who doesn't wear a watch. Even the clocks on our car dashboards are actually functional these days. So it's not too surprising that you can put clocks and other time-oriented add-ons on your Web pages. In addition to simple date and time programs, countdown timers are available. (Many people, for instance, have put countdowns to the year 2000 on their sites.) You can also add a variety of calendars to your site. Table 16-4 can save you time in finding these add-ons.

Table 16-4	Clocks, Timers, and Calendars
Program	**Web Address**
calendar.pl	http://kuoi.asui.uidaho.edu/~collinf/calendar/index.html
Countdown	http://www.worldwidemart.com/scripts/countdown.shtml
Date Stamp	http://www.freecode.com/cgi-bin/viewproduct.pl?4213
Event Calendar!	http://www.covesoft.net/script.htm
Quantum Date and Quantum Time	http://www.q-west.com/scripts/
Selena's Date and Time Scripts	http://www.extropia.com/Scripts/date.html
Text Clock	http://www.worldwidemart.com/scripts/textclock.shtml

A-One an' A-Two

How many people have visited your site? Access counters keep track for you and let you proudly display the total for anyone who wants to see. These counters are probably the most popular single add-on. You see them all over the place. Wherever you see a message such as "You are the 32nd visitor to this popular site," you're encountering an access counter.

You can find lots of variations on the simple access counter. Some of them are plain text; others use fancy graphics. Some even use roman numerals instead of the usual arabic numerals. You can count on the data in Table 16-5 to help.

Table 16-5	Access Counters
Program	**Web Address**
AXS Access Counter	http://www.xav.com/scripts/axs/index.html
DBasics Statistical Counter	http://www.getscript.com/counter/
Digee Counter	http://www.pica.army.mil/orgs/fsac/eod/examples/counter.cgi
Roman Numeral Text Counter	http://www.xav.com/scripts/roman/index.html

Program	Web Address
Simple Counter	http://dreamcatchersweb.com/ scripts/simplecounter.html
Text Counter	http://www.worldwidemart.com/ scripts/textcounter.shtml
Text Hit Counter	http://www.halcyon.com/sanford/ cgi/text_counter/

 If you're going to use a graphical access counter, some of them require you to supply the images of the numbers. Even the ones that come with images supplied may not meet your graphical tastes. You can find a whole bunch of numerical graphics at Digit Mania (http://www.digitmania.holowww.com/) — everything from odometer style to that scoreboard look.

Disorganize Your Site

One of the biggest problems with any Web site is keeping it fresh and new — which is what keeps people coming back again and again. Randomizing different aspects of your site is a good way to keep your visitors from getting bored with it. There are programs for generating random quotes, random images, and random hypertext links. Table 16-6, even though it isn't random, takes you to some of these programs.

Table 16-6	Randomizers
Program	Web Address
jarandom.pl	http://www.aquapal.co.uk/perl/ jarandom.html
Random Image Displayer	http://www.worldwidemart.com/ scripts/image.shtml
Random Link Generator	http://www.worldwidemart.com/ scripts/rand_link.shtml
Random Page	http://www.tardis.ed.ac.uk/~angus/ Computing/Programming/Perl/Samples/ PerlCGIRandom.html
Random Quote	http://www.freescripts.com/html/ quote_main.shtml

(continued)

Table 16-6 *(continued)*

Program	Web Address
Random Text	`http://www.worldwidemart.com/` `scripts/rand_text.shtml`
Rotating Link	`http://dreamcatchersweb.com/scripts/`
URLoRAMA	`http://www.middlebury.edu/~otisg/` `Scripts/URLoRAMA.shtml`

Minding the Store

If you're running an online store, you have special needs. You have to have a lot more going for you than just a good-looking site or lots of good links. You need to be able to do business, and that means selling things. Chapter 11 covers the methods of setting up secure online commerce, but you still need to let your customers see and buy your merchandise. If you're not set up with an existing online mall, you have two basic options: pay a fortune for custom database development or use a shopping cart program.

Shopping carts enable your customers to browse through your offerings, choosing what they want. As the name implies, these programs use the metaphor of a person walking through a store, adding some items to their cart, possibly changing their minds at times and putting something back "on the shelf," and then taking their purchases to the checkout counter to pay for them.

You may also want to use a credit-card verifier program. This type of program does not actually check to see whether the person making the order has available credit, nor do they see whether the card is stolen. They simply check to see whether the credit-card number that was entered follows the pattern the credit-card companies have established (you didn't know they did that, didja?). Some shopping carts include a credit-card verifier program.

If you have established online credit-card processing, you probably won't need a credit-card verifier program. However, if you're running on a shoe-string and punching in orders by hand every day as you receive the information from your site, a credit-card verifier program can save you a lot of time. Table 16-7 shows you where to shop for them.

Table 16-7	Online Commerce Programs
Program	**Web Address**
Credit Card Verifier	http://www.worldwidemart.com/scripts/ccver.shtml
CyberCart	http://www.lobo.net/~rtweb/
Database Shopping Cart!	http://www.covesoft.net/script.htm
PerlShop	http://www.arpanet.com/perlshop/

Form Processing

When someone fills out a form on your site, you can do two things with the data from it. You can have a program process the data in some way, or you can have the information sent to you via e-mail. The e-mail option is a fairly simple matter if the person filling out the form is using a browser that supports mailto links, but not all browsers do. Fortunately, some programs will transform the form data into an e-mail message and send it to you, independently of the browser's capabilities. Table 16-8 shows you where to find these form mail processors.

Table 16-8	Form Mail Processors
Program	**Web Address**
Anonymous Web Form Mailer	http://www.halcyon.com/sanford/cgi/web2mail/
Form Mail	http://www.worldwidemart.com/scripts/formmail.shtml
Form-Processor	http://www.freescripts.com/html/form_main.shtml
Form Return	http://dreamcatchersweb.com/scripts/formreturn.html

Audience Participation

With most sites, the audience is a passive participant in a highly structured and relatively static situation. We already talked about randomizing events as a way of keeping a site on its toes, but that still leaves the visitors to your site in the position of waiting to see what happens. You can give visitors some degree of control over what they see on your site in several different ways. You can allow them to add links to your pages, thus adding the work of many hands to your Web connections. You can have guestbooks (one of the most popular things on the Web), which allow visitors to leave messages for you that other visitors can also read. And there's the ever popular graffiti wall, where anyone can "scribble" on your Web page. Table 16-9 shows links to these programs.

Table 16-9	User Participation Programs
Program	*Web Address*
Addlink	http://www.zonecoaster.com/shop/?Enter
Book of Guests	http://dreamcatchersweb.com/scripts/bookofguests.html
Dream Catchers Post It!	http://dreamcatchersweb.com/scripts/postit.html
Free Linkage	http://dreamcatchersweb.com/scripts/
GuestPost	http://www.stepweb.com/guestpost1.shtml
Trivia Quiz Guestbook	http://kuoi.asui.uidaho.edu/~collinf/trivia/index.html
Zone Coaster Guestbook	http://www.zonecoaster.com/shop/?Enter

You're giving up control of your site's content when you put these programs into play. With link adders, if someone wants to put in a link to a site you find objectionable, they can. With graffiti walls and guestbooks, anyone can leave obscene messages or hate mail for the world to see. Still, most people don't do that and guestbooks are one of the most popular add-ons on the Internet. Just to protect yourself, though, make sure that you post a message to the effect that you have no control over what other people say or do in these public access places and that visitors follow links or read messages at their own risk.

It's a Banner Day

Advertising banner rotators are close relatives of random-image generators, but they have a different purpose entirely. While a simple random image is designed to do nothing more than alleviate boredom, advertising banners need to be rotated so that ads from several different clients can be shown to different site visitors. Advertising banners are usually small images, and they're nearly always located at the top of a Web page. Unlike plain images, they have hypertext links associated with them so that anyone looking at the advertisement can just click on the image and go directly to the home page of the advertiser. Table 16-10 takes you to the home pages for some banner programs.

Table 16-10	Banner Advertising Programs
Program	*Web Address*
Advertise	`http://kuoi.asui.uidaho.edu/ ~collinf/advertise/`
BanEx	`http://www.stepweb.com/ bannerex.shtml`
BannerWheel	`http://www.freescripts.com/html/ bannerwheel_main.shtml`
Random Banner Generation!	`http://www.covesoft.net/script.htm`

Chapter 17

Ten More Easy Ways to Enhance Your Site

*T*his chapter continues in the grand tradition of Chapter 16. It includes several more CGI programs you can plug into your site to increase its functionality and enjoyability. In addition to CGI, we also suggest some other ways to enhance your site, such as by adding sound.

We've included as many of these programs as possible on the *Setting Up An Internet Site For Dummies* CD-ROM.

My Baby Sent Me a Letter

One of the just plain neatest things any site can have is the capacity to send electronic postcards. In Chapter 12, we show you how to use them to promote your site and include several examples of how other people are using postcards successfully. Electronic postcards work as follows: People come to your site, choose an image and a message (or they may be able to put in their own custom message), and then type in the name and e-mail address of the person they want to send the postcard to. They usually add their own name and e-mail address, too. The postcard generator then sends an e-mail message to the recipient, telling them that they have a postcard waiting at your Web site and giving them the URL and a password (or access code) to claim it.

The recipient then comes to your site, types or pastes in the access code, and gets to see the postcard. Most of these programs will keep the postcard for only a set period of time (a few days or a month), after which the postcard is deleted. Electronic postcards are very popular and have a tremendous advantage for the site builder because they generate double hits — one for the sender and one for the recipient. Table 17-1 will send you to some of these postcard programs.

Table 17-1	Postcard Programs
Program	*Web Address*
Personal Postcards Gold	`http://mypostcards.com/gold/`
Postcard	`http://www.freescripts.com/html/card_main.shtml`
Postcards	`http://kuoi.asui.uidaho.edu/~collinf/postcards/index.html`
Postcards from the Net	`http://www.rcbowen.com/perl/post.html`

Surveys and Voting

Election time? Just want to know what people think about something? Survey and voting programs are your answer to getting their answers — whether you want to conduct a straw poll to compare with real elections or just want to know how people feel about your new background image. Table 17-2 shows you where to get the programs that let the people's voice be heard.

Table 17-2	Survey and Voting Programs
Program	*Web Address*
MultiPoll	`http://www.cgi-world.com/` `multipoll.html`
Poll-It Lite	`http://www.cgi-world.com/pollit.html`
Vote	`http://www.freescripts.com/html/` `vote_main.shtml`
Zone Coaster Survey	`http://www.zonecoaster.com/shop/?Enter`

Databases

Databases have so many possible uses that it would take an entire library of books to just list them all. And databases have become so prevalent that there's practically no part of our lives that isn't involved in some way with retrieving information from them. Department stores already know your address when you buy something because you're in their database. Telephone operators used to flip through phone books but now key directory information requests into their database retrieval systems. And on and on and on. You can use databases on your site, too, for everything from catalogues to phone books. And, as the simple-to-use programs listed here prove, you don't have to spend a fortune or become a programmer specializing in the arcane arts of JDBC, SQL, and all that other alphabetical whatnot. Table 17-3 has the information you need to get your own simple database set up.

Table 17-3	Database Programs
Program	*Web Address*
Database Manager	`http://www.gossamer-threads.com/` `scripts/dbman/`
Internet Phone Book	`http://www.cyberwhiz.com/cgi/` `databases.shtml`
Selena Sol's Database Manager and Search	`http://www.extropia.com/Scripts/` `database_manager.html`
WODA	`http://audrey.fagg.uni-lj.si/~zturk/` `works/wb/`

Fake Autoresponder

We cover e-mail autoresponders in Chapter 8. In case you missed that one, autoresponders are special e-mail programs designed to send a preprogrammed response back to anyone who sends an e-mail message to a particular address. The Fake Autoresponder program does the same thing without you having to bother with all the details of setting one up. You just plug this little wonder into your Web page and tell it what to send to people, and you're finished. You can get the program at `http://www.stepweb.com/fakemail.shtml`.

Password Protection

Password protection is another one of those relatively complex topics we cover in another chapter (in this case, Chapter 9). As with autoresponders, though, you can add programs to your Web site that will do the same thing without all the complexity. Table 17-4 shows some programs that make visitors give their name and a password before they can get into your site.

Table 17-4	Password Programs
Program	**Web Address**
Icheck	`http://www.upstatepress.com/perl/programs/story.cfm?id=9`
Login Pro	`http://netlinkworld.com/snud/cgi-bin/scripts.cgi?loginpro`
Password Authorization	`http://www.cyberwhiz.com/cgi/passwords.shtml`
Protect It	`http://www.cgi-world.com/protect_it.html`

Entertainment

Sometimes it's nice to have some plain old-fashioned fun. Table 17-5 lists three programs you can add to your site so that people can enjoy themselves. The first is the familiar game of checkers, the second is a fortune-telling program, and the last is similar to the game MadLibs.

Table 17-5	Entertainment Programs
Program	*Web Address*
KewlCheckers	http://user.mc.net/~twagner/kewlcheckers.htm
Selena's Fortune Cookie Script	http://selena.mcp.com/Scripts/fortune.html
WebLibs	http://awsd.com/scripts/weblibs/index.shtml

File Upload

You've probably been downloading files from Web sites for as long as you've been on the Web. Did you know that you can upload files to a Web site, too? Both of the major Web browsers support this capability, and the programs in Table 17-6 assist you in setting up a special directory where your users can upload files for everyone to share.

Table 17-6	File Upload Programs
Program	*Web Address*
File Upload!	http://www.terminalp.com/scripts/file_upload.shtml
HTTP File Transfer System	http://www.e.aarhus.ih.dk/~knudris/filetrans/
Upload	http://www.webcom.se/projects/freeware/upload/
Zone Coasters Upload	http://www.zonecoaster.com/shop/?Enter

Caller ID

Caller ID is a handy little program that, just like caller ID on telephone systems, tells you who's "calling" your Web site. It'll snag as much information as it can about your visitors and tell you what browsers they're using and where they were referred from, among other things. You can get it at http://www.tardis.ed.ac.uk/~angus/Computing/Programming/Perl/Samples/PerlCGIInfo.html#CallerID.

Animated GIFs

The easiest way to add animation to your site is with animated GIFs. (See Chapter 5 for information on adding images to your HTML pages.) As far as your Web page is concerned, an animated GIF is just like a regular, static image. There's an important difference, though. An animated GIF is actually a series of images contained in a single file that, when shown in a Web browser, appear one after another, looking as if they're in motion. Animated GIF files are much smaller than traditional animation files, which means faster download time, which means less strain on your server. You can create your own animated GIF file with one of the animation tools discussed in Chapter 18, or you can lay your hands on thousands of free ones that are readily available for download. Some of them are just average, but others are designed by talented professional artists such as Brandi Jasmine. Table 17-7 shows you where to find lots of animated GIF files.

Table 17-7	Animated GIF Sources
Program	*Web Address*
Badger's Animated GIF Gallery	`http://www.vr-mall.com/anigifpd/anigifpd.html`
Brandi Jasmine's Digital Art Gallery	`http://web.idirect.com/~bjasmine/gallery/`
The Wagon Train	`http://dreamartists.com/animated.htm`
Web GraFX-FX	`http://www.webgrafx-fx.com/`
Web Wizard's Animation Station	`http://www.geocities.com/SiliconValley/Park/8100/animfram.htm`
XOOM	`http://xoom.com/xoom/web_clip_empire`

Sound

We've tried to keep the enhancements section limited to things that will work on any Web browser without the need for your site's visitors to use plug-in programs in their browsers. However, if you want to add music or sound effects to your Web page, you're probably best off asking your visitors to use either Crescendo or RealAudio plug-ins. Crescendo is a program that plays MIDI files (a common and popular music file format). RealAudio requires that you have their server installed on your system, but is capable of playing a wide variety of sound files. You can get the details on using either system from their home pages. The Crescendo Web site is located at `http://www.liveupdate.com/crescendo.html`, and you can find RealAudio at `http://www.real.com/publisher/index.html`.

Chapter 18

Ten Tools for Web Development

This chapter presents a selection of tools you'll need or want for developing your Web page. Most of these tools are graphics oriented, but we list a few really good HTML editors, too. You can put together a really useful Web site development toolbox with these programs.

We've included as many of these programs as possible on the *Setting Up An Internet Site For Dummies* CD-ROM.

GIF Animation Tools

If you want to add animated GIFs to your site, you'll want a GIF animation tool. True, you can create animated GIFs manually, but why bother when the little beauties in Table 18-1 will do most of the work for you?

Table 18-1	GIF Animation Programs
Program	**Web Address**
Animagic GIF Animator	`http://rtlsoft.com/animagic/index.html`
GIF Construction Set	`http://www.mindworkshop.com/alchemy/gifcon.html`
Ulead GIF Animator	`http://www.ulead.com/webutilities/`

3-D Font Creation

A program called Font F/X, available at `http://www.dcsifx.com/`, will knock your socks off (unless you're wearing sandals, of course). Font F/X enables you to extrude and manipulate TrueType fonts in three dimensions to create some truly wonderful text designs. Use it for logos, labels, or whatever, but use it somewhere!

Image Managers

Sooner or later, you'll end up with a large collection of images for use on your Web sites. When it comes to managing your images, the three programs in Table 18-2 are some of the most useful, powerful, and friendly you will find. They all have slightly different features, but in general they allow you to manage your images by cataloguing, viewing, changing from one file type to another (for instance, from GIF to JPG), resizing, and just about anything else you can imagine.

Table 18-2	Image Management Programs
Program	**Web Address**
Graphic Workshop	`http://www.mindworkshop.com/alchemy/gww.html`
IrfanView 32	`http://stud1.tuwien.ac.at/~e9227474/`
SuperJPG	`http://www.midnightblue.com/superjpg/`

HTML Editors

When it comes to writing HTML code, any text editor will do the trick, but specialized HTML editors can make things a lot easier on you. They can help you in so many ways, it would take an entire book just to scratch the surface. Want to add an image? Just click the image button and the code is typed for you. Some HTML editors can also color code your HTML, so you can keep straight which parts of a line of code are tags and which are variable names. Try one of the HTML editors in Table 18-3, and you'll probably never touch Notepad again.

Table 18-3	HTML Editing Programs
Program	*Web Address*
CoffeeCup HTML Editor++	http://www.coffeecup.com/products.html
HomeSite	http://www.allaire.com/products/homesite/30/index.cfm
HotDog	http://www.sausage.com/hotdog32.htm

Paint Programs

If you're just going to use other people's images from clip-art collections and the like, you don't need a paint program, which is used to draw bitmapped images, such as GIFs. But if you want to make your own images, or if you need to modify clip art, two of the best tools to use are Paint Shop Pro (http://www.jasc.com/psp.html) and Lview Pro (http://www.lview.com/).

Image Map Creators

Image maps (see Chapter 6) can be coded manually, it's true, but you'll be a candidate for a long rest if you try that approach. With image map creators, however, you just load the image you want to use and then mark the areas you want to use for links. The program asks you where to link that area to — and instant image map! As with the other programs in this chapter, you can find many different ones. If you can't make an image map with either CoffeeCup Image Mapper++ (http://www.coffeecup.com/) or LiveImage (http://www.mediatec.com/), however, it can't be done.

GIF Wizard

One of the biggest problems for any Web designer is the size of GIF images. Fortunately, a solution to this problem exists. It's not a program you keep in your own computer; it's a Web site called GIF Wizard (http:// gifwiz2.gifwizard.com/). GIF Wizard is free for noncommercial users; others pay a fee based on usage. You feed GIF Wizard the URL of an image on your site. Then GIF Wizard fetches a copy of the image, processes the copy in various ways (such as removing unused colors from the palette), and presents you with several samples showing how it would look if you chose various options. You don't have to understand one bit of the process — just choose the image you like best, save it to your hard drive, and replace the old (original) image at your leisure.

POV-Ray

The Persistence of Vision raytracer (POV-Ray for short) is not the easiest program in the world to work with, but you can use it to create some truly stunning images. *Ray tracing* is a specialized type of 3-D graphics that produces images so true to life that they're known as *photorealistic*. The official Web site at http://www.povray.org/ has lots of examples, as well as links to tutorials and guides to plenty of utilities that make working with the raytracer an easier prospect. There are utilities to create flashes of light, trees, books, and all sorts of other items to include in your images.

Dr. Jack's HTMLView

Dr. Jack's HTMLView is a specialized image viewer designed for use by Webmasters. It is different than normal image viewers in several ways. HTMLView recognizes that Web designers often have many different images in different directories, and allows you to load images from many directories at a time instead of just one. HTMLView also has a tile preview feature that lets you see how any image will look if you use it as a background image on a Web page — before you commit to using the image. The tile preview includes a lot of text in dozens of different colors overlaying the background image so you can see which text color would look best with it. You can get a look at HTMLView on their Web site at http://www.drjack.com/ htmlview/.

Hidden 3D

The Hidden 3D program isn't a necessity for Web design, but it's a fascinating toy to play with — and you just might end up with something you'll want to share with your site's visitors. If you've ever seen a picture that appears to be a meaningless jumble of colored dots until you look at it just right, you know what Hidden 3D is all about. The program takes two images, scrambles one and tiles it, and then adds information from a second image that is not apparent. The image that results looks like abstract art. If you focus your eyes just beyond the surface, however, the second image springs out, appearing to hover in the air. You can download a copy from `http://energy.ece.uiuc.edu/CesarPascual/Hidden3D.zip`.

Appendix A

Preparing a Personal Computer for the Internet

· ·

You have two ways to connect your personal computer to the Internet. One way is to use a modem to connect your computer to an Internet access provider through a telephone line. The other way is to use a network card to connect directly to your own private computer network, called a *LAN* (local area network), and then connect your LAN to the Internet. Remember that the Internet is just a very large network of smaller computer networks. If you build your own computer network, you can make your network a part of the Internet so that each computer on your network can communicate with every other computer on the Internet. This process is how the Internet grows. Figure A-1 compares a network connection to the Internet with a modem connection.

Remember, too, that every telephone or ISDN modem connection requires a separate phone line, which isn't free, and you may need to pay usage fees to the phone company for each minute that each of your computers is connected through a telephone line to the Internet. We highly recommend that you build your own computer network instead and connect it to the Internet so that you pay one fixed monthly fee for unlimited Internet access, regardless of the number of computers in use at your site. We understand, however, that not everyone who wants to set up an Internet site has more than one computer or can afford the additional expense associated with connecting a LAN to the Internet. This appendix, therefore, shows you how to prepare a personal computer to connect to the Internet by using either a modem or your own LAN. Chapter 2 shows you how to link computers together to form a LAN and then connect your LAN to the Internet. Chapter 2 also shows you how to connect a single computer to the Internet over a dedicated link so that you can avoid the higher costs associated with connecting an entire LAN to the Internet.

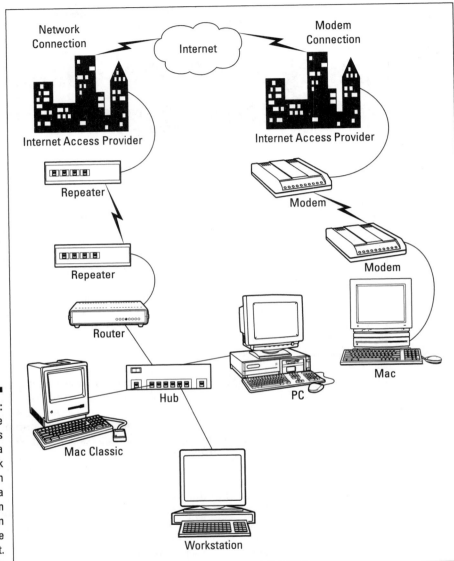

Figure A-1: Study the differences between a network connection and a modem connection to the Internet.

Installing Data-Communications Hardware

For the most part throughout this book, we assume that you know how to install hardware and software on your computer. In the past, hardware installation could prove so difficult and complicated if you used an IBM-compatible PC, that trying to explain how to install hardware would have been almost pointless in a book such as this one. Today, however, installing new hardware can be so simple that nothing's left for us to write about. Therefore, we just present the most critical, if somewhat obvious, points about hardware installation necessary to prepare your personal computer for the Internet.

For your computer to communicate with other computers, your computer must have a way to transmit data to and receive data from other computers. The two most common technologies that enable computer data communications are the *modem,* which is short for *modulator-demodulator,* and the *network adapter.* A modem modulates and demodulates a signal carried by wire or by radio wave so that you can encode, transmit, receive, and decode information without using a purely digital optical or electronic communications network. A network adapter, on the other hand, transmits and receives electrical or optical pulses over a digital computer network. A network adapter doesn't need to modulate or demodulate a carrier signal, so it can operate at much higher speeds and with much greater reliability than a modem.

Installing a modem or a network adapter

Modems come in three types: *internal modems,* which you must plug into an expansion slot inside your computer; *external modems,* which you must plug into one of the communication ports on the outside of your computer; and credit-card-sized *PC card modems* (PC/MCIA), which you usually use with a notebook computer and plug into a PC/MCIA card slot the way that a floppy disk fits into your disk drive.

A fourth kind of modem also exists that's really neat: a *network modem.* Network modems don't plug into your computer at all. Instead, they plug into your computer network and communicate with your computer digitally over the network. Because of special software device drivers provided for use with the network modem, your computer doesn't know the difference between a network modem and a modem that's physically connected to a communications port. Network printers, network fax machines, and network scanners work the same way — by communicating digitally with your computer over a data network. You enjoy many advantages in using network devices such as these, but the most pronounced advantage is that any computer on the network can use the network device, thereby saving unnecessary expense for additional peripheral devices for each computer.

Network adapters are generally internal, which means you must open your computer and plug the adapter into an available expansion port. The big difference between network adapters is in the network cabling and communications standard they use. One network adapter may use twisted-pair cable and a communications standard known as *Ethernet* to interface to the network; another may use fiber-optic cable and a communications standard known as *Asynchronous Transfer Mode* (ATM). The two most common cabling types for computer networks are *twisted-pair* and *coaxial cable*. If you have lots of extra money sitting around that you'd like to use for something worthwhile, spend it buying network adapters and cabling that use fiber-optic technology and the ATM communications standard. Otherwise, do as most new site builders do and purchase Ethernet network adapters that use twisted-pair cable. See Chapter 2 for a more in-depth understanding of how to use network cable to connect all the computers in your network.

Using Windows 95 Plug and Play to install hardware

If you use the Windows 95 Plug and Play feature, installing a new modem or network adapter is a snap. Literally. Just snap the modem or network adapter into an expansion slot or plug the modem into a communications port and then turn on your computer. Windows 95 automatically detects and configures the new hardware for you. Figure A-2 shows the New Hardware Found window that Windows 95 displays after it finds new hardware such as a network adapter or a modem connected to your computer.

Figure A-2:
Use Plug
and Play
so that
installing
new
hardware
is a snap.

For Plug and Play to work correctly on your Windows 95 computer, you need to be aware of two things. First, not all hardware supports Plug and Play. If you have an old modem or network adapter that doesn't support Plug and Play, Windows 95 may not be capable of configuring the device automatically. Second, not all IBM-compatible PC motherboards support Plug and Play. If you own an old 386 or 486 computer that doesn't support Plug and Play, Windows 95 may not be capable of configuring your modem or network adapter for you even if the device does support Plug and Play. (The moral of this story is to sell your old computer equipment and buy hardware that supports Plug and Play.)

As you can see in Figure A-2, Windows 95 gives you several options for locating a software device driver for your new hardware. If Windows 95 already has a default driver available for the hardware that you're adding, the first item in the list is available. Otherwise, you must use a software driver disk provided by the manufacturer of your hardware. Click the Driver from Disk Provided by Hardware Manufacturer option, and then click OK.

The window shown in Figure A-3 appears on-screen, prompting you to insert the disk containing the software driver provided by your hardware manufacturer. After the disk is in the drive that the Copy Manufacturer's Files From list box indicates, click OK.

Figure A-3:
Insert the disk containing the software driver for your new hardware.

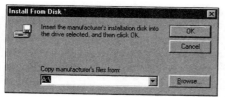

In addition to copying the software driver for your new hardware from the disk that your hardware manufacturer provides, Windows 95 may need to copy files from the Windows 95 CD-ROM or floppy disks. A prompt may appear on-screen if Windows 95 needs to copy additional files from a Windows 95 disk. Insert the disk indicated or insert the Windows 95 CD-ROM, and then click OK.

If Windows 95 needs help locating the files that it needs to copy, a window similar to the one shown in Figure A-4 appears. Specify the drive and directory locations of the Windows 95 system files, and then click OK to continue copying files.

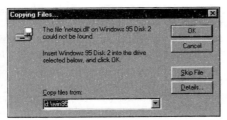

Figure A-4:
Use this
window if
Windows 95
needs help
locating the
system
files.

As Windows 95 copies files, it displays a status window. If any problems
arise during file copying, Windows 95 stops and asks you for help. (For
being so expensive and powerful, computers sure need a lot of help from a
human to do simple things correctly.) One common problem occurs if
Windows 95 tries to copy from the system disks a file that already exists on
your computer. Sometimes, the file on your computer is newer than the file
on the Windows 95 disks.

Figure A-5 shows what happens if Windows 95 discovers a file on your
computer that's newer than a file it's trying to copy. To avoid any problems,
you should always keep the newer file. Click the Yes button to keep the
newer copy of the file and prevent Windows 95 from copying the older file.

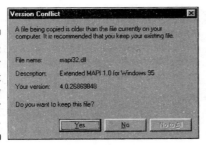

Figure A-5:
Keep newer
files that
are already
on your
computer.

After Windows 95 finishes copying files and asking you questions, you need
to reboot your computer so that the changes made to your system can take
effect. The window that appears enables you to reboot immediately by
clicking the Yes button.

After your computer reboots, you can verify that your modem or network
adapter was installed correctly by using the Control Panel. In the Control
Panel, find an icon labeled Modems and one labeled Network. Double-click
the Modems icon in the Control Panel to open the Modems Properties

window, as shown in Figure A-6. The modem that you just installed should be listed. If it isn't shown in the Modems Properties window, Windows 95 didn't successfully install and configure your modem. Try removing the device physically from your computer and rebooting your computer. Then shut down your computer again and restart the hardware installation from scratch.

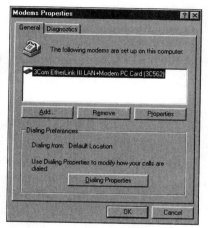

Figure A-6:
Verify the configuration of your modem by checking the Modems Properties window.

If you have trouble installing your modem or want to view more detailed information about what Windows 95 did as it installed and configured your modem, click the Diagnostics tab in the Modems Properties window. The Diagnostics tab shows you which device is presently configured to use which COM port and enables you to obtain additional information about the hardware configuration, such as the device drivers installed.

If you're installing a network adapter, double-click the Network icon in the Control Panel window. Figure A-7 shows the Network window, which displays network configuration information for your Windows 95 computer. You should see at least one entry in the Configuration tab's list box for your network adapter if Windows 95 Plug and Play succeeded in installing and configuring your hardware. You may also see an entry for Dial-Up Adapter, as shown in Figure A-7. Windows 95 installs the Dial-Up Adapter automatically if you install a modem for use with dial-up networking. In the figure, the entry for a 3Com EtherLink III modem/network adapter combination PC card appears above the Dial-Up Adapter entry. If you don't see an entry for your network adapter in the Network window, Windows 95 Plug and Play didn't successfully install and configure your adapter.

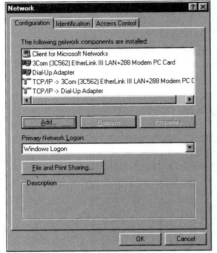

Figure A-7:
Use the
Control
Panel to
view your
computer's
Network
configuration.

If things don't go smoothly with your hardware installation, get help from a computer technician. On Windows-based IBM-compatible PCs, hardware installation is either Plug and Play or frustrating, time-consuming, unpleasant, costly, and overly complicated. If you stick with brand-name hardware products and replace all your older hardware with equipment manufactured after 1996, you should have no trouble installing the hardware yourself. By doing so, you save hundreds of dollars in payments to a computer technician over the life of your computer.

Installing hardware on a Macintosh

Nothing in the computer world is simpler than installing hardware on a Macintosh computer: Turn off your Macintosh, plug the hardware into the right connector in your computer, and then turn on your computer again. The Macintosh Operating System automatically detects and configures your new hardware. That's all you need to do. You can buy an internal modem, an external modem, or an internal network adapter. (Remember that you plug internal devices into an expansion port inside your computer, and connect external devices to one of the ports on the outside of your computer.) If you experience trouble installing hardware in your Macintosh, you can use the only thing in the computer world that's as simple as installing hardware on a Macintosh: the Apple support line, at 1-800-SOS-APPL.

Configuring TCP/IP on Your Computer

All computers on the Internet rely on a common protocol, called *TCP/IP* (Transmission Control Protocol/Internet Protocol), to exchange information packets. TCP/IP is the standard way to relay data around the world on the Internet, but not all computers on the Internet speak TCP/IP directly. Some computers speak a different language that you must translate into TCP/IP before the data can travel across the Internet. Actually, it is quite common for two computers that don't speak TCP/IP to communicate with each other over the Internet; the two machines rely on translators at either end to convert the conversation to and from TCP/IP. To construct new Internet sites using anything other than TCP/IP, however, is most uncommon, so we do in this section what most people do these days: try to forget that anything other than TCP/IP exists on the Internet.

The technology that enables a Macintosh or an IBM-compatible PC computer to speak TCP/IP is now commonplace and easy to configure. Windows 95 and the new versions of Mac OS (such as System 7.5.5 and later) come with TCP/IP ready for configuring, so you don't need to worry about getting additional software. You have only a few steps to follow to set up the TCP/IP networking software for Windows 95 or Mac OS, and the following sections show you what you need to know to configure both.

Your computer can speak TCP/IP through a modem or through a network adapter. If your computer speaks TCP/IP through a network adapter, information packets are "carried" on top of another networking protocol such as Ethernet. If your computer speaks TCP/IP through a modem, however, information packets are "carried" on top of a networking protocol designed to work with modems, such as Point to Point Protocol, or PPP. Keep in mind as you read the following instructions that two ways exist for your computer to speak TCP/IP, and the method your computer uses depends on whether you install a modem or a network adapter.

Macintosh Open Transport TCP/IP

You have two ways to set up TCP/IP on a Macintosh computer: the old way and the new way. The old way is to install MacTCP, a Control Panel component that adds TCP/IP communications capability to Mac OS versions such as System 7. The new way, using MacOS versions such as System 7.5 and on all Power Macs, is to use a technology called *Open Transport*. Mac OS System 7.5.5 and later versions include Open Transport 1.1.1 built in. A few Open Transport upgrades are available from Apple on the Internet (at http://www.apple.com/) that work with versions of MacOS before System 7.5.5, but the best way to install Open Transport on your Mac is to upgrade your operating system to System 7.5.5 or later. You can also find Open Transport 1.1.1 on Apple sites within America Online (keyword: APPLECOMPUTER) and CompuServe (shortcut: GO APLSUP).

After you upgrade your operating system to System 7.5.5 or later, configuring TCP/IP on your Macintosh is simple. Start by choosing Apple⇨TCP/IP Control Panel from the menu bar. If this time is your first time opening the TCP/IP Control Panel, a window appears on-screen alerting you to the fact that TCP/IP is currently inactive. Click the Yes button so that TCP/IP becomes active after you finish with the TCP/IP Control Panel.

The next window that appears on-screen is shown in Figure A-8. This window, entitled TCP/IP, is where you configure TCP/IP settings for your Macintosh. Select your network adapter from the Connect via drop-down list box. Also select Manually from the Configure drop-down list box so that your TCP/IP window looks something like the one shown in Figure A-8. Now enter your computer's IP address, subnet mask, the address of the network router to use, the addresses of name servers to use, and the domain of which your computer is a part.

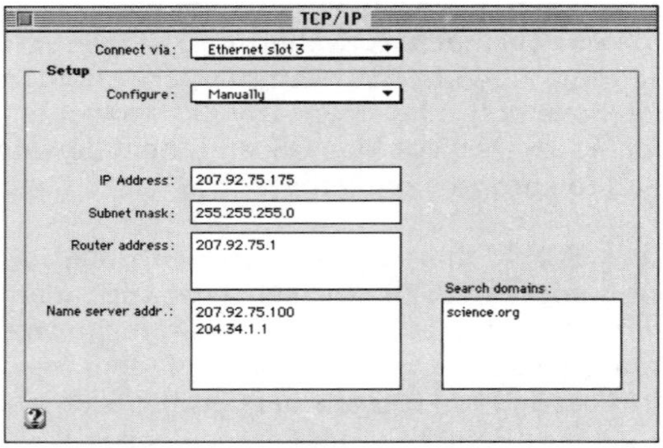

Figure A-8:
Configure
TCP/IP
settings
for your
network
adapter.

	TCP/IP	
Connect via:	Ethernet slot 3 ▼	
— Setup —		
Configure:	Manually ▼	
IP Address:	207.92.75.175	
Subnet mask:	255.255.255.0	
Router address:	207.92.75.1	
		Search domains:
Name server addr.:	207.92.75.100 204.34.1.1	science.org

Your Internet access provider supplies all this information after you sign up for service. If you're building your own computer network for your Internet site, your Internet access provider gives you a range of IP addresses to use for the computers in your network. Choose an unused IP address from the ones supplied by your IAP and enter that address in the IP Address text box. Which of the addresses you use for each of your computers doesn't matter as long as you don't use the same address more than once.

If you don't have a network adapter and instead intend to connect to the Internet through a modem, select PPP from the Connect via drop-down list box (see Figure A-9). Select Manually from the Configure drop-down list box so that your TCP/IP window looks something like the one shown in Figure A-9. Enter your computer's permanent IP address, the addresses of name servers to use, and the domain name of which your computer is a member.

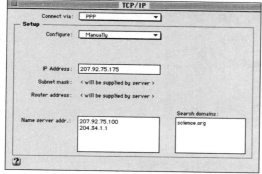

Figure A-9:
Configure
TCP/IP
settings
for your
dedicated
PPP
connection.

When you're finished, close the TCP/IP Control Panel by clicking the Close box in the upper-left corner. A window appears, asking you to confirm that you want to save changes to your current TCP/IP configuration. Click the Save button to save the new TCP/IP settings for your Macintosh. After the save is complete, TCP/IP is ready for your Macintosh to use, either over a modem or through a network adapter, depending on the hardware you installed.

If you have any trouble installing or configuring Open Transport or a new version of MacOS, somebody at Apple is available to help you at no charge during the week. Call the following number and explain your problem, and the Apple support engineer can assist you: 1-800-SOS-APPL.

Windows 95 Windows Sockets 1.1

Before the release of Windows 95, getting TCP/IP to work with your Windows-based PC required a lot of effort. Now, thanks to Plug and Play and Windows Sockets 1.1 for Windows 95, you can configure TCP/IP for your PC in only a few minutes and with few complications. Start by installing your network adapter or modem as described earlier in this appendix and then open the Windows 95 Control Panel. Double-click the Network icon. After the Network Configuration window appears on-screen, click the Add button. The Select Network Component Type window appears, as shown in Figure A-10. Select Protocol from the list and then click the Add button.

The Select Network Protocol window appears, as shown in Figure A-11, and enables you to choose from a list of manufacturers and network protocols. Choose Microsoft as the manufacturer and TCP/IP as the network protocol; then click OK. This action instructs Windows 95 to add Windows Sockets 1.1 with TCP/IP support to your computer.

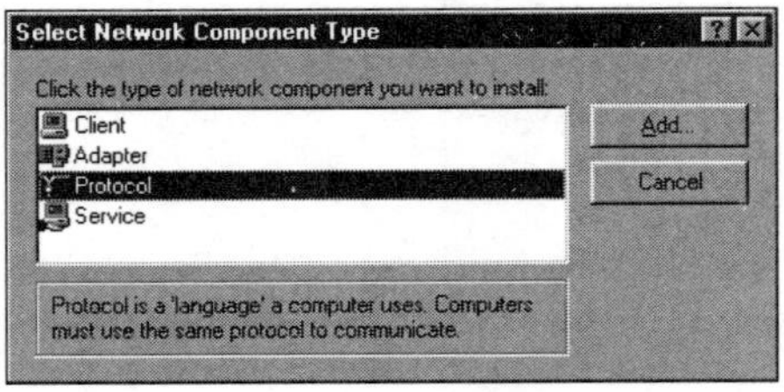

Figure A-10:
Select
Protocol
to begin
adding the
TCP/IP
component.

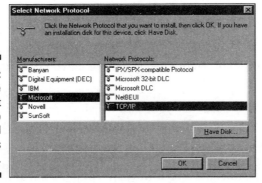

Figure A-11:
Choose
Microsoft
TCP/IP to
install
Windows
Sockets.

Windows 95 automatically binds the TCP/IP network protocol to your modem or network adapter, whichever is installed in your computer. You don't need to do anything special to tell Windows 95 about the communications hardware with which you intend to use the TCP/IP network protocol. As long as your hardware is correctly installed, the TCP/IP protocol is available for use with the hardware when you finish the installation.

The only thing left to do now is to configure TCP/IP settings for your computer. Figure A-12 shows the first TCP/IP configuration screen, which Windows 95 displays for you automatically, in which you type the IP address and subnet mask that your computer will use. Your Internet access provider can tell you what your computer's permanent IP address is; make sure that you type this address accurately in the IP Address text box.

Next, click the DNS Configuration tab to reveal the screen shown in Figure A-13. Click the Enable DNS radio button so that your computer can resolve domain names to IP addresses. Type the host name of your computer in the Host text box, and type the Internet domain name of which your computer is a member in the Domain text box. Together, your host and domain names are considered your *fully qualified domain name* (FQDN). Other people use your FQDN if they want to refer to your computer by name instead of by IP address.

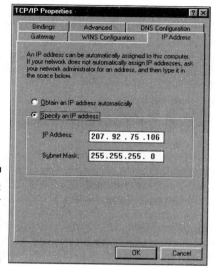

Figure A-12:
Give your
computer a
unique IP
address.

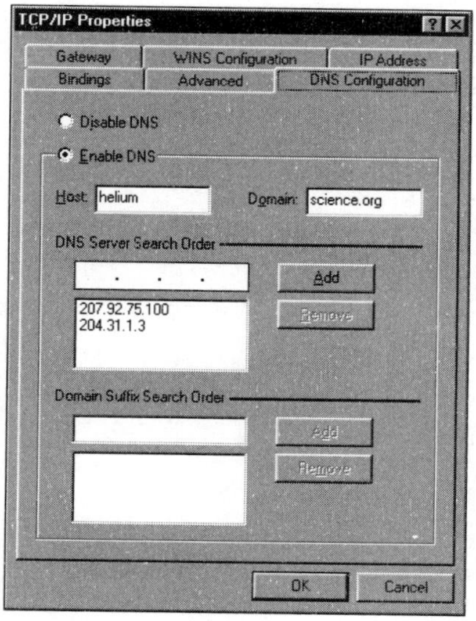

Figure A-13:
Provide
DNS
Configuration
information
for name
resolution.

The FQDN of the configuration shown in Figure A-13 is as follows:

```
helium.science.org
```

To add the addresses of the DNS servers that your computer uses to resolve domain names to IP addresses, enter these addresses one at a time in the DNS Server Search Order text box and click the Add button. The IP address you enter is added to the list box beneath the entry field. Your Internet access provider can tell you which IP addresses to use here. If you decide to set up your own DNS server, enter the IP address of the computer on which your DNS server is running. Enter the IP address of your own computer if you intend to install and run your DNS server on the computer that you're now configuring.

Finally, click the Gateway tab to reveal the screen shown in Figure A-14. In this screen, you must type the IP address of the computer or router that relays TCP/IP packets to and from your computer and the rest of the Internet. If you use a modem to establish your dedicated Internet connection, you should leave the Gateway screen blank. If your modem connects to your Internet access provider by using PPP, a new gateway is normally added to your system automatically. If you enter a gateway IP address manually in the Gateway tab and then connect to your IAP by using a modem, this action can cause problems and prevent your computer from communicating with the Internet at all. If you aren't going to use a modem to connect to the Internet, you must enter a gateway IP address in the New gateway text box. Click the Add button to add the IP address of your new gateway to the list of Installed gateways. Click OK to complete your installation of Microsoft TCP/IP.

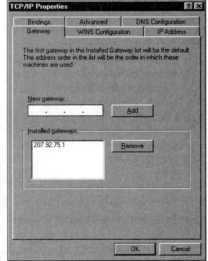

Figure A-14:
Enter a gateway IP address if you don't use a modem to your access provider.

Your computer is now fully prepared to communicate with the Internet, either through a dial-up PPP connection to your access provider or through your own computer network, depending on the communications hardware you decided to use. Chapter 2 shows you how to connect your computer or computer network to the Internet so that you can internetwork with others on the Internet.

This LAN Is Your LAN, This LAN Is My LAN

We strongly suggest that you build your own computer network as you set up your Internet site. Although you could connect each of your computers to the Internet through a separate modem and phone line and thereby avoid creating your own computer network, such an approach has several serious drawbacks. First, you sink a significant amount of money into modems. For the same price as an average modem, about $150, you can purchase a 10 Mbps Ethernet card. Consider the amount of money you spend for each kilobit-per-second of communications potential. By using a 28.8 Kbps modem, you spend about $5 for each kilobit of communications speed. By using a standard 10 Mbps Ethernet adapter, on the other hand, you spend only about 15 cents for each kilobit. Modems are a terrible communications investment compared to network adapters.

Assuming that you already have modems in each of your computers, think about the cost of Internet access for all of them. You pay at least $20 per month to your Internet access provider for each computer, and you pay at least $15 per month to the phone company for a telephone line for each computer. As soon as you connect more than three computers to the Internet through modems, you start paying more per month to various service providers than you'd pay if you built a computer network and connected the network to the Internet through a single communications link. Consider also how much more you'd need to spend to upgrade the speed of your Internet connection if you relied on modems and phone lines. You'd need to replace every modem and every phone line with a faster communications technology, such as ISDN, if you set up your Internet site by connecting each computer to the Internet through a standard modem and phone line. If you build a 10MB Ethernet computer network and connect it to the Internet, however, you need to replace only one piece of communications equipment and one Internet access service to upgrade your Internet connection for every one of your computers.

Appendix B

About the CD

● ●

*H*ere's some of what you can find on the *Setting Up An Internet Site For Dummies* CD-ROM:

✔ Paint Shop Pro, a great shareware graphics program for Windows

✔ BBEdit Lite, a freeware text editor for Mac OS computers that is useful for HTML editing

✔ Lots of CGI programs that add capabilities to your Web site

System Requirements

Make sure your computer meets the minimum system requirements listed here. If your computer doesn't match up to most of these requirements, you may have problems in using the contents of the CD.

✔ A PC with a 486 or faster processor, or a Mac OS computer with a 68030 or faster processor.

✔ Microsoft Windows 3.1 or later, or Mac OS system software 7.5 or later.

✔ At least 8MB of total RAM installed on your computer. For best performance, we recommend that Windows 95-equipped PCs and Mac OS computers with PowerPC processors have at least 16MB of RAM installed.

✔ At least 150MB of hard drive space available to install all the software from this CD. (You'll need less space if you don't install every program.)

✔ A CD-ROM drive — double-speed (2x) or faster.

✔ A monitor capable of displaying at least 256 colors or grayscale.

✔ A modem with a speed of at least 14,400 bps.

If you need more information on the basics, check out *PCs For Dummies,* 4th Edition, by Dan Gookin; *Macs For Dummies,* 4th Edition, by David Pogue; *Windows 95 For Dummies,* by Andy Rathbone; or *Windows 3.11 For Dummies,* 3rd Edition, by Andy Rathbone (all published by IDG Books Worldwide, Inc.).

How to Use the CD with Microsoft Windows

To install the items from the CD to your hard drive, follow these steps:

1. **Insert the CD into your computer's CD-ROM drive.**

2. **Windows 3.1 or 3.11 users: From Program Manager, choose File⇨Run.**

   Windows 95 users: Click the Start button and click Run.

3. **In the dialog box that appears, type** D:\SETUP.EXE.

   Replace *D* with the proper drive letter if your CD-ROM drive uses a different letter. (If you don't know the letter, see how your CD-ROM drive is listed under My Computer in Windows 95 or File Manager in Windows 3.1.)

4. **Click OK.**

   A license agreement window appears.

5. **Read through the license agreement, nod your head, and then click the Accept button if you want to use the CD.**

   (After you click Accept, the License Agreement window will never bother you again.) The CD interface appears. The interface is a little program that shows you what is on the CD and coordinates installing the programs and running the demos. The interface basically lets you click a button or two to make things happen.

6. **The first screen you see is the Welcome screen. Click anywhere on this screen to enter the interface.**

   Now you are getting to the action. This next screen lists categories for the software on the CD.

7. **To view the items within a category, just click the category's name.**

   A list of programs in the category appears.

8. **For more information about a program, click the program's name.**

   Be sure to read the information that appears. Sometimes a program might require you to do a few tricks on your computer first, and this screen will tell you where to go for that information, if necessary.

9. **If you don't want to install the program, click the Go Back button to return to the previous screen.**

   You can always return to the previous screen by clicking the Go Back button. This allows you to browse the different categories and products and decide what you want to install.

10. **To install the program, click the appropriate Install button.**

   The CD interface drops to the background while the CD begins installation of the program you chose.

11. **To install other items, repeat Steps 7 through 10.**

12. **When you're finished installing programs, click the Quit button to close the interface.**

   You can eject the CD now. Carefully place it back in the plastic jacket of the book for safekeeping.

How to Use the CD with the Mac OS

To install the items from the CD to your hard drive, follow these steps:

1. **Insert the CD into your computer's CD-ROM drive.**

   In a moment, an icon representing the CD you just inserted appears on your Mac desktop. Chances are, the icon looks like a CD-ROM.

2. **Double-click the CD icon to show the CD's contents.**

3. **Double-click the License Agreement icon.**

   This is the end-user license that you agree to by using the CD.

4. **Double-click the Read Me First icon.**

   This text file contains information about the CD's programs and any last-minute instructions you need to know about installing the programs on the CD that we don't cover in this appendix.

5. **The software on the CD is organized into category folders, so double-click the folder icon to open the category you are interested in.**

   Inside the category folder you will find the program files or folders.

6. **To install most programs, just drag the program's folder from the CD window and drop it on your hard drive icon.**

7. **Some programs come with installer programs — with those you simply open the program's folder on the CD, and double-click the icon with the words "Install" or "Installer."**

   After you have installed the programs you want, you can eject the CD. Carefully place it back in the plastic jacket of the book for safekeeping.

What You'll Find

Here's a summary of the software on the *Setting Up An Internet Site For Dummies* CD-ROM. If you use Windows, the CD interface helps you install software easily. (If you have no idea what we're talking about when we say "CD interface," flip back a page or two to find the section, "How to Use the CD with Microsoft Windows.")

If you use a Mac OS computer, you can enjoy the ease of the Mac interface to quickly install the programs.

CGI scripts

We have included over 40 CGI scripts designed to run on Web servers with Perl that you can use on your own Web site. You can browse these scripts in Windows Explorer and select the ones you want to place on your hard drive or Web server, or you can copy all of them to your hard drive using the self-extractor we created just for that purpose. All CGI scripts are in a folder called CGISCRIP (CGI Scripts on the Mac side) on the CD. If you are using Windows and you have trouble accessing the files in the CGISCRIP folder, run the self-extractor CGISCRIP/CGISCRIP.EXE. This self-extractor places all of the CGI script files on your hard drive, in a folder called C:\CGISCRIP, maintaining the same directory structure as on the CD.

Advertise, from Collin Forbes

CGISCRIP/ADVRTISE on your CD. Advertise is a CGI script that puts an advertising banner on your Web page. Check out `http://kuoi.asui.uidaho.edu/~collinf/advertise/` on the World Wide Web for a full description.

AXS Access Counter, from Fluid Dynamics

CGISCRIP/AXS on your CD. Free Perl script for gathering information about your site's visitors. More than just another counter script, AXS gives you full data concerning origin, pages accessed, browser used, and where the visitor went when he or she left. A variety of charts and graphs keep you informed about what's going on at your site. Check out `http://www.xav.com/scripts/axs/index.html` on the World Wide Web for a full description.

BanEx, from StepWeb.Com

CGISCRIP/BANEX on your CD. CGI script that loads rotating banners with links. Check out `http://www.stepweb.com/bannerex.shtml` on the World Wide Web for a full description.

BannerWheel, from Command-O Software

CGISCRIP/COBANNER on your CD. Free Perl script that loads rotating banners. Includes the capability to set the probability of a particular banner being shown. Check out `http://www.freescripts.com/html/bannerwheel_main.shtml` on the World Wide Web for a full description.

calendar.pl, from Collin Forbes

CGISCRIP/CALENDAR on your CD. Calendar program in Perl that lets you put a calendar on your site for any month from January, 1970 to December, 2049. Check out `http://kuoi.asui.uidaho.edu/~collinf/calendar/index.html` on the World Wide Web for a full description.

CallerID.pl, from Angus McIntyre

CGISCRIP/CALLERID on your CD. Free Perl script that tells you who's dropping in on your Web page. Check out `http://www.tardis.ed.ac.uk/~angus/Computing/Programming/Perl/Samples/PerlCGIInfo.html#CallerID` on the World Wide Web for a full description.

Chat 2.0, from Command-O Software

CGISCRIP/COCHAT on your CD. Free CGI real-time chat program. A simplified version of the commercial program, ChatPro, Chat allows only a single chat room. Check out `http://www.freescripts.com/html/chat_main.shtml` on the World Wide Web for a full description.

Database Manager, from Gossamer Threads

CGISCRIP/DBMAN on your CD. Very nice Web interface to a flat file database. Allows add, delete, sort, search, and so on. Check out `http://www.gossamer-threads.com/scripts/dbman/` on the World Wide Web for a full description.

Digee Counter, from Rick Watkins of the USATECHDET WWW Development Team

CGISCRIP/DIGEE on your CD. Quick and easy graphical access counter script. Check out `http://www.pica.army.mil/orgs/fsac/eod/examples/counter.cgi` on the World Wide Web for a full description.

Dream Catchers Book of Guests, from Dream Catchers Technologies

CGISCRIP/DCBOOKGU on your CD. Free guestbook that e-mails you when a guest signs in. It also e-mails the guest a thank-you message. Check out `http://dreamcatchersweb.com/scripts/bookofguests.html` on the World Wide Web for a full description.

Dream Catchers Form Return, from Dream Catchers Technologies

CGISCRIP/DCFORMRE on your CD. Free CGI form-processing software that e-mails you the results and e-mails a confirmation to the form user. Check out `http://dreamcatchersweb.com/scripts/formreturn.html` on the World Wide Web for a full description.

Dream Catchers Free Linkage, from Dream Catchers Technologies

CGISCRIP/DCFREELI on your CD. Free CGI program that lets your Web site visitors instantly put links into any of ten categories on your Web page. Check out `http://dreamcatchersweb.com/scripts/freelinkage.html` on the World Wide Web for a full description.

Dream Catchers Message Board, from Dream Catchers Technologies

CGISCRIP/DCMESSAG on your CD. Free message board that allows your visitors to post their own messages and respond to the postings of others. Check out `http://dreamcatchersweb.com/scripts/messageboard.html` on the World Wide Web for a full description.

Dream Catchers Post it!, from Dream Catchers Technologies

CGISCRIP/DCPOSTIT on your CD. Free graffiti wall that e-mails you when a guest signs in. It also e-mails the guest a thank-you message. Check out `http://dreamcatchersweb.com/scripts/postit.html` on the World Wide Web for a full description.

Dream Catchers Rotating Link, from Dream Catchers Technologies

CGISCRIP/DCROTATI on your CD. Perl CGI script for putting a different link on your Web page for each visitor. Check out `http://dreamcatchersweb.com/scripts/rotatinglink.html` on the World Wide Web for a full description.

Dream Catchers Simple Counter, from Dream Catchers Technologies

CGISCRIP/DCSIMPLE on your CD. Access counter that lets you use plain text or graphics. Check out `http://dreamcatchersweb.com/scripts/simplecounter.html` on the World Wide Web for a full description.

Fake Autoresponder, from StepWeb.Com

CGISCRIP/FAKEAUTO on your CD. CGI script that simulates an autoresponder. Can automatically e-mail an ASCII file to anyone who selects options from your form. Check out `http://www.stepweb.com/fakemail.shtml` on the World Wide Web for a full description.

File Upload!, from Terminal Productions

CGISCRIP/FILEUPLD on your CD. Free Perl script that lets you upload files via your browser. Check out `http://www.terminalp.com/scripts/file_upload.shtml` on the World Wide Web for a full description.

Form-Processor, from Command-O Software

CGISCRIP/COFORMPR on your CD. This freeware CGI form processor goes beyond simply e-mailing you the results of a user's form input. It can also save the results in a database and even send a message to the person who used the form. Check out `http://www.freescripts.com/html/form_main.shtml` on the World Wide Web for a full description.

GuestPost, from StepWeb.Com

CGISCRIP/GUESTPST on your CD. Guestbook CGI script that lets guests leave not just a message but also a picture. Check out `http://www.stepweb.com/guestpost1.shtml` on the World Wide Web for a full description.

ICheck from Dave Palmer

CGISCRIP/ICHECK on your CD. CGI script to require visitors to log in before getting access to your site. Not as secure as .htaccess methods, but simpler. Check out `http://www.upstatepress.com/perl/programs/story.cfm?id=9` on the World Wide Web for a full description.

Intermediate Search, from Fluid Dynamics

CGISCRIP/INTERMED on your CD. Free Perl CGI script for searching Web sites. Check out `http://www.xav.com/scripts/search/index.html` on the World Wide Web for a full description.

jarandom.pl, from Jason Anthony

CGISCRIP/JARANDOM on your CD. Perl CGI script for creating a link that sends users to random Web locations. Check out `http://www.aquapal.co.uk/perl/jarandom.html` on the World Wide Web for a full description.

KewlCheckers, from Tom Wagner

CGISCRIP/KEWLCHCK on your CD. Two-player real-time checkers game that you can add to your Web site. Check out `http://user.mc.net/~twagner/kewlcheckers.htm` on the World Wide Web for a full description.

LoginPro 2.0, from SNUD

CGISCRIP/LOGINPRO on your CD. Free CGI logon script that lets you specify what page is displayed. Check out `http://netlinkworld.com/snud/cgi-bin/scripts.cgi?loginpro` on the World Wide Web for a full description.

MessageBulletin 3.1, from StepWeb.Com

CGISCRIP/MSGBULTN on your CD. Free CGI message board with unlimited threads and expiration dates on posts. Check out `http://www.stepweb.com/messagebulletin.shtml` on the World Wide Web for a full description.

PerlShop, from ARPAnet Corp.

CGISCRIP/PERLSHOP on your CD. Shopping cart script written in Perl. It's adverware, which means the only cost involved is to accept the advertising that comes with it. Check out `http://www.arpanet.com/perlshop/` on the World Wide Web for a full description.

Poll-It Lite, from CGI World

CGISCRIP/POLLIT on your CD. CGI script that lets you add voting to your Web site. Gives running totals and grand totals. Check out `http://www.cgi-world.com/pollit.html` on the World Wide Web for a full description.

Postcard, from Command-O Software

CGISCRIP/COPSTCRD on your CD. Lets visitors to your site send electronic postcards. Check out `http://www.freescripts.com/html/card_main.shtml` on the World Wide Web for a full description.

Postcards from the net, from Richard Bowen

CGISCRIP/POSTNET on your CD. Lets visitors to your site send electronic postcards. Check out `http://www.rcbowen.com/perl/post.html` on the World Wide Web for a full description.

RandomPage.pl, from Angus McIntyre

CGISCRIP/RANDOMPG on your CD. Perl CGI script for selecting random Web jumps. Check out `http://www.tardis.ed.ac.uk/~angus/Computing/Programming/Perl/Samples/PerlCGIRandom.html` on the World Wide Web for a full description.

Random Quote, from Command-O Software

CGISCRIP/CORNDMQT on your CD. Perl CGI script for inserting random quotations into your Web page. Check out `http://www.freescripts.com/html/quote_main.shtml` on the World Wide Web for a full description.

Roman Numeral Text Counter, from Fluid Dynamics

CGISCRIP/ROMANCT on your CD. Clever twist on standard access counters. This one uses Roman numerals instead of the usual digital system. Check out `http://www.xav.com/scripts/roman/index.html` on the World Wide Web for a full description.

Site Search 1.02, from Krishnan Jayakrishnan

CGISCRIP/SITESRCH on your CD. Very nice search engine. Provides various search options such as "search by any term." Check out `http://www.agl.uh.edu/~saljxk/site_Search/` on the World Wide Web for a full description.

SWAT, from Chris Knight

CGISCRIP/SWAT on your CD. Perl CGI search engine. Check out `http://www.chriscrawler.com/swat/Overview.html` on the World Wide Web for a full description.

Trivia Quiz GuestBook, from Collin Forbes

CGISCRIP/TRIVIAQ on your CD. Guestbook with a twist. Site visitors must answer trivia questions to get access to the guestbook. Check out http://kuoi.asui.uidaho.edu/~collinf/trivia/index.html on the World Wide Web for a full description.

Upload, from WebCom datakommunikation

CGISCRIP/UPLOAD on your CD. Free CGI script that lets you upload files from your browser. Check out http://www.webcom.se/projects/freeware/upload/ on the World Wide Web for a full description.

Vote, from Command-O Software

CGISCRIP/COVOTE on your CD. Lets your site visitors rate anything on a scale of 1 to 10. Produces running totals. Check out http://www.freescripts.com/html/vote_main.shtml on the World Wide Web for a full description.

WODA, from Dr. Ziga Turk

CGISCRIP/WODA on your CD. Perl CGI script for Web database applications. Check out http://audrey.fagg.uni-lj.si/~zturk/works/wb/ on the World Wide Web for a full description.

Xavatoria Indexed Search, from Fluid Dynamics

CGISCRIP/XAVATORI on your CD. Search engine for text-intensive Web sites. Check out http://www.xav.com/scripts/xavatoria/index.html on the World Wide Web for a full description.

Zone Coaster Addlink

CGISCRIP/ZCADLINK on your CD. Free Perl script that allows your site visitors to add their own links. Check out http://www.zonecoaster.com/shop/?Enter on the World Wide Web for a full description.

Zone Coaster Chat

CGISCRIP/ZCCHAT on your CD. Free Perl script that lets you set up multiple chat rooms on your site. Has advanced features such as private messaging and private chat rooms. Check out http://www.zonecoaster.com/shop/?Enter on the World Wide Web for a full description.

Zone Coaster Guestbook

CGISCRIP/ZCGUESTB on your CD. Free Perl script that lets users create their own guestbook with a custom look. Check out http://www.zonecoaster.com/shop/?Enter on the World Wide Web for a full description.

Zone Coaster Search

CGISCRIP/ZCSEARCH on your CD. Free Perl script for site searching. Can search multiple directories, and supports case-sensitive and case-insensitive searches. Shows the number of keyword matches per file found. Check out http://www.zonecoaster.com/shop/?Enter on the World Wide Web for a full description.

Zone Coaster Survey

CGISCRIP/ZCSURVEY on your CD. Free Perl script that can handle multiple survey forms. Uses browser interface for survey setup. Check out http://www.zonecoaster.com/shop/?Enter on the World Wide Web for a full description.

Zone Coaster Upload

CGISCRIP/ZCUPLOAD on your CD. Free Perl script that lets you upload files via your browser. Check out http://www.zonecoaster.com/shop/?Enter on the World Wide Web for a full description.

Graphics tools

Animagic GIF Animator, from Right to Left Software

For Windows 3.1/95/NT. Premier GIF animation program has special effects such as wipe, spiral, and blind. Features include cropping, color reduction, and local and global palette optimization. 30-day evaluation version. Check out http://rtlsoft.com/animagic/index.html on the World Wide Web for a full description.

GraphicConverter, from Lemke Software

For Mac OS. GraphicConverter is a powerful shareware graphic viewing and conversion program. You can also make retouches, perform batch conversions for Mac and PC graphic formats, and more. Check out http://members.aol.com/lemkesoft on the World Wide Web for a full description.

Hidden 3D, from César Pascual

For Windows 95/NT. Creates hidden 3-D stereogram images. Check out http://energy.ece.uiuc.edu/CesarPascual/Hidden3D.zip on the World Wide Web to download the latest version only. *Note:* You can run this program from the CD interface or install it by copying the folder GRAPHICS\IRFANVW to your hard drive. To use the program, just run IRFANVW\I_VIEW32.EXE.

IrfanView32, from Skiljan Irfan

For Windows 95/NT. Impressive file viewer and converter. Fast and easy to use. Check out http://stud1.tuwien.ac.at/~e9227474/ on the World Wide Web for a full description. *Note:* You can run this program from the CD interface or install it by copying the folder GRAPHICS\HIDDEN3D to your hard drive. To use the program, just run HIDDEN3D\HIDDEN3D.EXE.

LiveImage from LiveImage Corporation

For Windows 95/NT. This is a 14-day trial version of the new image-mapping program from the author of the classic Map This!. Check out `http://www.mediatec.com/` on the World Wide Web for a full description.

Paint Shop Pro, from JASC Inc.

For Windows 3.1/95/NT. Paint Shop Pro is a shareware graphics viewing and editing tool. A version is available on the CD for Windows 3.1 and Windows 95. Check out `http://www.jasc.com/` on the World Wide Web for a full description.

SuperJPG, from Midnight Blue Software

For Windows 95. Fast image management program for Windows 95. Includes TWAIN scanner support. Check out `http://www.midnightblue.com/superjpg/` on the World Wide Web for a full description.

Internet tools

Adobe Acrobat Reader, from Adobe Systems Inc.

For Windows 3.1/95/NT. Adobe Acrobat Reader enables you to view the graphics and formatting contained in Portable Document Format (PDF) files — without having the original application. Miraculous! Acrobat Reader also includes a plug-in for Netscape Navigator, which enables you to view Acrobat Reader documents within a Web page. The documentation for Hidden 3D is in PDF files.

Allaire HomeSite

For Windows 95/NT. Full-featured Web page development program. Check out `www.allaire.com/products/homesite/30/index.cfm` on the World Wide Web for a full description.

BBEdit Lite 4.0.1, from Bare Bones Software

For Mac OS. BBEdit Lite 4.0.1, from Bare Bones Software, Inc., is a Macintosh freeware text editor with powerful features that make creating HTML scripts for your Web pages easy. The commercial version of this program, BBEdit 4.5, has stronger HTML editing features. We've included a demo version of BBEdit 4.5 on the CD. This demo is fully featured but cannot save files. Check out `http://web.barebones.com/free/free.html` on the World Wide Web for a full description.

CoffeeCup HTML Editor++, from CoffeeCup Software

For Windows 95. A classy HTML editor with support for JavaScript, style sheets, and CGI. Features include a table wizard, a color wizard, and spell checking. Check out `http://www.coffeecup.com/editor/` on the World Wide Web for a full description.

CoffeeCup Image Mapper++, from CoffeeCup Software

For Windows 95. Image mapping program with wizards to assist you in creating image maps. One very nice feature of this program is that it displays the map code while you are creating it. Check out `http://www.coffeecup.com/mapper/` on the World Wide Web for a full description.

CyberSpyder link test, from Aman Software

For Windows 3.1/95/NT. Broken link checker that has a report manager and can be scheduled to run at a specified time. Check out `http://www.cyberspyder.com/index.html` on the World Wide Web for a full description.

DNews News Server, from NetWin LTD

For Mac OS and Windows NT. A full-featured news server. Check out `http://www.netwinsite.com/dnews.htm` on the World Wide Web for a full description.

Dr Jack's HTMLview, from JC Associates

For Windows 95. Program that solves a few annoying problems Web designers have to deal with. A graphics viewer specifically designed for Web developers, it can load images from multiple directories simultaneously. It can also display tiled background images behind a selection of text in lots of different colors to help you make those tricky design decisions. Check out `http://www.drjack.com/htmlview/` on the World Wide Web for a full description.

HotDog Pro, from Sausage Software

For Windows 95/NT. The old standard just keeps getting better. Way beyond most other HTML editors, HotDog Pro now has more tools and options than ever. Check out `http://www.sausage.com/hotdog32.htm` on the World Wide Web for a full description.

Infolink Link Checker, from BiggByte Software

For Windows 95/NT. Full-featured link checker. Unlike some programs, Infolink can check more than just http links. The program has the capability to check either individual pages or full sites. Check out `http://www.biggbyte.com/` on the World Wide Web for a full description.

Linkbot, from Tetranet Software

For Windows 95/NT. Broken link checker, and a lot more. Linkbot also looks for pages with slow download times, outdated pages, and other key points that can mess up your site. Check out http://www.tetranetsoftware.com/ on the World Wide Web for a full description.

LISTSERV Lite

For Windows 95/NT. The Free Edition of the LISTSERV® Lite mailing list manager, licensed by L-Soft International, Inc. The Free Edition may not be used for commercial purposes. Check out http://www.lsoft.com/ listserv-lite.html on the World Wide Web for the full policy as well as a complete description of the program.

NetPresenz 4.1, from Stairways Software

For Mac OS. A useful FTP server program for Macintosh. Check out http://www.stairways.com/netpresenz/index.html on the World Wide Web for a full description.

Pegasus Mail, from David Harris

For Mac OS and Windows 3.1/95/NT. A friendly and very popular e-mail client program for Windows and Macintosh. Check out http://www.pegasus.usa.com/ on the World Wide Web for a full description.

SLMail, from Seattle Lab

For Windows 3.1/95/NT. A full e-mail server program for Windows 95/NT. Check out http://www.seattlelab.com/ on the World Wide Web for a full description.

WFTPD, from Texas Imperial Software

For Windows 95/NT. An FTP server for Windows 95/NT. Check out http://www.wftpd.com/index.html on the World Wide Web for a full description.

WS_FTP LE, from Ipswitch

For Windows 3.1/95/NT. Powerful but easy-to-use FTP client for Windows. (Portions of this software Copyright 1991-97, Ipswitch, Inc.) Check out http://www.ipswitch.com/ on the World Wide Web for a full description.

Compression tools

StuffIt Lite, from Aladdin Systems

For Mac OS. Compression utility for the Macintosh. Check out http://www.aladdinsys.com/stuffitlite/index.html on the World Wide Web for a full description.

WinZip, from Nico Mak Computing

For Windows 3.1/95/NT. The old standard for file compression. Check out http://www.winzip.com on the World Wide Web for a full description.

If You Have Problems (Of the CD Kind)

We tried our best to compile programs that work on most computers with the minimum system requirements. Alas, your computer may differ, and some programs may not work properly for some reason.

The two likeliest problems are that you don't have enough memory (RAM) for the programs you want to use, or you have other programs running that are affecting installation or running of a program. If you get error messages such as Not enough memory or Setup cannot continue, try one or more of these methods and then try using the software again:

- ✓ **Turn off any anti-virus software that you have on your computer.** Installers sometimes mimic virus activity and may make your computer incorrectly believe that a virus is infecting it.

- ✓ **Close all running programs.** The more programs you're running, the less memory is available to other programs. Installers also typically update files and programs. So if you keep other programs running, installation may not work properly.

- ✓ **Have your local computer store add more RAM to your computer.** This is, admittedly, a drastic and somewhat expensive step. However, if you have a Windows 95 PC or a Mac OS computer with a PowerPC chip, adding more memory can really help the speed of your computer and enable more programs to run at the same time. This may include closing the CD interface and running a product's installation program from Windows Explorer.

With the CGI scripts, you might have problems if your server is using an older version of Perl than the programs are written for. Check the program's documentation (often found at the beginning of the script instead of in a separate file) to see what version of Perl the program needs. Make sure you have changed any variables in the script to those that apply to your own server setup. You also must have the authority to run CGI scripts on the server. If you are using an ISP's server, you may have to ask your ISP to okay and install the scripts for you.

If you still have trouble with installing the items from the CD, please call the IDG Books Worldwide Customer Service phone number: 800-762-2974 (outside the U.S.: 317-596-5430).

Glossary

Aardvark. A type of anteater whose name means *earth pig*.

Alias. An e-mail address that has no mailbox of its own, but simply relays messages sent to it to another address that does have a mailbox.

Anonymous FTP. File access via the File Transfer Protocol, which is open to the public and does not require a registered user name and password. The user name is given as *anonymous* and the password is either the user's e-mail address or the word *guest*.

Attachment. A file that is sent along with an e-mail message. Most e-mail clients place attachments into a separate directory from the one where e-mail messages are stored.

Authentication. Verifying the identity of a person or a service, usually through digital IDs.

Autoresponder. Program that automatically responds to an e-mail message by sending back a preprogrammed e-mail message of its own. Autoresponders are useful, for example, for providing price lists and newsletters.

Banner. An image with an associated link that appears on a Web page (generally at the top of the page) and contains advertising for a sponsor.

Bertie Wooster. The employer of the famed fictional butler, Jeeves.

Binary file. A program file. When transferring files via FTP, you must be careful to send program files as binary files rather than text files, because text files have a different format.

Browser. *See* Web browser.

Carbon copy. Sending an e-mail message to more than one person at a time. The person you are sending the e-mail message to is aware of this. If you want to send a carbon copy without the original recipient knowing about it, you send a blind carbon copy. The regular kind is usually abbreviated *cc* and the blind version is abbreviated *bcc*.

Cat. A creature that deigns to allow humans to inhabit the same planet.

CGI. *See* Common Gateway Interface.

Client/server. A computer that provides resources to other computers over a network is said to be providing a network *service* and is referred to as a *server*. The computers that use the services of a server are called *clients*. The term *server* is used also to refer to the software that provides the service; the software that accesses the server is also called the *client* or *client agent*.

Common Gateway Interface (CGI). A technique for passing to a program for processing information gathered by a Web form.

Configuration. The process of setting options in a program. Also, the set of options chosen.

Dedicated connection. A permanent, 24-hours-a-day, Internet connection. A dedicated connection can be a telephone line that is used solely for a modem that connects to a local ISP but is usually a high-speed connection installed specifically for Internet usage.

Dedicated server. A computer reserved for the use of a single person, company, or organization. *See* virtual server.

Default. Failure to pay bills. Seriously, defaults are the normal settings that software and hardware come with. In most cases, you can change the default settings to suit yourself.

Demographics. Literally, "writing about people." Information you gather from the people who visit your site. Commonly, demographics includes such things as computer system used, income level, and any other information you think you require to understand your audience. Be careful about gathering data on age, race, sex, ethnicity, religious persuasion, and the like because this can lead to discrimination charges. Make sure that, if you do ask for this type of information, you make it clear that such disclosures are purely optional. And never, never, never, make any of this information available to anyone else, except as a lump sum total. Individual input should be held absolutely confidential.

Denmark. A country in eastern Europe, of which about 75% is composed of farms.

Dial-up connection. A telephone line by which occasional connections are made to the Internet via a modem call to a local ISP.

Digital ID. An encrypted identifier kept on file at a central repository (called a *certificate authority*) that certifies that you are who you say you are (just in case you were beginning to wonder).

DNS. *See* Domain Name System.

Domain Name System (DNS). DNS enables computers on the Internet to have names that are easier than IP addresses for people to remember. The names assigned to computers through DNS are called *domain names*. The term *domain name* has two meanings, depending on the context in which the term is used. A domain name such as `science.org` refers to the Internet site run by a particular organization, whereas a domain name such as `titanium.science.org` refers to a particular network node within the `science.org` domain. The longer domain name is sometimes referred to as the network node's *fully qualified domain name* to differentiate it from the larger domain, but the term usually is shortened to *domain name*. Therefore, both `titanium.science.org` and `science.org` are domain names. The former, however, refers to a particular computer named `titanium` that exists within the `science.org` domain; the latter refers generally to a group of related computers that belong to a single organization.

Download. To get a file transferred from another computer to yours. Also, the file which is downloaded. *See also* upload.

E-mail. Messages sent via a local network or the Internet from one computer user to another. When sent across the Internet, e-mail is addressed to the user as *username@hostname.* The *username* part is — you guessed it — the person's user name, and the *hostname* part is the fully qualified domain name of the user's host computer. So, if you wanted to send an e-mail message to someone whose user name was ralph123 and who maintained an account on toymouse.com, you'd address it to `ralph123@toymouse.com` (the @ means *at*).

Emerald City. The home base of the Wizard of Oz.

EtherNet. A common network standard.

Fargo. A city in North Dakota.

Feed. The transmission of messages from one news server to another.

File Transfer Protocol (FTP). A method for transferring files from one computer to another across a network or the Internet.

Flame. A message containing insults or inflammatory material.

Flame war. An extended exchange of messages containing flames. Flame wars disrupt the normal process of communication in mailing lists or newsgroups. *See also* flame.

FTP. *See* File Transfer Protocol.

GIF. An image stored in a file that follows the standards of the Graphics Interchange Format. GIFs are commonly used for limited animation.

Gopher. An early method, predating the World Wide Web, for locating and accessing resources on the Internet. The name comes from the fact that you would tell it what resources you wanted to see and it would "go for" them.

Guillemot. A type of sea bird famous for waddling.

Header. The top part of an e-mail message, which contains information showing the date and time the message was sent, what path it took to reach you, and lots of other information of interest only to the true e-mail maniac. Most e-mail client programs enable you to set an option that relieves you of ever having to see header information.

Hit. A single access of a Web page.

Horace Greeley. Newspaper editor, most famous for the phrase, "Go west, young man, go west." He wasn't the person who said that, but nobody remembers John Soule, who did.

HTML. *See* Hypertext Markup Language.

HTML editor. Specialized text editor for writing Web pages.

HTTP. *See* Hypertext Transfer Protocol.

Hyperlink. *See* link.

Hypertext. Text available on a computer that includes links to other text, images, sound, and so on.

Hypertext Markup Language (HTML). The native language of the World Wide Web, used to construct Web pages.

Hypertext Transfer Protocol (HTTP). A system for transferring files across the World Wide Web.

IANA. *See* Internet Assigned Numbers Authority.

IETF. *See* Internet Engineering Task Force.

Image. General term for any picture or artwork included on a Web page. Images are stored usually in GIF or JPEG format.

Image map. An image that contains multiple links. Users viewing an image map select different links by (with mouse-oriented systems) moving the pointer to different parts of the image and clicking. The images used with image maps must be carefully designed to provide visual clues to the contained links.

Inactivity timeout. The period of time after which a connection will be automatically severed if no activity occurs.

Internet. Short for *internetwork,* which means to link many networks. Sometimes called the "network of networks," the Internet was created — and continues to grow — by linking computer networks so that they can all communicate with one another.

Internet access. The capability to connect to the Internet. Usually provided by an ISP.

Internet Assigned Numbers Authority (IANA). The group that makes port-number assignments on a first-come, first-served basis. Only developers of network software need to worry about having a port number reserved for their software, but the IANA Web site, at `http://www.iana.org/iana/`, is an important place for you to visit anyway, to understand more about how Internet software works.

Internet Engineering Task Force (IETF). The group responsible for keeping track of existing Internet standards and helping create new ones. Anyone can join the IETF for free and participate directly in the creation of new Internet standards. Visit their Web site at `www.ietf.org` for more information.

Internet presence provider (IPP). A company that provides servers for the use of paying customers. Most IPPs are also ISPs.

Internet relay chat (IRC). Live, online interaction between people. The interaction takes place as a kind of live e-mail, with the participants typing messages that are instantly seen by all others who are in a particular chat room. You first need to use a program such as mIRC or Microsoft Chat to log on to an IRC server, and then choose a chat room from the list of available ones (or create your own).

Internet service provider (ISP). A company that provides Internet access, usually by dial-up connections, though many also offer high-speed dedicated connections.

Internet site. A collection of computers that are permanently connected to the Internet and that appear to the outside world to be related to one another.

Internet standards. Worldwide agreements about how Internet technology should function.

Internet telephony. The Internet is essentially a telephone system connecting computers. With the addition of a microphone, speakers, and a sound card to your computer, programs such as Internet Phone and FreeTel make it possible to carry on conversations with anyone who has a similarly equipped computer anywhere in the world over the Internet. Although the sound quality falls short of what you're accustomed to on a regular telephone, unlimited worldwide telephone service for the price of a local Internet connection is hard to beat. And the sound quality is improving all the time as Internet telephony catches on. It goes without saying that the telephone companies are somewhat upset about this development.

IP address. A unique numerical identifier for Internet sites. An IP address is a set of four numbers separated by periods, or dots (also called a *dotted quad*): 207.92.75.100, for example.

IPP. *See* Internet presence provider.

IRC server. *See* Internet relay chat.

Isopoda. A type of crustacean with a small head.

ISP. *See* Internet service provider.

John of Lancaster. Admiral of the British fleet in 1422.

JPEG. Also called *JPG*. An image stored in a file that follows the standards of the Joint Photographic Experts Group. JPEG files are generally smaller than other file formats, but maintain a high-quality image nonetheless.

JPG. *See* JPEG.

Jukebox. A CD-ROM drive that holds multiple disks simultaneously.

Keyword. A search term supplied by a person to a search engine, which then looks for Internet resources that contain that term. Also, such terms that are included on a Web page so that search engines can properly categorize the page.

Klondike. An area in Alaska where gold was discovered in the late nineteenth century.

Link. Also called a *hyperlink,* a connection between a Web page and another Internet resource. Usually, a link contains the URL (Internet address) of another Web page, but it can also link to other resources, such as images. By convention, links are displayed as blue, underlined text that, when activated (usually by a mouse click), causes a Web browser to load the linked resource. Images are also often used as links; by convention, such image links are surrounded by a thin blue border to differentiate them from normal images. Image maps, which are images that contain more than one link, are an exception to the blue border rule.

List owner. The person who manages a mailing list. Usually, the list owner is the person who conceived and launched the list. Also called *list manager,* and may be the *moderator. See* moderator.

List server. A program that processes the e-mail messages that compose a mailing list. The list server usually also handles such routine administrative matters as subscribing and unsubscribing list members when they send a message containing the appropriate commands.

Locomotive. A specialized type of railroad car, also known as an *engine,* that propels other railroad cars along the track.

Log file. A file that records activity. A Web server log file, for instance, records the origin of anyone who looks at a Web page, the type of browser they were using, and so on. Log file analyzer programs such as Statbot are useful to Webmasters in figuring out peak times of usage, the number of hits per day, where visitors were referred from, and so forth.

Mail filtering. The process of automatically taking action on e-mail messages as they come in. You might set rules that put all mail with a particular word in the subject into a different folder, for instance, or that delete mail from a particular person before you see it.

Mail server. A program that receives, stores, and forwards e-mail messages.

Mailbox. A storage area where your e-mail messages are kept until you retrieve them.

Mailing list. A discussion group, the members of which post messages that are relayed via e-mail by a list server. Mailing list membership can be either open or closed.

Message board. Similar to a newsgroup, but operates on an individual Web site. Message boards, sometimes called graffiti walls, allow site visitors to leave messages for other visitors to read. The more sophisticated message board programs include such niceties as message threading and keyword search capabilities.

Modem. *M*odulator/*Dem*odulator. Device that allows a computer to send signals over a telephone line.

Moderator. A person who controls the content of a mailing list or newsgroup. In extreme cases, this can amount to censorship, but moderate moderation simply results in the removal of extraneous material such as sales pitches for products and services unrelated to the topic of the mailing list or newsgroup. A moderator may also play peacemaker, attempting to keep tempers in check among the members of the mailing list or newsgroup, thus avoiding flame wars.

Modesty Blaise. A popular adventure character first introduced in a 1962 comic strip, later the subject of about a dozen novels and at least one movie.

Name server. A computer that maintains a database of domain names and IP addresses. *See* Domain Name System.

Netiquette. Internet etiquette. A series of customs that has evolved to enable people to get along while living together in cyberspace. Basically, be nice and consider how other people might be affected by your actions.

Network. A collection of computers and other devices (such as printers) that are connected for the purpose of sharing resources.

Network adapter. A computer card that allows a computer to be connected to a network.

Network hub. A device that is the central point for relaying signals between parts of a network.

Network News Transfer Protocol (NNTP). The system by which newsgroup messages are transferred between news servers.

Network node. Any device on a network.

Network repeater. A signal amplifier that allows devices on a network to be located farther apart than usual.

News reader. A program that is used to connect to a news server. News readers allow people to read messages and download images from newsgroups.

News server. A program that receives, stores, and forwards newsgroup messages. The server that is sending is called the *upstream* server; the one that is receiving is called the *downstream* server.

Newsgroup. A discussion group, the members of which post messages relayed via a news server. Newsgroups can be either local or global. Global newsgroups are open to the public.

NNTP. *See* Network News Transfer Protocol.

Northwest Passage. The channel leading from the Atlantic to the Pacific Ocean north of North America. Much sought after since the fifteenth century, but not successfully negotiated until 1906.

Ogdensburg. A city in New York State at the meeting of the Oswegatchie and Saint Lawrence rivers.

Online service. Sort of a mini-Internet, services such as CompuServe and America Online provide many of the functions that the Internet does, but on a smaller scale. In recent years, the online services lost much business to the Internet and decided to provide Internet access as part of their services.

Packet. Like little envelopes sent by traditional mail. Each packet contains an address, just as any paper envelope does, and some amount of information.

Page-generation program. Software that uses a WYSIWYG (what you see is what you get), point-and-click interface for creating Web pages.

Password. A secret word used to gain computer access. Passwords are sometimes chosen, sometimes assigned. Two schools of thought on passwords exist. One says that passwords should be so difficult to imagine that no one else could possibly guess yours in a million years. These people want everyone to have a password like *109834akjd30d9dfnap33o78dsjfa23sdorf*. Although it's true that it's not a good idea to use your dog's name for your password, this approach seems a bit extreme. (Most passwords are between 4 and 10 characters, anyway.) The other school of thought says that you should be able to remember your password. If you have only one or two, this is no big deal, regardless of their complexity; you'd be surprised how quickly a random series of numbers can become familiar. One technique favored by many people is to combine two unrelated but easy to remember words, putting a few numbers between them, such as *music42bank*. Just make sure the terms have no connection to you. The *music42bank* password would be a fine password for a dog breeder, but a lousy one for a banker who played jazz gigs after hours, especially if he or she was 42 years old.

Pausanias. General of the Greek army in the Battle of Plataea in 479 B.C.

POP. *See* Post Office Protocol.

Port numbers. Part of the IP address, port numbers are unique for a particular IP address, meaning that two information services can't both use port 80 on network node 207.92.75.100. But port numbers are not unique globally. The network node at IP address 207.92.75.100 can provide an information service by using port 80, and at the same time, IP address 207.92.75.101 can provide a service by using port 80. Together, an IP address and a port number identify a unique network node and a unique information service on the network node, respectively.

Post Office Protocol. The method by which e-mail clients pick up e-mail from a mail server.

Privileges. Limitations on access or the types of commands available given to various people or groups. *Root privileges,* for example, are available only to the person in charge of a server, because they allow anyone who has them to totally change the system.

Protocol. An agreed-upon set of commands for accomplishing a particular purpose.

Quimper. A French city on the Odet River.

Ray tracing. A method of producing images that follows rays of (theoretical) light as they pass through a (hypothetical) scene and reproduces the effects that would be produced by those light rays if the scene actually existed.

Reciprocal link. A link to a Web page that also has a link back to your own Web page. Hyperlinking is a common practice for building traffic among Web sites. If you want to establish reciprocal links with someone's site, put in a link to their site on your own, and then send them an e-mail message asking them to reciprocate.

Ring. A series of Web sites connected with links that lead from one to the other such that visitors who follow all the links can go full circle and return to their starting place.

Runic alphabet. The characters used by Teutonic peoples of early Europe, also called *futhark.*

Samuel Langhorne Clemens. The real name of a writer known to history as *Mark Twain.*

Search engine. A program that checks through a database of terms to see which Internet resources contain them. Local search engines are a variant on this; they actually read every page in a Web site to see if it contains the search term.

Server. *See* Client/server.

SGML. *See* Standard Generalized Markup Language.

Shopping cart. A program that permits people visiting your site to choose which items they will purchase. The shopping cart metaphor extends to the ability to put items into the cart and remove them before making the final purchasing decision.

Simple Mail Transfer Protocol (SMTP). A common method for sending e-mail between mail servers.

Sleep. A common practice utterly unknown to authors trying to meet a deadline.

SMTP. *See* Simple Mail Transfer Protocol.

Spam. Unsolicited e-mail messages, sent in bulk quantities to several addresses. Also, the same message posted to multiple newsgroups simultaneously.

Standard. A generic term for just about anything that lots of people agree on. A standard may be a way to transfer files from one system to another one, the exact structure and function of a computer language, or a method of compressing video images. If a recognized, organized group develops a standard, it's called an *official standard*. If a standard is developed by the market leader and is used by most of the people in a particular field, it's called a *de facto standard*.

Standard Generalized Markup Language (SGML). A method for describing markup languages such as HTML.

Subscriber. A member of a mailing list. Also called, amazingly enough, *list member*.

TCP/IP. *See* Transmission Control Protocol/Internet Protocol.

Telecommuting. Working from home via remote computer access.

Telepathy. The capability to transfer thoughts from one mind to another.

Telnet. A method of remote access to a computer. Allows users to type commands as though they were at the terminal of the remote computer.

Text editor. A simple form of word processor that saves text files without formatting.

Text file. A file of text. (No kidding.) When transferring text files via FTP, be careful to send them as text rather than as binary files because text files often need to be converted between Windows and UNIX systems, which have slightly different text formats.

Traffic. The number of visits to an Internet site, as in "Our traffic increased by 100,000 visitors last week."

Transmission Control Protocol/Internet Protocol (TCP/IP). The standard way for data to be relayed around the world on the Internet. Many, but not all, computers on the Internet speak TCP/IP directly. Other computers speak a different networking language and rely on translation equipment to convert between TCP/IP and their native network language.

Uncertainty principle. A fundamental theorem of quantum physics, which states that it is impossible to know both the direction of travel and the location in space-time of an atomic particle.

Uniform Resource Locator (URL). Each bit of information on the Internet is known as a *resource*. A URL specifies the type of software used to handle the resource, the computer on which the resource is located, and the name of the resource. The URL adds a specific resource name, such as a filename, to the IP address and port-number combination. The first part is called a *prefix*. Following are some common prefixes.

Prefix	Information Service	Example URL
http://	World Wide Web	http://www.science.org/
ftp://	File Transfer Protocol	ftp://ftp.science.org/
gopher://	Gopher	gopher://science.org/
mailto:	E-mail address	mailto:info@science.org

UNIX. A common operating system on the Internet.

Upload. To get a file transferred from your computer to another one. Also, the file that is uploaded. *See also* download.

URL. *See* Uniform Resource Locator.

User name. Also called *user ID*. The name by which a person is identified on a particular computer system. Usually some variant on the person's given name.

Van de Graaff generator. A primitive device that can generate millions of volts of static electricity.

Virtual server. A directory on a computer that simulates the existence of a separate computer. *See also* dedicated server.

Web. *See* World Wide Web.

Web browser. A program that displays Web pages and follows links to allow a user to traverse the World Wide Web.

Web page. Also called *HTML page*. A display composed with the Hypertext Markup Language that is viewable with a Web browser.

Web site. Any presence on the World Wide Web. Usually applied to a collection of Web pages.

Webmaster. The person in control of a Web site. A Webmaster may be an individual with only a single Web page, or the manager of a large team of developers who create and maintain Web sites.

William Kidd. Eighteenth-century English privateer who went down in history as the pirate "Captain Kidd." He provided documents to political authorities that showed he had attacked only ships carrying papers that revealed they were at war with England, but the papers were lost until the 1970s.

World Wide Web (WWW). The total selection of Web sites interconnected via the Internet.

WWW. *See* World Wide Web.

Xylem. The central core of plant roots.

Ytterbium. A rare earth element often found in combination with gadolinite.

Zymurgy. The study of the fermentation process.

Index

(continued)

(continued)

● *P* ●

(continued)

IDG Books Worldwide, Inc., End-User License Agreement

Note: The GNU (General Public License) may apply to individual programs on the *Setting Up An Internet Site For Dummies* CD-ROM. Please see the individual progrms for details.

READ THIS. You should carefully read these terms and conditions before opening the software packet(s) included with this book ("Book"). This is a license agreement ("Agreement") between you and IDG Books Worldwide, Inc. ("IDGB"). By opening the accompanying software packet(s), you acknowledge that you have read and accept the following terms and conditions. If you do not agree and do not want to be bound by such terms and conditions, promptly return the Book and the unopened software packet(s) to the place you obtained them for a full refund.

1. **License Grant.** IDGB grants to you (either an individual or entity) a nonexclusive license to use one copy of the enclosed software program(s) (collectively, the "Software") solely for your own personal or business purposes on a single computer (whether a standard computer or a workstation component of a multiuser network). The Software is in use on a computer when it is loaded into temporary memory (RAM) or installed into permanent memory (hard disk, CD-ROM, or other storage device). IDGB reserves all rights not expressly granted herein.

2. **Ownership.** IDGB is the owner of all right, title, and interest, including copyright, in and to the compilation of the Software recorded on the disk(s) or CD-ROM ("Software Media"). Copyright to the individual programs recorded on the Software Media is owned by the author or other authorized copyright owner of each program. Ownership of the Software and all proprietary rights relating thereto remain with IDGB and its licensers.

3. **Restrictions on Use and Transfer.**

   (a) You may only (i) make one copy of the Software for backup or archival purposes, or (ii) transfer the Software to a single hard disk, provided that you keep the original for backup or archival purposes. You may not (i) rent or lease the Software, (ii) copy or reproduce the Software through a LAN or other network system or through any computer subscriber system or bulletin-board system, or (iii) modify, adapt, or create derivative works based on the Software.

   (b) You may not reverse engineer, decompile, or disassemble the Software. You may transfer the Software and user documentation on a permanent basis, provided that the transferee agrees to accept the terms and conditions of this Agreement and you retain no copies. If the Software is an update or has been updated, any transfer must include the most recent update and all prior versions.

4. **Restrictions on Use of Individual Programs.** You must follow the individual requirements and restrictions detailed for each individual program in the "About the CD" appendix of this Book. These limitations are also contained in the individual license agreements recorded on the Software Media. These limitations may include a requirement that after using the program for a specified period of time, the user must pay a registration fee or discontinue use. By opening the Software packet(s), you will be agreeing to abide by the licenses and restrictions for these individual programs that are detailed in the "About the CD" appendix and on the Software Media. None of the material on this Software Media or listed in this Book may ever be redistributed, in original or modified form, for commercial purposes.

5. **Limited Warranty.**

   (a) IDGB warrants that the Software and Software Media are free from defects in materials and workmanship under normal use for a period of sixty (60) days from the date of purchase of this Book. If IDGB receives notification within the warranty period of defects in materials or workmanship, IDGB will replace the defective Software Media.

   (b) IDGB AND THE AUTHORS OF THE BOOK DISCLAIM ALL OTHER WARRANTIES, EXPRESS OR IMPLIED, INCLUDING WITHOUT LIMITATION IMPLIED WARRANTIES OF MERCHANTABILITY AND FITNESS FOR A PARTICULAR PURPOSE, WITH RESPECT TO THE SOFTWARE, THE PROGRAMS, THE SOURCE CODE CONTAINED THEREIN, AND/OR THE TECHNIQUES DESCRIBED IN THIS BOOK. IDGB DOES NOT WARRANT THAT THE FUNCTIONS CONTAINED IN THE SOFTWARE WILL MEET YOUR REQUIREMENTS OR THAT THE OPERATION OF THE SOFTWARE WILL BE ERROR FREE.

   (c) This limited warranty gives you specific legal rights, and you may have other rights that vary from jurisdiction to jurisdiction.

6. **Remedies.**

   (a) IDGB's entire liability and your exclusive remedy for defects in materials and workmanship shall be limited to replacement of the Software Media, which may be returned to IDGB with a copy of your receipt at the following address: Software Media Fulfillment Department, Attn.: *Setting Up An Internet Site For Dummies,* 3rd Edition, IDG Books Worldwide, Inc., 7260 Shadeland Station, Ste. 100, Indianapolis, IN 46256, or call 800-762-2974. Please allow three to four weeks for delivery. This Limited Warranty is void if failure of the Software Media has resulted from accident, abuse, or misapplication. Any replacement Software Media will be warranted for the remainder of the original warranty period or thirty (30) days, whichever is longer.

   (b) In no event shall IDGB or the authors be liable for any damages whatsoever (including without limitation damages for loss of business profits, business interruption, loss of business information, or any other pecuniary loss) arising from the use of or inability to use the Book or the Software, even if IDGB has been advised of the possibility of such damages.

   (c) Because some jurisdictions do not allow the exclusion or limitation of liability for consequential or incidental damages, the above limitation or exclusion may not apply to you.

7. **U.S. Government Restricted Rights.** Use, duplication, or disclosure of the Software by the U.S. Government is subject to restrictions stated in paragraph (c)(1)(ii) of the Rights in Technical Data and Computer Software clause of DFARS 252.227-7013, and in subparagraphs (a) through (d) of the Commercial Computer–Restricted Rights clause at FAR 52.227-19, and in similar clauses in the NASA FAR supplement, when applicable.

8. **General.** This Agreement constitutes the entire understanding of the parties and revokes and supersedes all prior agreements, oral or written, between them and may not be modified or amended except in a writing signed by both parties hereto that specifically refers to this Agreement. This Agreement shall take precedence over any other documents that may be in conflict herewith. If any one or more provisions contained in this Agreement are held by any court or tribunal to be invalid, illegal, or otherwise unenforceable, each and every other provision shall remain in full force and effect.

Installation Instructions

• •

Using the CD with Microsoft Windows

To install the items from the CD to your hard drive, follow these steps:

1. **Insert the CD into your computer's CD-ROM drive.**

2. **Windows 3.1 or 3.11 users: From Program Manager, choose File⇨Run.**

   Windows 95 users: Click the Start button and click Run.

3. **In the dialog box that appears, type** D:\SETUP.EXE.

   Replace *D* with the proper drive letter if your CD-ROM drive uses a different letter. (If you don't know the letter, see how your CD-ROM drive is listed under My Computer in Windows 95 or File Manager in Windows 3.1.)

4. **Click OK.**

   A license agreement window appears.

5. **Read through the license agreement, nod your head, and then click the Accept button if you want to use the CD.**

   (After you click Accept, the License Agreement window will never bother you again.) The CD interface appears. The interface is a little program that shows you what is on the CD and coordinates installing the programs and running the demos. The interface basically lets you click a button or two to make things happen.

6. **The first screen you see is the Welcome screen. Click anywhere on this screen to enter the interface.**

   Now you are getting to the action. This next screen lists categories for the software on the CD.

7. **To view the items within a category, just click the category's name.**

   A list of programs in the category appears.

8. **For more information about a program, click the program's name.**

   Be sure to read the information that appears. Sometimes a program might require you to do a few tricks on your computer first, and this screen will tell you where to go for that information, if necessary.

9. **If you don't want to install the program, click the Go Back button to return to the previous screen.**

   You can always return to the previous screen by clicking the Go Back button. This allows you to browse the different categories and products and decide what you want to install.

10. **To install the program, click the appropriate Install button.**

    The CD interface drops to the background while the CD begins installation of the program you chose.

11. **To install other items, repeat Steps 7 through 10.**

12. **After you're finished installing programs, click the Quit button to close the interface.**

    You can eject the CD now. Carefully place it back in the plastic jacket of the book for safekeeping.

Using the CD with the Mac OS

To install the items from the CD to your hard drive, follow these steps:

1. **Insert the CD into your computer's CD-ROM drive.**

   In a moment, an icon representing the CD you just inserted appears on your Mac desktop. Chances are, the icon looks like a CD-ROM.

2. **Double-click the CD icon to show the CD's contents.**

3. **Double-click the License Agreement icon.**

   This is the end-user license that you agree to by using the CD.

4. **Double-click the Read Me First icon.**

   The Read Me First text file contains information about the CD's programs and any last-minute instructions you may need to install the programs correctly.

5. **The software on the CD is organized into category folders, so double-click the folder icon to open the category that you are interested in.**

   You will find program files or folders inside each category folder.

6. **To install most programs, just drag the program's folder from the CD window and drop it on your hard drive icon.**

7. **Some programs come with installer programs — with these, you simply open the program's folder on the CD and double-click the icon with the words "Install" or "Installer."**

   After you have installed the programs you want, you can eject the CD. Carefully place it back in the plastic jacket of the book for safekeeping.

We hope you enjoy the book and CD-ROM and that your site-building projects are a success!

WWW.DUMMIES.COM

YOUR
ONLINE
RESOURCE

Discover Dummies Online!

The Dummies Web Site is your fun and friendly online resource for the latest information about ...*For Dummies*® books and your favorite topics. The Web site is the place to communicate with us, exchange ideas with other ...*For Dummies* readers, chat with authors, and have fun!

Ten Fun and Useful Things You Can Do at www.dummies.com

1. Win free ...*For Dummies* books and more!
2. Register your book and be entered in a prize drawing.
3. Meet your favorite authors through the IDG Books Author Chat Series.
4. Exchange helpful information with other ...*For Dummies* readers.
5. Discover other great ...*For Dummies* books you must have!
6. Purchase Dummieswear™ exclusively from our Web site.
7. Buy ...*For Dummies* books online.
8. Talk to us. Make comments, ask questions, get answers!
9. Download free software.
10. Find additional useful resources from authors.

Link directly to these ten fun and useful things at
http://www.dummies.com/10useful

For other technology titles from IDG Books Worldwide, go to
www.idgbooks.com

Not on the Web yet? It's easy to get started with *Dummies 101*®: *The Internet For Windows*®*95* or *The Internet For Dummies*®, *4th Edition,* at local retailers everywhere.

IDG
BOOKS
WORLDWIDE

Find other ...*For Dummies* books on these topics:

Business • Career • Databases • Food & Beverage • Games • Gardening • Graphics • Hardware
Health & Fitness • Internet and the World Wide Web • Networking • Office Suites
Operating Systems • Personal Finance • Pets • Programming • Recreation • Sports
Spreadsheets • Teacher Resources • Test Prep • Word Processing

IDG BOOKS WORLDWIDE BOOK REGISTRATION

We want to hear from you!

Visit **http://my2cents.dummies.com** to register this book and tell us how you liked it!

- Get entered in our monthly prize giveaway.

- Give us feedback about this book — tell us what you like best, what you like least, or maybe what you'd like to ask the author and us to change!

- Let us know any other *...For Dummies*® topics that interest you.

Your feedback helps us determine what books to publish, tells us what coverage to add as we revise our books, and lets us know whether we're meeting your needs as a *...For Dummies* reader. You're our most valuable resource, and what you have to say is important to us!

Not on the Web yet? It's easy to get started with *Dummies 101*®: *The Internet For Windows*® *95* or *The Internet For Dummies*®, 4th Edition, at local retailers everywhere.

Or let us know what you think by sending us a letter at the following address:

...For Dummies Book Registration
Dummies Press
7260 Shadeland Station, Suite 100
Indianapolis, IN 46256-3945
Fax 317-596-5498

BUSINESS AND
GENERAL
REFERENCE
BOOK SERIES
FROM IDG

COMPUTER
BOOK SERIES
FROM IDG